SACRED AND
HISTORICAL PLACES
HAWAI'I

A GUIDE TO LDS HISTORIC SITES IN HAWAI'I

Mary Jane Woodger
Riley M. Moffat
Fred E. Woods

Jonathan Napela Center for Hawaiian and Pacific Island Studies
Brigham Young University–Hawaii
Mormon Historic Sites Foundation

MOUNTAIN
PRESS

ISBN 978-0-8425-2974-7

Printed in the United States of America

Contents

Preface

Historian LaMar C. Berrett wrote the following as an introduction to his *Sacred Places* series:

When Moses came to the mountain of God and the burning bush, the Lord said unto him, "Put off thy shoes from off thy feet, for the place whereon thou standest is holy ground" (Exodus 3:5).

Through the ages, the locations of sacred historical events have traditionally become holy. How holy or sacred a site is depends on the understanding of those beholding it. Elizabeth Barrett Browning wrote:

> Earth's crammed with heaven,
> And every common bush afire with god;
> But only he who sees, takes off his shoes—
> The rest sit round it and pluck blackberries.
> (*Aurora Leigh*, Book 7, 820–23)

On April 6, 1830, the Lord revealed to Joseph Smith in Fayette, New York that "there shall be a record kept among you" upon the organization of the Church (D&C 21:1). Consequently in 1838, a commandment was given, "Let the city, Far West, be a holy and consecrated land unto me; and it shall be called most holy, for the ground upon which thou standest is holy" (D&C115:7). From this time forward, it was recognized and accepted among Church members that specific "places and events" intertwined in the Church's history were to be both "sanctified and recorded." The *Sacred Places* series was written to "bring the history and geography . . . of the Church to life."[1]

Sacred and Historical Places: Hawai'i provides detailed maps, interesting narratives, and numerous photographs in its effort to document the many places where historical events took place and had significance in the collective memory of the people. Other

---

1 LaMar C. Berrett, ed., *Sacred Places: New England and Eastern Canada* (Salt Lake City: Bookcraft, 1999), vii.

locations we identify are made sacred by the faith and testimonies of past generations of Island Saints. Conscious of the admirable strength of Mormon pioneers from all over the world, The Church of Jesus Christ of Latter-day Saints has a long tradition of recognizing and recording the many sacred places and events of its history. "Each country where Mormonism has established itself has its own separate history of pioneers, leaders, persecution, and response to challenge."[2] The comprehensive nature of this guide encourages readers to follow in the footsteps of George Q. Cannon, Jonathan Napela, Joseph F. Smith, David O. McKay, and other Church leaders, or to seek out the paths of their own ancestors.

2 Davis Bitton and Leonard J. Arrington, *Mormons and Their Historians* (Salt Lake City: University of Utah Press, 1988), 169.

Introduction

During the spring of 2007, a few members of the Department of Church History and Doctrine in the College of Religious Education at Brigham Young University took a regional studies scouting trip to the Hawaiian Islands. Two incidents caused us to think about writing this book about sacred places in the Hawaiian Islands. The first incident took place while we were trying to identify the place where Hawaiʻi was dedicated for the preaching of the gospel. William Farrer, an early missionary, had recorded the dedication as happening on December 13, 1850.

> We . . . went onto a mountain about three miles from the wharve [sic] and about 1,000 feet above the level of the sea; there on a small round knoll that rose several feet above the rest of the land around, and was about four or five rods across with a smooth flat surface: there each of us carried a stone and all built an alter [sic]; we then sung a Hymn and each one then expressed his feelings and desires in regard to the mission we are now on. Bro. Clark then offered up a prayer to the Lord that he would open the way that we might be enabled to preach the gospel on these Islands, and that we might have his spirit to be with us at all times to guide us in the way of truth and be preserved from the power of the adversary and from every evil, and that the honest in heart might embrace the truth when they heard it, and that all who should oppose the truth might be confounded.[1]

We spoke with Church Educational System personnel, missionaries, ecclesiastical leaders, etc., but no one we asked knew the location of King's Falls, also known as Kapena Falls. We found the closest identification of the dedication location to be somewhere in the large housing subdivision of Pacific Heights. (We should have contacted Riley Moffat or one of the other excellent

---

1 William Farrer, *Biographical Sketch, Hawaiian Mission Report and Diary, 1821–1906*, December 13, 1850, typescript, 45, L. Tom Perry Special Collections, Harold B. Lee Library, Brigham Young University, Provo, Utah.

historians at BYU–Hawaii.) Finally, after wandering about for a few hours, we called retired Brigham Young University History Professor Lanier Britsch in Orem, Utah. He explained that King's Falls and the pool where the early Hawaiian Saints were baptized were located behind a Buddhist temple. Following his directions, we walked a short distance on a path and came to the spot where the missionaries, in 1850, had bathed before ascending the hill where they built an altar and dedicated the Hawaiian Islands for preaching the gospel. We felt we were on sacred ground, and we wanted to share this sacred Church history site with others.

The second incident that prompted the creation of this book as part of the *Sacred Places* series happened on the small island of Lanaʻi. We had been told that the *Mormon Historic Sites Foundation* had placed a marker identifying the site to commemorate the early gathering of Latter-day Saints to that place. We were also told that it would be necessary to rent a Jeep to view the marker, because it could only be reached by an all-terrain vehicle. After we rented a Jeep we found that the marker was easily accessible—it was right on the main road. We did not need to incur the extra expense of renting an all-terrain vehicle.

These two incidents suggested to us that a guidebook for Latter-day Saint sacred spots on the Hawaiian Islands was sorely needed. Little has been done to preserve the location of sites where significant happenings in our Church history took place in the Hawaiian Islands. We learned that much of the history of the Church in this region was being lost with the passing of each generation.

The Church of Jesus Christ of Latter-day Saints has always sought to preserve sacred places and to record sacred events. As Latter-day Saints, we are a people who commemorate and celebrate important events in our history, and as we do so our collective memory is enlarged (see Alma 37:8). Sacred or holy places are an important part of our history. We hope that *Sacred and Historical Places: Hawaiʻi* will bring the history and geography of the sacred places of Church history in Hawaiʻi to life, and that by bringing that history and geography to life, we will increase the understanding and appreciation of Hawaiʻi's historical and sacred places of interest to Latter-day Saints.

Following the history of The Church of Jesus Christ of Latter-day Saints in Hawai'i from the first missionaries and converts to the construction of a temple in Kona, Hawai'i, this book will serve as a valuable resource for academic historians and amateur Church history enthusiasts alike; yet, we will not identify every location of all Latter-day Saint Church congregations. During the first hundred years of the Church in Hawai'i, upwards of some eighty branches in Hawai'i at any one time served a mostly rural Hawaiian population, each group with its own chapel, though some chapels were simply thatched or simple wooden structures; to try to describe each one is unnecessary, though we have appended lists of former branches (see appendices A, B, C, D). Instead we focus on those sites that are significant to the history of the Church in Hawai'i.

In selecting sites to be included in this guide, the authors proposed a simple acid test. The guidebook being a guide for visitors, we first asked "Is there something to see when you get there? Has the site been described in published accounts? And last, if the site is not accessible to the average visitor, we acknowledge that fact. Private land in Hawai'i often has a "KAPU" sign attached, meaning "No Trespassing." Unless you have specific permission from the landowner, please respect these signs, for your own safety. The authors admit that, depending on the reader's perspective, we may have fudged a bit in applying the acid test in an effort to be more inclusive. Just as in Church history elsewhere, many sites may not be particularly sacred but did have significant historical or cultural importance to the history of the Church and to members of that locality.

Over the past century and a half there have been nearly one hundred branches, most with their own chapels, and other historic sites around the islands, and most are now gone without a trace. The members who worshiped there have left descendants and memories; many stories remain to be discovered and recorded. The faith and service of these Saints need to be preserved as a testament to their sacrifice in accepting and living the restored gospel of Jesus Christ. All of this took place across the beautiful landscape that is the Hawaiian Islands.

This book also includes a few points of interest not directly related to Church history. However, this book is not a guide to popular non-LDS tourist sites, lodging, or food. For this information, we suggest travelers consult commercial travel guides, such as those from *Fodor's, Frommer's, Lonely Planet, Moon, National Geographic, Eyewitness*, or Andrew Doughty's Ultimate Guidebooks. The best published maps to use in finding sites are those by James A. Bier from the University of Hawai'i.[2] The comprehensive nature of the book encourages readers to follow in the footsteps of early Hawaiian Saints and missionaries and to seek out the paths of their own ancestors. It also enables armchair tourists to vicariously visit the many magnificent places related to Church history in Hawai'i.

In Hawai'i, directions are commonly given as *mauka* (toward the mountains) or *makai* (toward the sea). Directions are also sometimes given by mentioning some place along the coast one way or another, since most main roads follow the coast rather than north, south, east or west directions.

2 See James A. Bier, *O'ahu, Hawai'i: The Gathering Place* (Honolulu: University of Hawai'i Press, 2007); James A. Bier, *The Friendly Isle, Moloka'i; the Pineapple Isle, Lana'i* (Honolulu: University of Hawai'i Press, 2002); James A. Bier, *Hawai'i: Maui, the Valley Isle* (Honolulu: University of Hawai'i Press, 2008); James A. Bier, *Hawai'i: The Big Island* (Honolulu: University of Hawai'i Press, 2011); and James A. Bier, *Kaua'i, The Garden Isle* (Honolulu: University of Hawai'i Press, 2015).

Acknowledgments

So many individuals have contributed to *Sacred and Historical Places: Hawai'i* that it is impractical, even impossible, to give personal credit to all those who deserve it. However, the following individuals and institutions were particularly helpful.

Brigham Young University's College of Religious Education, Department of Church History and Doctrine, and the Religious Studies Center, represented by Thomas A. Wayment, Arnold K. Garr, Richard Bennett, Richard Neitzel Holzapfel, Kent S. Jackson, Devan Jensen; and BYU–Hawaii's Jonathan Napela Institute for Hawaiian and Pacific Islands Studies represented by Phillip H. McArthur have all been instrumental in the realization of *Sacred and Historical Places: Hawai'i* by supplying funding for research. Also, through various means—time, student assistants, secretarial help, research grants, and various other forms of financial aid—these organizations and the people associated with them have been indispensable to the completion of this project.

A special thanks also goes to the writers, researchers, journal keepers, Church historians, and others who laid the groundwork upon which *Sacred and Historical Places: Hawai'i* has been constructed. We are indebted to local historians and Church members, without whose research, writing and memories of the islands, this look back in time and place would not have been possible: Linda Gonsalves on Kaua'i, Roy Horner and Lorraine Pescaia on Moloka'i, Oscar Aguilar on Lana'i; Dwayne Wada on Maui; Roy Bauer, Rhea Akoi, Gail Kaapuni, Jacob and Luana Keanaaina, Earl Veloria, and Carolyn Depp on the Big Island; and Gloria Cronin, who added invaluable accuracy and expertise to this study. In addition, we are grateful for the oral traditions passed down by native Hawaiians and Polynesians, which have contributed to the transfer of both culture and history. We wish to acknowledge the incredible research of historians Lanier R. Britsch, Ken Baldridge, and Grant Underwood. We express gratitude to our research assistants from BYU–Hawaii, Kaitlin Zeller and Carl Canlas, for their excellent work on photography and the directions to various sites. Eric Perkins, Teodora Hristova, Daniel Anderson, Scott Baxter, Haylee Chournos, Alice Beesley, Jessica Christensen, Wendy Vardeman, Michelle Vanegas, and Emily Jane Rule—all were surely some of the most cheerful, dependable, and intelligent of assistants. We also thank Kurt Laird, Camber Agrelius, and especially Don E. Norton for their excellent editing expertise contributed to this work and Marny K. Parkin for preparing the index. We are also indebted to cartographer Luke Moffat and their ThinkSpatial team in the Department of Geography at BYU for creating the maps.

We are also grateful to the staffs and administrators of the many repositories who have been so helpful in our research. Especially gracious were the staffs of the Brigham Young University Harold B. Lee Library Faculty Delivery; Brigham Young University–Hawai'i Joseph F. Smith Library and Archives; and the Church History Library.

Finally, we are grateful to Phillip H. McArthur, editor-in-chief of publications for the Jonathan Napela Institute for Hawaiian and Pacific Islands Studies, and Devan Jensen of the Brigham Young University Religious Studies Center, for making this guide available.

Introduction to Hawai'i

In The Book of Mormon: Another Testament of Jesus Christ, we are told that the Lord will remember "those who are upon the isles of the sea" (2 Nephi 29:7), and "great are the promises of the Lord to those who are upon the isles of the sea" (2 Nephi 10:21). These memories and promises are also apparent in both the preface and the appendix of the Doctrine and Covenants (D&C 1:2; 133:8). Included among God's children upon the isles of the sea are those who live or have lived on the islands now known as Hawai'i, an island chain consisting of volcanic peaks formed over the past six million years.

The Hawaiian Islands were first settled by Polynesians who arrived via sailing canoes from Polynesian islands to the south, according to archaeological investigations.[1] However, some Mormon Hawaiians who have compiled their genealogy from

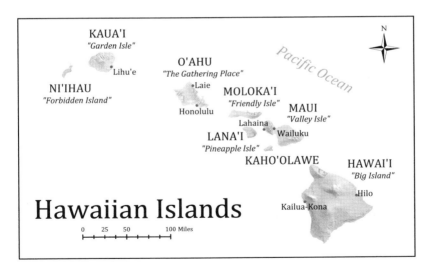

KAUA'I
"Garden Isle"

O'AHU
"The Gathering Place"

•Lihu'e

NI'IHAU
"Forbidden Island"

•Laie

MOLOKA'I
"Friendly Isle"

Honolulu

Lahaina

MAUI
"Valley Isle"

LANA'I
"Pineapple Isle"

Wailuku

KAHO'OLAWE

HAWAI'I
"Big Island"

•Hilo

Hawaiian Islands

Kailua-Kona

Pacific Ocean

N

0   25   50   100 Miles

---

1 See Patrick Vinton Kirch, *Unearthing the Polynesian Past: Explorations and Adventures of an Island Archaeologist* (Honolulu: University of Hawai'i Press, 2015).

traditional oral histories claim to go back to the name of Hagoth, a sailor in the Book of Mormon dating from around 55 BC.

After human occupation, the population grew as they adapted to the islands' limited resources. What early history we have concerning the people of Hawai'i comes from chants or legends memorized and passed down through generations of Hawaiians. The Hawaiian language was not written until Protestant missionaries arrived from New England in 1820 and created a written alphabet.[2]

The Hawaiian Islands were settled hundreds of years before any European set foot on them. One common belief concerning the genesis of early settlers in Hawai'i is that they came from the east, and the only lands east of the Hawaiian Islands are the Americas. This belief was popular among the Hawaiian people long before a priest named Pa'ao came to Hawai'i from central Polynesia and introduced new and sometimes violent ways of worship that conflicted with the ways of early inhabitants.[3]

Some Book of Mormon geographers propose that Book of Mormon peoples settled in Hawai'i and the Pacific Islands. While archaeologists agree that culturally and linguistically Hawaiians are most closely related to the eastern Polynesian islands of Tahiti and the Marquesas Islands,[4] some Church scholars propose that Book of Mormon character Hagoth made contact with Hawai'i about 55 BC, according to Alma chapter 63 in the Book of Mormon. Following the example of Thor Heyerdahl's *Kon Tiki* in 1958, Latter-day Saint explorer DeVere Baker demonstrated that a raft could float from Southern California to Hawai'i.[5] A few scholars go

---

2 Albert J. Schutz, *The Voices of Eden: A History of Hawaiian Language Studies* (Honolulu: University of Hawai'i Press, 1994), 122; and George Armitage, *A Brief History of Hawai'i* (Mililani, HI: The Islander Group, 1961), 33–34.

3 E. S. Craighill Handy et al., *Ancient Hawaiian Civilization* (Rutland, VT: Charles E. Tuttle Co., 1965), 32.

4 See Patrick Vinton Kirch, *Feathered Gods and Fishhooks* (Honolulu: University of Hawai'i Press, 1985), 68; John L. Culliney, *Islands in a Far Sea: The Fate of Nature in Hawaii*, 2nd ed. (Honolulu: University of Hawai'i Press, 2006), 313; DeVere Baker, *The Raft Lehi IV: 69 Days on the Pacific Ocean* (Long Beach: Whithorn Publishing Co, 1959); Bruce S. Sutton, *Lehi, Father of Polynesia: Polynesians are Nephites* (Orem, UT: Hawaiki Publishing, 2001); and Russell T. Clement, "Apostle in Exile: Joseph F. Smith's Third Mission to Hawaii, 1885–1887," *Dialogue: A Journal of Mormon Thought* 13, no. 4 (1980): 53–62.

5 See Baker, *The Raft Lehi IV*; Sutton, *Lehi, Father of Polynesia*; and Clement, "Apostle in Exile," 53–62.

Captain James Cook. Courtesy of National Maritime Museum.

so far as to equate the traditional god of peace and fertility, Lono, with Jesus Christ, whose return Hawaiians confused with Captain Cook in 1778. Others, such as Bruce S. Sutton, feel the links between Hagoth and the Hawaiians are much clearer.[6] Church leaders have, since 1851, stated that the blood of Israel flows through the veins of Hawaiians and other Polynesians and that they are descendents of Lehi.[7]

God prepared the Hawaiian people by various means for the introduction of the gospel of Jesus Christ. One of the first steps of preparation occurred when Captain James Cook became the first European to encounter Hawai'i in 1778.[8] His three major Pacific voyages provided new information about the Pacific Ocean and the people who inhabited its islands. His third voyage to the Pacific resulted in his discovery of the Hawaiian Islands. The primary goal of Cook's voyage was to determine whether there was a Northwest Passage above the North American continent. Sailing north from Tahiti, Cook encountered Kaua'i on January 18, 1778, and decided to name the island group the Sandwich Isles, after a friend and supporter, John Montague, the Earl of Sandwich.

After a fruitless summer searching for a northwest passage, Cook returned to the Hawaiian Islands to replenish and repair his ships. Searching for a safe harbor, he anchored in Kealakekua Bay on the Kona coast of the Big Island. Cook arrived during the Hawaiian *makahiki* season, when all wars ceased and games

6 See Alan C. Miner, *Step by Step Through the Book of Mormon* (Springville, UT: Self-published, 1996), http://stepbystep.alancminer.com.
7 Russel T. Clement, "Polynesian Origins: More Word on the Mormon Perspective," *Dialogue: A Journal of Mormon Thought* 13, no. 4 (Winter 1980): 88–98; and Marjorie Newton, *Tiki and Temple: The Mormon Mission in New Zealand, 1854–1958* (Draper, UT: Greg Kofford Books, 2012), 129–31.
8 Richard Tregaskis, *The Warrior King: Hawaii's Kamehameha the Great* (Toronto, Ontario: Macmillan, 1973), 85–87.

were held to honor Lono, the native god of fertility and harvest. When the Hawaiians saw Captain Cook, they mistook him for Lono. A young chief named Kamehameha, along with other chiefs of the Big Island, traveled to Kealakekua Bay to meet Captain Cook. Treating Cook like a god, the chiefs lavished him with gifts and held ceremonies in his honor.

Kamehameha the Great. Courtesy of National Park Service.

Shortly after Cook and his crew departed Hawai'i, a storm damaged the *Resolution*, forcing it to return to Kealakekua. The natives could not understand how a god could have allowed this to happen. Awe of Cook waned, and relations between the Hawaiians and the foreigners grew tense. A misunderstanding led to an altercation in which Cook was killed by angry natives, and thus ended the life of the first known European to visit Hawai'i. Cook's discovery opened the door for others to visit and influence the course of Hawaiian history.

The next major event in Hawaiian Island history began when Kamehameha I (c. 1758–1819) devised a plan to conquer all his rivals and unite all the Hawaiian Islands under his rule. Kamehameha was aided by British and American traders, who sold guns and ammunition to him. Armed with this modern weaponry, Kamehameha felt confident enough to begin his conquest. Setting sail from the island of Hawai'i with an armada of war canoes, he set out to conquer the islands of Maui, Moloka'i, and O'ahu. In 1810, after many bloody battles, he successfully united all the Hawaiian Islands under his rule.

During his lifetime King Kamehameha controlled Hawai'i's commerce with the outside world. His firm control of the islands of Hawai'i established a strong monarchy that ensured the kingdom's independence for nearly a hundred years.

*Kamehameha II. Courtesy of
Wikimedia Commons.*

To help prepare the kingdom for Christianity, King Kamehameha ended human sacrifice and was the last monarch to follow traditional Hawaiian religious practices and traditions. Kamehameha's son Liholiho, or Kamehameha II, however, would institute measures in his reign that would not only radically change many of Hawai'i's deeply entrenched traditions, but would also create an environment in which a new religion, Christianity, could take root.

One of the hallmarks of the native Hawaiian religion was the concept of *kapu*, the Hawaiian version of the term *taboo*, meaning "forbidden" or "set aside." Certain things in Hawaiian culture were *kapu* to certain groups of people on a permanent basis or at different times of the year. For instance, men and women eating together was *kapu*, as well as women eating certain foods, like pork or bananas; and catching certain types of fish at the wrong time of the year was *kapu*. Kamehameha I's favorite wife, Ka'ahumanu, who particularly opposed these traditional rules, used her position of considerable influence with the new king to see that they were done away with. Following the death of Kamehameha I in 1819, Liholiho, acting under the guidance of Ka'ahumanu, began abolishing the *kapu* system by publicly eating with women. Following the meal, Liholiho announced that all the *kapus* were abolished, and that all *heiau* (traditional temples) and god images should be destroyed throughout the kingdom. Although many of the *kapus*, practices, and traditions continued to be observed, the native religion was shaken by this edict of the king. This paved the way for the first Protestant missionaries, who arrived the following year.[9]

---

9 Tregaskis, *The Warrior King*, 304–6. See also Ralph S. Kuykendall, *The Hawaiian Kingdom, Volume 1, 1778–1854: Foundation and Transformation* (Honolulu: University of Hawai'i Press, 1938), 65–70.

In 1820, the first American Protestant missionaries arrived in Hawai'i aboard the ship *Thaddeus* from New England. Although Liholiho entertained those missionaries, he was not interested in their religion. However, his subjects *were* interested in the missionaries' message. The Protestants also taught reading and writing, and the Hawaiians responded enthusiastically to this education. Soon, the native Hawaiian population boasted a higher rate of literacy than the United States.[10]

The Protestant missionaries brought many Western ideas to Hawai'i, including the concept of privatized land ownership, Western economics, and Western ideas about politics. Some of these missionaries and their children worked as advisors in the king's government and influenced his ideas about the future of Hawai'i. In 1840, Kamehameha III established the first constitution; and in 1848 a law was passed that created the *mahele*, which allowed privatized land ownership for the first time in Hawaiian history. Before this, all lands were managed by the king as a stewardship from the gods. The intent of this measure was to put land into the hands of native Hawaiians and move Hawai'i into a more modern age. Much of the land nevertheless eventually ended up in the hands of non-Hawaiians as a succession of monarchs attempted to develop a governmental land tenure and economic system modeled after those of western nations.

The first Christian missionaries, who arrived in the spring of 1820 from New England, were "determined to Christianize [the] Heathen Hawaiians." This was at the same time that Joseph Smith experienced his First Vision. These Protestant missionaries opened the way for the arrival of Latter-day Saint missionaries in Hawai'i by introducing Christianity to the Hawaiian people. The Protestant missionary efforts produced a shift from chiefdoms to a constitutional monarchy in the Kingdom of Hawai'i, a literate society, and a growing Christian nation.[11] However, "the native Hawaiian population was being decimated by foreign diseases. As the native population decreased, Protestants and Catholics became well entrenched and very protective of their converts. This

10 Edward Joesting, *Kauai: The Separate Kingdom* (Honolulu: University of Hawai'i Press, 1984), 118, 126–27.
11 See also Britsch, *Moramona*, 10–12, for contributions of the Protestants.

was the condition of Hawai'i just before the first LDS missionaries arrived."[12]

In the meantime, foreign influences had become much stronger in Hawai'i. American and European missionaries, having gained a significant foothold in the islands, succeeded in converting many islanders to Christianity. They were extremely protective of their congregations, which proved to be a source of friction between these Protestant missionaries and the Mormon elders as well as the Catholic priests; nevertheless, the early work of these Congregationalists paved the way for the first Latter-day Saint missionaries.[13]

By 1850, Hawai'i had changed significantly. Whaling was at a peak, sandalwood harvesting was depleted, and the sugarcane industry was just getting started.[14] The land of many native Hawaiians who had fallen victim to diseases brought by foreigners let their land lay fallow, and many early LDS island converts died of smallpox during the early years of the establishment of the Church in Hawai'i. Early native Hawaiian Church members who died of disease were seen as opening up the gospel in the spirit world to their people. For example, in 1853, when a serious smallpox epidemic swept the Hawaiian Islands, a number of Latter-day Saint converts died. Elder Benjamin F. Johnson, heartbroken to see these new proselytes suffering, tried to make sense of why the Lord would cause them to be taken. He wrote, "I pondered the subject prayerfully until the light of the Lord shone upon my understanding, and I saw multitudes of their race in the spirit world who had lived before them, and there was not one there with the priesthood to teach them the gospel. The voice of the Spirit said to me, 'Sorrow not, for they are now doing that greater work for which

12 Edward Joesting, *Kauai: The Separate Kingdom* (Honolulu: University of Hawai'i Press, 1984), 118, 126–67.
13 On the conflict between the different Christian faiths, Guy M. Bishop, "Waging Holy War: Mormon-Congregationalist Conflict in Mid-Nineteenth Century Hawaii," *Journal of Mormon History* 17 (1991): 100–19; and William Kauaiwiulaokalani Wallace III, "The Church of Jesus Christ of Latter-day Saints in the Hawaiian Islands from 1850–1900; An Abridgement" (presentation, La'ie Hawai'i Stake, Laie, Hawaii, 2000). Transcription in authors' possession.
14 Robert K. Min, F. Karl Teshima, Jr., and Dwayne Y. Wada, *Stewards of the Promise: The Heritage of the Latter-day Saints on Hawaiian Islands of Maui, Molokai, and Lanai* (Kahului, Hawai'i Stake, 1995), 2.

they were ordained, and it is all of the Lord.'"[15]

Beginning in the 1850s, various interests in Hawai'i and Washington began lobbying for annexation of Hawai'i by the United States. This precipitated the overthrow of the monarchy in 1893, when the last reigning Hawaiian royal, Queen Lili'uokalani (1838–1917), proposed a new constitution that would restore powers to the monarch that had been lost. In response to the queen's proposal, a group of American businessmen sought to overthrow the monarchy. This

Queen Lili'uokalani. Courtesy of Wikimedia Commons.

group convinced the American minister in Hawaii, John L. Stevens, to land U.S. troops to support them in taking control of the government. Queen Lili'uokalani was deposed and the monarchy dissolved. On July 4, 1894, the Republic of Hawai'i was established, with Sanford B. Dole as president.[16]

Hawai'i was annexed to the United States on July 7, 1898, when Congress passed the Newlands Resolution. This was seen as part of America's expansionist agenda during the Spanish-American War.

At annexation, Hawai'i's economy was based on sugar. The large Hawaiian sugar plantations needed to import foreign agricultural laborers. These laborers, coming from places like China, Japan, Portugal, and later the Philippines, offset the declining population of Hawaiians and fueled the growing multiculturalism of the Islands.

---

15 See Benjamin F. Johnson, *My Life's Review* (Independence, MO: Zion's Printing and Publishing Co., 1947), 157–58.

16 W. D. Alexander, *A Brief History of the Hawaiian People* (New York, Cincinnati, Chicago: American Book Company, 1899), 319.

The biggest event in the history of the United States Territory of Hawai'i was the attack on Pearl Harbor on December 7, 1941, by the Japanese military, and the subsequent entry of the United States into World War II. Immediately after the Pearl Harbor attack, Hawaiian Governor John Poindexter declared martial law, which remained in force until October 24, 1944.

After World War II, proponents of Hawaiian statehood made great efforts for many years to convince residents of the Islands, as well as citizens of the United States, that Hawai'i should become a state.[17] Hawai'i was finally admitted as the 50th state on August 21, 1959, by a proclamation of U.S. President Dwight D. Eisenhower. The sugar industry in Hawai'i began to decline after statehood. Today the Hawaiian economy is based largely on tourism.[18]

Latter-day Saints in Hawai'i

In the spring of 1843, Joseph Smith called Addison Pratt on a mission. When he was younger, Pratt had been a sailor and had spent time in the Sandwich Islands. In addition to Pratt, three other Latter-day Saints—Benjamin F. Grouard, Noah Rogers, and Knowlton F. Hanks—were also assigned to take the restored gospel to the peoples of Oceania.[19]

The four LDS missionaries sought a ship in New Bedford, Massachusetts, bound for the Sandwich Islands;[20] however, the ship they boarded was a whaling ship, the *Timoleon*, bound for the Society Islands. Their voyage, which began on October 9, 1843, took them around the Cape of Good Hope. Just three weeks into the voyage, Elder Hanks died of consumption at sea. After six months of sailing, the other three missionaries arrived on the

---

17 Ralph S. Kuykendall and A. Grove Day, *Hawaii: A History* (New York: Prentice-Hall, 1948), 291.

18 For more information on Hawaiian history, see Gavan Daws, *Shoal of Time* (Honolulu: University of Hawaii, 1968), or Ralph Kuykendall, *The Hawaiian Kingdom*, vol. 1–3 (Honolulu: University of Hawaii, 1967).

19 R. Lanier Britsch, *Unto the Islands of the Sea: A History of the Latter-day Saints in the Pacific* (Salt Lake City: Deseret Book, 1986), 3.

20 This is evidenced in *Wilford Woodruff's Journals*, ed. Scott G. Kenney (Midvale, UT: Signature Books, 1983), 2:233, for the date May 23, 1843, wherein Elder Woodrufff notes, "we set apart Elders Noah Rogers, Addison Pratt, Benjamin F. Grouard & Knowlton Hanks to take a mission to the Sandwich Islands."

island of Tubuai, 350 miles south of Tahiti. Though the elders never made it to the Sandwich Islands, their journey to Tubuai marked the beginning of LDS missionary work in the Pacific Islands.[21]

In 1850, Brigham Young called another group of missionaries who would eventually bring the gospel to Hawai'i. Originally, these young men were sent to California as gold-mining missionaries. In the fall of 1850, Elder Charles C. Rich, a member of the Quorum of the Twelve, rode into a mining camp in California, arriving as "Brigham Young's personal representative to all Latter-day Saints in the Pacific Coast area."[22] Coming into the camp, Elder Rich decided to ask some of the Latter-day Saint miners to fill missions to the Sandwich Islands.

Brigham Young. Courtesy of BYU–Hawaii Archives.

Because of the gold rush, it was excessively expensive to stay in California. In fact, it was cheaper to have one's laundry sent to Hawai'i to be washed than it was to have it done locally. Miners also had difficulty working in the winter, so it seemed reasonable to send some of them to the Islands as missionaries during that season.[23] In mid-October 1850. Elder Rich selected and set apart ten men to fill missions in Hawai'i: Henry William Bigler, George Q. Cannon, John Dixon, William Farrer, James Hawkins, James

21 Fred E. Woods, "The Mormon Voyage of the Whaleship Timoleon: Launching Latter-day Saint Missionary Work in the Pacific," *The Log of Mystic Seaport*, Spring 2005, 12–21; see also Fred E. Woods, "Launching Mormonism in the South Pacific: The Voyage of the *Timoleon*," in *Go Ye into All the World: The Growth and Development of Missionary Work*, ed. Reid L. Neilson and Fred E. Woods (Provo, UT: Religious Studies Center; Salt Lake City: Deseret Book, 2012), 191–216 and S. George Ellsworth, ed., *The Journals of Addison Pratt* (University of Utah Press: Salt Lake City, 1990) for the complete story of this early mission among the islanders of the South Pacific.

22 R. Lanier Britsch, *Moramona: The Mormons in Hawai'i* (Laie, HI: The Institute for Polynesian Studies, 1989), 3.

23 Ibid., 3.

Keeler, Thomas Morris, Thomas Whittle, Hiram H. Blackwell, and Hiram Clark, who was appointed president.[24] In early November all of the missionaries except for Hiram Clark traveled from Sacramento to San Francisco, where they boarded the *Imaum of Muscat*. While on the voyage, George Q. Cannon reported having a dream that would greatly affect his future service in Hawai'i:

> I dreamed one night that this party of brethren were heaving at the windlass, having a rope attached to it reaching forward to the anchor at the bow of the vessel. We were working with all of our might endeavoring to raise the anchor, but seemingly we made little progress. While thus engaged I thought the Prophet Joseph came from the after part of the vessel dressed in his temple clothes, and tapping me on the shoulder told me to go with him. I went, and he climbed on to the forecastle and there he knelt down, also telling me to kneel down with him. He prayed according to the order of prayer which is revealed. After prayer, he arose upon his feet. "Now," said he, "George, take hold of that rope"—the rope we had been pulling with all of our might. I took hold of it, and with the greatest ease and without the least effort, the anchor was raised. "Now," said he, "let this be a lesson to you; remember that great things can be accomplished through the power of prayer and the exercise of faith in the right way."[25]

After nearly a month at sea, on December 12, 1850, the missionaries landed at Honolulu, the first Latter-day Saint missionaries to visit Hawai'i.[26]

Some of the first conversions to the Latter-day Saint Church took place on the island of Maui, where the first branch was organized in the Kula District, near Pulehu, on August 6, 1851. Membership grew quickly, and by the end of 1854 there were more than four thousand Hawaiian converts in fifty-three branches, meeting in several small Latter-day Saint schoolhouses and meetinghouses. The Book of Mormon was translated into the Hawaiian language

---

24 Marba C. Josephson, "A Glance at Hawaiian Mission History," *Improvement Era*, 53 (August 1950), 619.
25 George Q. Cannon, in *Journal of Discourses* (Liverpool, England: Albert Carrington, 1882), XXII, 289.
26 Britsch, *Moramona*, 4.

by Elder Cannon and early convert Jonathan H. Napela and published in Hawaiian in 1855.[27]

Many missionaries served in Hawai'i after the initial introduction of the gospel in 1850. Most notable among these early missionaries was future Church President Joseph F. Smith, who at the age of fifteen began a mission in the Sandwich Islands in 1854, serving until 1857.

In 1854, Latter-day Saints in Hawai'i attempted to gather to a local Zion, called the City of Joseph, on the island of Lana'i. This City of Joseph failed, at least in part because of environmental conditions, which included great difficulty in raising crops. In addition, with the removal of the most devoted Hawaiian Saints to Lana'i, branches on other islands were weakened, and the membership of the Church declined in Hawai'i. In the words of Latter-day Saint historian Richard Bennett, "there was more plucking than planting." This trend of decline became even more severe when missionary leaders were called back to Utah in 1858 because of the Utah War.[28]

The leadership vacuum left by the departure of mission leaders opened the way for the adventurer and supposed missionary Walter Murray Gibson to assume leadership over the Church in Lana'i and elsewhere. He used the organization of the Church in Hawai'i as his personal political kingdom from September 1861 to April 1864. During these years, Gibson introduced many false doctrines into the Church in Hawai'i, and he even sold priesthood offices to local members.[29]

---

27 For more information on the life of Jonathan H. Napela, see Fred E. Woods, "A Most Influential Mormon Islander: Jonathan Hawai'i Napela," *The Hawaiian Journal of History* 42 (2008): 135–57; Fred E. Woods, "An Islander's View of a Desert Kingdom: Jonathan Napela Recounts his 1869 Visit to Salt Lake City," *BYU Studies* 45, no. 1 (2006): 23–34; Fred E. Woods, "Jonathan Napela: A Noble Hawaiian Convert," *Regional Studies in Latter-day Saint Church History: The Pacific Isles*, ed. Reid L. Neilson et al. (Provo, UT: Religious Studies Center, 2008): 23–36.

28 The Utah War was a dispute between the Mormons in Utah Territory and the U.S. government, which was misled into believing the Mormons were in rebellion against U.S. authority.

29 Fred E. Woods, "The Palawai Pioneers of the Island of Lanai: The First Hawaiian Latter-day Saint Gathering Place (1854–1864), *Mormon Historical Studies* 5, no. 2 (Fall 2004): 3–35.

In the spring of 1864, Brigham Young sent Ezra T. Benson and Lorenzo Snow, with former missionaries Joseph F. Smith, Alma Smith, and W. W. Cluff as translators, on a mission to Hawai'i to straighten out the problems created by Gibson.[30]

Once in Hawai'i, the group visited Gibson on Lana'i, and he was excommunicated from the Church on April 7, 1864.[31] Joseph F. Smith was then left in charge of reorganizing the mission, since membership had fallen to about four hundred, while the other elders returned to Utah. Joseph F. Smith followed his companions home in the fall of 1864.

Shortly thereafter, President Brigham Young sent Francis Asbury Hammond and George Nebeker to Hawai'i to buy property for a new gathering place. They looked at properties at Kealia on Kaua'i, Hana on Maui, and Papa'ikou on Hawai'i, but settled on La'ie. On January 26, 1865, the Church purchased a 6,500-acre plantation at La'ie on O'ahu for $14,000.[32] La'ie then became the focal point of Church activities in Hawai'i, though strong congregations also developed in Honolulu and in other areas. Throughout his career in Church leadership, Joseph F. Smith kept his relationship to Hawai'i close to his heart. On June 1, 1915, he dedicated a site in La'ie for a temple in Hawai'i. Four and a half years later, on November 27, 1919, his successor, President Heber J. Grant, dedicated the first LDS temple outside the North American continent in La'ie.

Many small branches were organized every five or ten miles around the islands to accomodate the membership. There were

---

30 Britsch, *Moramona*, 56–57.

31 Ralph S. Kuykendall, *The Hawaiian Kingdom, 1854–1874* (Honolulu: University of Hawai'i Press, 1953), 104.

32 On February 21, 1865, Francis Hammond sent a telegraph to President Brigham Young from San Francisco, stating among other things the following: "Six thousand five hundred 6500 acres fourteen thousand 14000 dollars entire cost bought of T. L. Dougherty land with improvements six hundred 600 head of cattle. Five hundred 500 sheep twenty 20 horses two hundred and fifty 250 native houses furnished all inside of a stone enclosure of four 4 acres. Five 5 acres of cotton doing well situated on the weather side of Oahu names of Land Laie—Seventy 70 Natives belonging to the church now living on the land five thousand 5000 dollars to be paid in ten 10 weeks from the eighteenth 18 of January three thousand 3000 by July six thousand 6000 in 2 years." See Brigham Young incoming correspondence, February 21, 1865, telegraph by Francis Hammond to Brigham Young Church History Library, The Church of Jesus Christ of Latter-day Saints, Salt Lake City.

some eighty or more branches in the Hawaiian Islands. Mission President Samuel E. Woolley reported in 1915 that of the eighty-odd branches at that time, fifty-two had their own chapels, mostly on deeded land.[33] At first the edifices were usually *pili* grass thatch huts, sometimes with rock walls, often evolving into wood-frame buildings, located generally in rutal areas where native Hawaiians lived. Many were in areas that had been set aside as homestead lands for Hawaiians from the 1890s to 1920s, particularly as part of the Hawaiian Homes Act of 1921, sponsored by Hawai'i's delegate to Congress Prince Jonah Kuhio Kalanianaole, who used La'ie as a model of a successful Hawaiian community. As transportation and economics improved after World War II, they were consolidated into larger branches, and later into wards.[34] Beginning in about 1960 under Mission President Harry V. Brooks, these small rural branches were consolidated, and concrete block chapels were built, often by the labor missionary program, which are still in use today.[35]

President Grant organized the Oahu Stake on June 30, 1935, with Ralph E. Woolley as president. Two years later, President Grant formed the Japanese Mission in Hawai'i, with Hilton A. Robertson as mission president; this mission's name was changed to the Central Pacific Mission in 1942 because of World War II. By 1950, when the Central Pacific Mission was combined with the Hawaiian Mission as missionary work was reestablished in Japan (1948), missionaries in the Japanese/Central Pacific Mission had baptized 671 Americans of Japanese ancestry into the Church. Many of these early converts and their children have held import-ant church positions. Adney Y. Komatsu was the first of that group to be called as a General Authority in 1975, and Hawaiian-born Chieko Okazaki was called as first counselor in the General

---

33 Andrew Jenson, Manuscript History of the Hawaiian Mission of The Church of Jesus Christ of Latter-day Saints, 6 volumes, typescript, Church History Library, April 4, 1915, n.p. (hereafter cited as Manuscript History).
34 See appendices A, B, C, and D.
35 See David W. Cummings, *Mighty Missionary of the Pacific: The Building Program of the Church of Jesus Christ of Latter-day Saints, Its Scope, and Significance* (Salt Lake City: Bookcraft, 1961); and Alice C. Pack, *Building Missionaries in Hawaii, 1960–1963* (Laie: Church College of Hawaii, 1963); Adele F. Feinga, "Labor Missions in Tonga and Hawaii," in *Pioneers of the Pacific*, ed. Grant Underwood (Provo, UT: Religious Studies Center, 2005).

Relief Society presidency in 1990.[36] However, until World War II, the Latter-day Saint Church in Hawai'i was viewed by the rest of Hawai'i as a Hawaiian church. Before the organizing of the Central Pacific Mission, proselytizing was limited largely to the Hawaiian community.[37] Missionaries needed to know the Hawaiian language, and church services were often conducted in Hawaiian, expecially in rural areas, up until the 1950s.

It was also important that the Church establish education in the Islands. In September 1955, the Church College of Hawai'i was founded under the direction of President David O. McKay. Initially a junior college, it was made a four-year school in 1959, and was renamed Brigham Young University–Hawai'i Campus in 1974.[38] In conjunction with the Church College of Hawaii, the Church founded the Polynesian Cultural Center (PCC) in La'ie, in October 1963. The purpose of the PCC is to preserve and present the cultures of Polynesia and to provide employment for the students of BYU–Hawaii. The PCC has become Hawai'i's number-one paid tourist attraction.[39]

The Church of Jesus Christ of Latter-day Saints continued to flourish and grow throughout the twentieth century in the Hawaiian Islands. These Latter-day Saints comprise native Hawaiians and many other ethnicities and nationalities, some 5.3 percent of Hawaii's population.[40] The *Church Almanac (2016)* for 2013 reported over 70,000 members in fifteen stakes. Today there are sixteen stakes, and The Church of Jesus Christ of Latter-day Saints is the second largest denomination in Hawai'i.[41]

---

36 Britsch, *Unto the Islands*, 167–70, 172.

37 In 1924, Elder Richard Lyman of the Quorum of the Twelve, in Hawai'i to dedicate the Kalihi chapel, estimated that 12,000 of the 13,000 members in Hawai'iwere Hawaiians, which constituted one-third of the 36,000 Hawaiians then living in the islands.

38 Alf Pratte and Eric B. Shumway, *BYU–Hawaii, Prophetic Destiny: The First 60 Years* (Laie: BYU–Hawaii, 2015).

39 Ibid., 182–84, 186–88. For a historical overview of the history of BYU–Hawaii as well as a concise history of the Polynesian Cultural Center, see Laura F. Willes, *Miracle in the Pacific: The Polynesian Cultural Center* (Salt Lake City: Deseret Book, 2012).

40 "Largest Latter-day Saint Communities (Mormon/Church of Jesus Christ Statistics)," April 12, 2005, http://www.adherents.com/largecom/com_lds.html.

41 *2013 Deseret News Church Almanac* (Salt Lake City: Deseret News, 2012), 349.

Oʻahu

Oʻahu, nicknamed the "Gathering Place," is the third largest of the Hawaiian Islands (604 square miles) and the most populous island in the State of Hawaii, with about one million residents. The island was created by two separate shield volcanoes: Waiʻanae and Koʻolau, which have eroded into parallel mountain ranges, with a broad "valley" or saddle between them.

Oʻahu was the first island sighted by Captain Cook on January 18, 1778, but was not visited until February 28, 1779, when Captain Clerke, assuming command after Captain Cook was killed, stopped briefly at Waimea Bay on Oʻahu's north shore. In 1795, Kamehameha I invaded Oʻahu and defeated the king of Oʻahu, Kalanikupule, at the Battle of Nuʻuanu and made his seat of government first at Waikiki and later Honolulu.

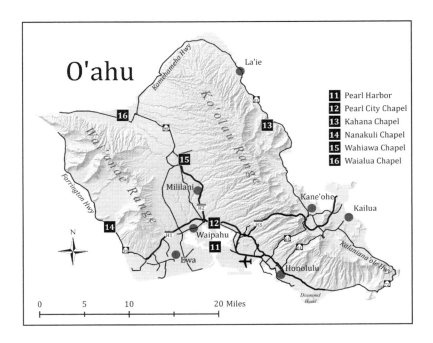

Honolulu

Honolulu grew up around a small basin hidden behind the reef that was not particularly important in precontact Hawai'i, but it became the best anchorage for foreign sailing ships. Its importance increased after Europeans arrived in 1793. By 1809, Kamehameha I moved his seat of government there for a few years. In 1845, Kamehameha III moved the permanent capital of the Hawaiian Kingdom from Lahaina, Maui, to Honolulu.[1] He and the kings that followed him transformed Honolulu into a modern capital, and it became the center of commerce in the Islands.

Most of the city's commercial and industrial developments are located on a narrow but relatively flat coastal plain, while numerous ridges and valleys located inland of the coastal plain divide Honolulu's residential areas into distinct neighborhoods: some spread along valley floors (for example, Manoa, Nu'uanu, or Kalihi), while others climb the elevated ridges. Within Honolulu

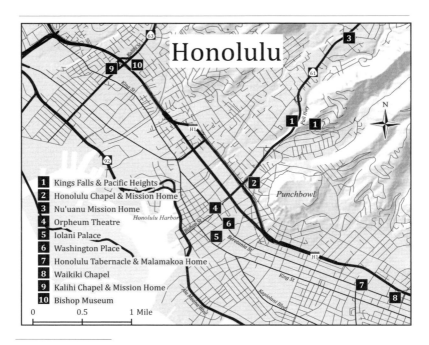

1 Kings Falls & Pacific Heights
2 Honolulu Chapel & Mission Home
3 Nu'uanu Mission Home
4 Orpheum Theatre
5 Iolani Palace
6 Washington Place
7 Honolulu Tabernacle & Malamakoa Home
8 Waikiki Chapel
9 Kalihi Chapel & Mission Home
10 Bishop Museum

0   0.5   1 Mile

---

1 Ruth M. Tabrah, *Hawaii: A Bicentennial History* (New York: Norton, 1980), 57. For more information on the early history of Honolulu, see Gavan Daws, *Honolulu: The First Century, the Story of the Town to 1876* (Honolulu: Mutual Publishing, 2006).

proper can be found several volcanic cones, including Diamond Head (Le'ahi) and Punchbowl (Puowaina).[2]

While Honolulu grew up around the little protected harbor as the commercial and political capital of Hawai'i, the tourism industry grew up around Waikiki Beach a few miles down the coast toward Diamond Head. In precontact Hawai'i, Waikiki was probably the most desirable location on O'ahu, with its sunny beaches backed by numerous taro patches.[3]

Latter-day Saint Historic Sites in Honolulu

1. King's Falls/Kapena Falls

The modern neighborhood of Pacific Heights above Nu'uanu Valley on O'ahu is the site where the first ten Latter-day Saint missionaries offered a dedicatory prayer on December 13, 1850.[4] They walked up Nu'uanu Valley to King's Falls (now known as Kapena Falls), where the elders bathed (their first real bath in a month), then hiked to the top of a nearby hill over-looking Honolulu. William Farrer describes what happened:

> We . . . went onto a mountain about three miles from the wharve and about 1,000 feet above the level of the sea; there on a small round knoll that rose that rose several feet above the rest of the land around, and was about four or five rods across with a smooth flat surface: there each of us carried a stone and all built an alter; we then sung a Hymn and each one then expressed his feelings and desires in regard to

Kapena Falls. Courtesy of BYU–Hawaii Archives.

2 Jeanette Foster, *Frommer's Hawai'i 2007* (Hoboken, NJ: Wiley Publishing, Inc., 2007), 98–99.

3 See Gary L. Fitzpatrick and Riley M. Moffat, *The Early Mapping of Hawai'i* (Honolulu: Editions Limited, 1986).

4 Britsch, *Moramona*, 4.

the mission we are now on. Bro Clark then offered up a prayer unto the Lord that he would open the way that we might be enabled to preach the gospel on these Islands.[5]

In that secluded place about five hundred feet above King's Falls, in what is now called Pacific Heights, they built a stone altar about three feet high and three feet around. In the prayer, President Hiram Clark dedicated Hawai'i for the preaching of the gospel. Clark asked "the Lord to open the way that they might be enabled to preach the Gospel on these islands, . . . have his spirit . . . to guide us, . . . preserve us from the adversary and from every evil, and that the honest in heart might embrace the truth."[6]

At sunset, the missionaries descended the hill. George Q. Cannon reported that their descent was quick and joyful, "and when men are joyful and the Spirit of the Lord rests upon them, they feel lithe and active. We had been in the prescience [*sic*] of the Lord, and had felt his power, and why should we not be happy?"[7] The missionaries then chose companions. Latter-day Saint historian R. Lanier Britsch explained:

> The missionaries assumed that they had been sent to the islands to preach the gospel only to white people; but surveying the situation later in the day they realized that very few whites were available for proselyting. Since there was obviously not enough work to be done among the *haoles* (whites) in and around Honolulu, the missionaries decided to divide into pairs and go to other islands to preach. It was decided that Blackwell and Hawkins would go to the "Big Island," Hawaii; Cannon, Keeler, and Bigler to Maui; Dixon and Farrer to Kauai; and that Clark, Morris, and Whittle would remain in Honolulu. President Clark, concerned about the safety of the elders, visited British Consul General William Miller, who told him the laws of the Kingdom would provide protection for the new missionary force. With this assurance they set sail to other islands of the chain. Thus

---

5 William Farrer, *Biographical Sketch, Hawaiian Mission Report and Diary, 1821–1906*, December 13, 1850, typescript, 45, L. Tom Perry Special Collections, Harold B. Lee Library, Brigham Young University, Provo, Utah.

6 Ibid.

7 George Q. Cannon, *My First Mission*, 17.

began the dissemination of the message of Mormonism among the people of the Sandwich Islands.[8]

Across Nu'uanu Street is the Oahu Cemetery, where Walter Murray Gibson's remains lie in the crypt of his son-in-law, Fred Hayselden, in the Old Columbarium section, lot 36.

Directions to the King's Falls or Kapena Falls:

From downtown Honolulu go up Nuuanu Avenue to Nuuanu Memorial Park at 2233 Nu'uanu Avenue. In the upper righthand corner of the cemetery you will find some mainte- nance buildings. Walk past those buildings, heading up the left bank of the Nu'uanu Stream. A good trail leads a couple of hundred yards up toward the falls. The location of the altar is somewhere on the ridge on the right in an area called Pacific Heights. Even George Q. Cannon could not identify its exact location when he returned for the Hawai'i Mission's Golden Jubilee in 1900.[9]

2. Honolulu Chapel and Old Mission Home

The first Honolulu Mis- sion Home, from 1879 to 1921, was on Lusitana Street. This bungalow-style mission home was home to the American elders assigned to the Hono- lulu-Waikiki area. Before the construction of the mission home, elders staying in Hono- lulu "had been obliged to put up with native Saints, some of

Honolulu Mission Home, 1899. Courtesy BYU–Hawaii Archives.

whom lived in places and in shacks not suited to the dignity of the visiting Elders."[10] Elder Henry P. Richards records that missionar- ies and members built the house next to the chapel in early 1879. An iconic LDS chapel was built next door in 1888, probably on the site of the earlier chapel, and was locally known as the "one-eyed"

8 Britsch, *Moramona*, 5.
9 George Q. Cannon, "Excerpts from the Journal of George Q. Cannon." *Improvement Era* v. 53 no. 8 (August 1950).
10 Jenson, Manuscript History, December 19, 1878.

church. It was the second largest Latter-day Saint building constructed on the island of O'ahu (the first was in La'ie). Missionaries in the 1870s, such as Henry P. Richards, mention that Queen Kapiolani would attend church often enough that the front right bench was called the "Queen's bench." Elder Matthew Noall, later mission president, was the head builder. The building was dedicated on April 27, 1888, with King Kalakaua and Queen Kapiolani in attendance. Queen Lili'uokalani would also occasionally attend branch and district conferences there.

Honolulu Chapel. Courtesy of BYU–Hawaii Archives.

It was not as large as the La'ie chapel (the Honolulu chapel seated two hundred), but it was a credit to the Church in that it provided a symbol of permanence for Church members on O'ahu. "The Honolulu branch, with its 891 members, was probably the largest branch of the Church west of the Rockies at that time."[11] The one-eyed church on Lusitana Street was later replaced as the main Honolulu chapel by the stone church in Kalihi.

Directions to the old Honolulu Chapel and Mission Home site:

Going up the Pali Highway (61) from downtown Honolulu, pass under the freeway one block and take the first right onto Kuakini Street. Proceed one block and turn right again on Lusitana Street to 1660, which is at the intersection of Lusitana and Puowaina Drive. This is the site of the 1888 Honolulu chapel; the 1879 mission home was on the south, or *makai,* side of the chapel. Going back up Lusitana Street about ½ mile you cross Pauoa Stream and see the current Awaiolimu Chapel on the right, built about 1952.

---

11 Britsch, *Moramona*, 98.

Nu'uanu Mission Home. Courtesy of BYU–Hawaii Archives.

3. Honolulu Mission Home

When D. Arthur Haycock became president of the Hawai'i Mission in 1954 he found the Malamakoa mission home to be termite eaten beyond repair (mentioned later), so he arranged with Ralph E. Woolley the purchase of a fine Tudor mansion on the Pali Highway in one of Honolulu's best neighborhoods. The move was made during the week of October 8, 1956. This large home still exists, even though the mission offices have been moved to the Church's office building next to the Honolulu Tabernacle.[12] The home is now the Queen Emma Preschool.

Directions to Honolulu Mission Home:
Going up the Pali Highway (61) from downtown Honolulu, go one block past the Queen Emma Summer Palace to the corner of Dowsett Avenue. The former mission home is on the right at 3019 Pali Highway.

4. Orpheum Theatre

The Church of Jesus Christ of Latter-day Saints held its Golden Jubilee Celebration at the new Orpheum Theatre on December 12, 1900. The planning "committee hoped that President George Q. Cannon, First Counselor in the First Presidency and the real leader of the first missionaries, would be able to attend." On December

---

12 D. Arthur Haycock, interview with Ken Baldridge, April 14, 1989, CR 329-7, transcription, Church History Library.

10, 1900, President Cannon, arrived in Hawai'i, accompanied by some of his family, much to the delight of the committee. President Cannon spoke at each of the six sessions held in the Orpheum Theatre. At first "he was able to speak a few words in Hawaiian, a language he had not used for forty-six years."[13] He was amazed, however, that by the end of the Jubilee he could speak for hours in Hawaiian.

> The language, also through the favor of the Lord, came to me in a manner to surprise me. When I was called upon this morning to speak, I did so principally in English and spoke with great power. The Spirit rested powerfully upon me but while speaking in English, the Spirit of the Lord would bring the native language back to me and I would break out in it to the surprise of myself and the delight of the people, for it was a great cause of wonder to them that I should be able to speak in the language at all after so long an absence from the Islands.[14]

The next four days were a whirlwind of meetings and receptions. Many of these anniversary activities were attended by former Queen Lili'uokalani.

Speeches, music, feasts, and receptions were held in the theatre, and George Q. Cannon gave many blessings to LDS members there. On Sunday, December 23, he spoke to the Saints at La'ie concerning the blessings the Lord still held in store for them. Mission President Samuel E. Woolley wrote, "He said if they would be faithful enough that the time would come when some would be given the power to seal husband and wife for time and eternity so that their children would be born under the New and Everlasting Covenant."[15] President Cannon discussed the same subject a week later in Honolulu. Taken together, these expressions later gave rise to the tradition that President Cannon had prophesied that a temple would be built in Hawai'i.[16] The Orpheum Theater, built in 1898, became in 1906 the first moving picture theater in Honolulu but burned down in April 1910.

---

13 Britsch, *Moramona*, 114.
14 Cannon, *My First Mission*, December 12, 1900.
15 Samuel E. Woolley, Journal, December 23, 1900, Church History Library.
16 Ibid.

Directions to Orpheum Theatre Site:

The site of the Orpheum Theater is 1234 Fort Street, just *mauka,* or mountain side, of Beretania Street on the right. It is now the parking structure for the Kukui Plaza apartment building.

5. Iolani Palace

Iolani Palace was the official residence of the Hawaiian Kingdom's last two monarchs— King Kalakaua and his successor and sister Queen Lili'uokalani.

Iolani Palace, 1887, with King Kalakaua and Queen Kapiolani. Courtesy of BYU–Hawaii Archives.

In 1882, after a round-the-world tour, King Kalakaua replaced an earlier royal residence, a wooden bungalow built in 1846 and named Hale Ali'i, with the magnificent stone Iolani Palace seen today as befitting a modern monarch.[17] It boasted electric lighting years before electricity came to the the U.S. president's residence, the White House.

King Kalakaua was known as a friend to the Latter-day Saints. On April 6, 1882, when the cornerstone of the I Hemolele (translated "Holiness to the Lord") chapel was laid in La'ie, King Kalakaua attended the ceremony and donated $100 to the project. Later, on October 6, 1882, when the chapel was dedicated, the king once again attended and was impressed with the large structure.[18] Britsch tells us that

> Kalakaua and his wife, Kapiolani, visited [The Church of Jesus Christ of Latter-day Saints in] Laie on many occasions. They made most of their visits as private citizens. Kapiolani attended Relief Society occasionally and was apparently pleased with

17 Walter F. Judd, *Palaces and Forts of the Hawaiian Kingdom* (Palo Alto, CA: Pacific Books, 1975), 66–95.
18 Britsch, *Moramona*, 91–92.

what she saw and heard; in fact, a government-sponsored "Female Relief Society" (the Hawaiian name is "Hui Hoola Lahui") was founded by the king and queen in an effort to assist the kingdom's poor.[19]

The reign of Kalakaua's successor, Lili'uokalani, was brief, lasting just over two years. The overthrow of January 17, 1893, brought an end to her reign and an end to the Hawaiian Kingdom. Lili'uokalani was well educated, a devoted Christian, and a strong leader.[20] Her motto was "Hawai'i for the Hawaiians," and her attempts to return power to the hands of native Hawaiians did not sit well with the white foreigners, who largely controlled the Kingdom.[21]

On many occasions Lili'uokalani visited Relief Society meetings in Honolulu and in La'ie. The Queen also requested that weekly Sunday LDS services be held at the Iolani Palace on March 13, 1892. After this, LDS services were regularly held in the Palace until the Queen was deposed. Lili'uokalani was a close friend of Libby Noall, wife of Mission President Matthew Noall, and sought her advice on a number of occasions. Another close associate was her cousin Minerva Fernandez, wife of Abraham Fernandez.

During the monarchy period, the palace was the center of social and political activity in the Kingdom of Hawai'i. Hawaiian historian Helena Allen records that

19 According to LDS Pacific historian Ken Baldridge, there are twenty-five known contacts between Kalakaua and the Mormons during his reign (1874–1891). Most of these contacts occurred when LDS Church leaders visited the Iolani Palace. See "The Monarchs and the Mormons: Kalakakua and the Latter-day Saints," Kalakaua, box 13 of the Ken Baldridge Oral History Collection, BYU–Hawaii Archives. Further, on October 31, 1888, the Noall couple visited the "Blue Room" in the Iolani Palace, where they met the king and queen, the queen's sister and Mrs. Dominis. Libbie wrote, "They were very social, more so than I expected, inquiring after affairs in Utah, how our temples were progressing, etc., which gave a favorable opportunity for a few words concerning the principles of our belief which Matthew gave. . . . He spoke for about 20 minutes. After our leave-taking we were kindly invited by the Treasurer [John Dominis] to call again and he would show us through the entire building." See "The Life and Missionary Journals of Matthew Noall, 1864–1950 and his wife Elizabeth DeEtte Laker," comp. Helen R. Gardner and Alice Gardner.
20 Ralph S. Kuykendall and A. Grove Day, *Hawaii: A History*, 174.
21 Tabrah, *Hawaii: A Bicentennial History*, 99.

Liliuokalani was baptized into the Church of Jesus Christ of Latter-day Saints in 1906. Her friend, Abraham Fernandez, performed the ordinance. At the time Fernandez was a counselor in the mission presidency and a convert of 10 years. She did not become an active member, however, and Mormonism never became her exclusive religion. Liliuokalani appreciated and affiliated with several different churches. It is likely that she included Mormonism in her religious life not only because of its affinity with old Hawaiian ways and because of her friendship with Mormons such as Libby Noall and Abraham Fernandez, but also because she, like many Hawaiians, deeply resented the role played by the sons of Protestant missionaries, the so-called "mission boys" in the revolutions of 1887 and 1893. It is possible that she sought company with a people and a church that were not so closely associated with her downfall.[22]

In 1896, she was released from house arrest at Iolani Palace and returned to her home at Washington Place, where she lived for the next two decades.[23] Queen Lili'uokalani wrote the song "Aloha Oe,"[24] which is widely known and loved, the symbol of Hawai'i for many. It has often been mistaken as Hawai'i's state song.[25] The former queen, beloved by the native Hawaiians, died in 1917.[26]

The Palace is open to the public for tours Mondays through Saturday from 9:00 a.m. to 4:00 p.m. and also for special community events. There is a charge for admission, and guided tours require a reservation. For more information, call 808-522-0832.[27]

Directions to Iolani Palace:

Iolani Palace is located at 364 South King Street between Punchbowl Street and Richards Street, *makai,* or toward the ocean, from the State Capitol.

---

22 Helena G. Allen, *The Betrayal of Liliuokalani, the Last Queen of Hawaii, 1838–1917* (Glendale, CA: Arthur H. Clark Company, 1982), 388; and Gavan Daws, *Shoal of Time: A History of the Hawaiian Islands* (Honolulu: University of Hawai'i Press, 1968), 291–92.

23 Edward Joesting, *Hawaii: An Uncommon History* (New York: W. W. Norton & Co, 1972), 244.

24 See appendix C.

25 Clifford Gessler, *Hawaii: Isles of Enchantment* (London: D. Appleton-Century Company, 1938), 108–9.

26 Ibid., 112.

27 Ibid., 234–35.

6. Washington Place

Named in honor of the first president of the United States, Washington Place was built by John Dominis in 1846. His son, John Owen Dominis, married Lydia K. P. Kapaʻakea (who later became Queen

Washington Place. Courtesy of BYU–Hawaii Archives.

Liliʻuokalani). Washington Place became the place of rendezvous for all who defended the monarchy and sought the restoration of the Kingdom's sovereignty. Washington Place is the oldest building in Honolulu that has been used continuously as a dwelling place. The queen, a baptized member of Latter-day Saint Church, made her home at Washington Place after her overthrow until her death in 1917. Washington Place is now the governor's official residence. Queen Liliʻuokalani's inscribed Book of Mormon, kept on her nightstand, can be viewed here.

During the Hawaiʻi Mission's golden anniversary celebrations, President George Q. Cannon records that on December 17, 1900:

> The ex-queen Liliuokalani sent me word that she would like to see me at one o'clock today as she expects to sail for Hilo. Sister Fernandez took me to the ex-queen's residence in her carriage. She welcomed me very cordially and expressed the pleasure it gave her at seeing me. She also dwelt on the good my visit had done and would do, how the people's feeling had been aroused and their love awakened and strengthened by my visit. Many more remarks of this character were made by her and when I arose to bid her goodbye, she said she would like me to give her a blessing, then she led the way to another room. Before I was aware of what she was doing she was on her knees before my feet to receive the blessing. I felt very free in blessing her and the Spirit rested upon us both.[28]

Tours may be arranged by appointment. Enter from Punchbowl Street. Phone 808-586-0240.

---

28 George Q. Cannon, "Excerpts from the Journal of George Q. Cannon." *Improvement Era,* vol. 53, no. 8 (August 1950).

Directions to Washington Place:
Washington Place is located at 320 South Beretania Street, Honolulu, across the street from the State Capitol.

7. Honolulu Tabernacle and the Malamakoa Home

When the Oahu Stake was organized in 1935, President Ralph Woolley and Mission President Castle Murphy felt the Church needed to be more visible. They proposed building a new stake center, or tabernacle. Good land was expensive in Honolulu, but Woolley, one of Honolulu's leading builders, found a good location and negotiated a sale far below mar-

Honolulu Tabernacle. Courtesy of BYU–Hawaii Archives.

ket value. Ground was broken on March 16, 1940, with Elders LeGrand Richards and Charles A. Callis in attendance. In a letter written by Elder Callis to his children he speaks of a stake conference held in conjunction with the groundbreaking as

Malamakoa Mission Home. Courtesy of BYU–Hawaii Archives.

follows: "The Oahu Stake Conference, held in Honolulu was the largest it was stated, of any conference ever held here. . . . Before we entered to the meeting, . . . the people placed leis, or wreathes of flowers, around our necks."[29]

29 Charles A. Callis Collection, April 9, 1940, MSS 22, box 1, folder 3, Church History Library, Salt Lake City.

This was the last tabernacle the Church ever built. Nothing similar in size or appearance had been constructed by the Church in Hawai'i before. Fundraisers, including *hukilaus* and Hawai'i's largest carnival, owned by Church member E. K. Fernandez and held at the jobsite, helped pay for it. In 1941, the Honolulu Tabernacle was impressive. It remains a beautiful architectural attraction. "The Tabernacle on Beretania Street," as it is generally referred to, did much to enhance the image of the Church both among Latter-day Saints and members of other faiths alike. It has often mistakenly been called a *temple* by visitors to the Islands.

Architects for the Tabernacle were Hyrum Pope and Harold Burton, the same men who designed the temple in La'ie. Ralph E. Woolley, the contractor, had supervised construction of the Laie Temple over twenty years before. The cost of the building was approximately $250,000, more than $60,000 of which was raised by the Hawaiian Saints.[30]

Of particular note is the mosaic mural of Christ above the front door of the Tabernacle. During the construction of the Tabernacle, its builder, Ralph Woolley, was sailing to California when he met on board the ship an artist named Eugene Savage, an art professor at Yale University, famous for his murals and paintings of Hawaiians. Professor Savage mentioned to President Woolley that he always hoped to have an opportunity to have Christ as a subject. It was then that President Woolley commissioned Savage to make a nineteen-foot-high glass tile mosaic of 100,000 pieces. Savage was so honored that he declined payment. This mosaic is unique among LDS buildings and remains a community landmark. It was not completed at the time of the dedication but was unveiled on March 1, 1942.

President David O. McKay, first counselor in the First Presidency, dedicated the Honolulu Tabernacle on August 17, 1941.[31] In the dedicatory prayer, President McKay blessed the tabernacle that it would not suffer any war-related damage. A few errant shells fell

---

30 Comfort Margaret Bock, *The Church of Jesus Christ of Latter-day Saints in the Hawaiian Islands* (Honolulu: University of Hawaii, 1941), 91; also Matthew O. Richardson, "The Last Tabernacle: A Refuge on Oahu," in *Regional Studies in Latter-day Saint Church History: The Pacific Isles*, 55–74.

31 Richard C. Harvey, *The Development of The Church of Jesus Christ of Latter-day Saints in Hawai'i* (Provo, UT: Brigham Young University, 1974), 77.

in Honolulu during the attack on Pearl Harbor, but nothing of any significance. There was, however, concern that the steeple, one of the highest points in Honolulu, would be used as a landmark or target.

World War II brought hundreds of Latter-day Saint servicemen and women to the Islands. A large home located on a lot adjoining the tabernacle became a recreation and rest center for these service people and their friends. This property had been purchased at the same time as the Tabernacle site, and at least one of its uses had been as a welfare cannery. On September 10, 1944, it was officially opened to hosting visiting military. This home was named *Malamakoa*, meaning "take care of the warrior." In addition to recreational and inspirational facilities, there were rooms for sleeping. After World War II, Malamakoa served as the Hawai'i mission home for a few years until termites made it unsafe in 1956. The Malamakoa home has since been replaced by a high-rise condominium, but the property's large banyan tree remains.

Directions to the Honolulu Tabernacle:

The address is 1560 South Beretania Street at its intersection with Kalakaua Avenue. Next door on the right on the corner of Beretania Street and Punahou Street is the Banyan Tree Plaza condominium on the site of the Malamakoa Home. On the left side of the Tabernacle are the Church's regional offices.

8. Waikiki Branch Chapel

From the early days of the Church in Honolulu there was a branch in the Waikiki area southeast of Honolulu Harbor which served the Hawaiian Saints living around the taro patches, rice paddies, and duck ponds behind the beach homes of royalty and Honolulu's elite. On June 22, 1908, Andrew Jenson's *Mission History* observes that the Waikiki Branch Saints felt they had outgrown their chapel. Another Waikiki Branch chapel was

Waikiki Chapel. Courtesy of BYU–Hawaii Archives.

built in 1913 for $5,500. A chapel built and dedicated by Mission President William M. Waddoups on February 2, 1930, still stands at 1902 South King Street. It is currently owned by the Tenrikyo Honolulu Church—Moiliili Chapel.

Directions to the Waikiki Chapel:

The old Waikiki Chapel is located at 1902 South King Street on the corner of Artesian Street.

9. Kalihi Chapel

The Kalihi area of Honolulu is north of downtown along Kalihi Stream and in Kalihi Valley. A wooden chapel was built here in 1913 for $1,700. This site was part of or near the estate of Abraham

Kalihi Chapel. Courtesy of BYU–Hawaii Archives.

and Minerva Fernandez. Albert N. Like spent his youth at this chapel, where he learned "the gospel principles and experienced faith promoting experiences." Like felt that "the general authorities must have been inspired by the lord to select [the

Kalihi Mission Home. Courtesy of BYU–Hawaii Archives.

site at Kalihi and Beckley St.] for a chapel." The chapel was built by the hard work of the Saints under the supervision of Mission President E. Wesley Smith, son of President Joseph F. Smith, and assisted by Paul Elia. It was "teamwork": "the sisters prepared the meals; the young people did the cleaning away of the debris or rubbish. . . . The brethren worked until late at night; . . . with no modern machinery or equipment, it was all done by manual labor."

The excavation of the two-acre area was eight feet deep and took several months of hard labor. On the first floor were six class-rooms, the clerk's office, and the baptismal font.[32]

When Elder Eugene Neff became mission president, he saw a need for a recreation and social center for the Honolulu youth, which was built in an open space next to the mission home. This recreational hall, completed in 1928, became the social center for dances and concerts for all of the O'ahu Saints. Along with sports, this recreation hall factored into the conversion of many non-member youth.

The large stone Kalihi Chapel (1922–1962) was the most impressive Latter-day Saint Church building in Honolulu before the Tabernacle was built in 1941 at a cost of $50,000 and served as the district headquarters, and after 1935 as the first stake center. It replaced the "one-eyed" chapel on Lusitana Street. It was a large and commodious structure capable of holding 650 people for meetings or conferences. It was a simple rectangle in shape, with a *lanai* (terrace) in front that served as a foyer; it had no spire. It had a meeting hall upstairs and classrooms and offices in the basement. The front porch faced Beckley Street. President Anthony W. Ivins of the First Presidency, along with Richard R. Lyman of the Quorum of the Twelve, dedicated this edifice on August 3, 1924, with over seventeen hundred people in attendance. Associated with this site was the Hawai'i Mission Home and headquarters, dedicated by Elder David O. McKay on February 22, 1921, and serving until after World War II, when the mission home was moved to Malamakoa next to the Tabernacle.

The stone Kahlihi Chapel was leveled in 1962 and replaced by a block chapel that still remains. The current chapel is an example of the many chapels built by labor missionaries in the early 1960s.[33] On the same property is the regional welfare center, constucted about where the former mission home was.

Directions to the Kalihi Chapel:
The Kalihi Chapel is located at 1723 Beckley Street at the intersection of Beckley Street and Kalihi Street near the Kalihi

---

32 Albert N. Like, "Kalihi Chapel," *Mormon Pacific Historical Studies, Proceedings* (1993): 1–3.
33 Britsch, *Moramona*, 150.

exit from the H-1 freeway on the *makai,* or ocean side. The mission home was on the corner of Beckley and Kalihi, where the regional welfare building is now, and had the address of 1124 Kalihi Street. The recreation hall was in the Diamond Head *maka'i* corner of the property.

10. Bishop Museum

The Bishop Museum was founded in 1889 by Charles R. Bishop, the American husband of Hawaiian Princess Bernice Pauahi (1831–1884), the last direct descendant of Kamehameha I.[34] The Bernice Pauahi Bishop Museum is dedicated to the study of Hawai'i's and the Pacific Islands' archaeology, natural history, and culture. It has been designated the State Museum of Natural and Cultural History.[35] The Bishop Museum exhibits Hawaiian and Polynesian arts, crafts, artifacts, flora, and fauna. Among items on display at Hawaiian Hall are royal jewelry, crowns, thrones, weapons, feather capes and cloaks, outrigger canoes, surfboards, artifacts of whalebone and tortoise shell. Its archives hold many treasured Hawaiian genealogies dating back hundreds of years and contain records pertaining to Latter-day Saint history in the Pacific. The museum is open from 9:00 a.m. to 5:00 p.m. daily except Tuesdays, and there is an admission fee. Access to the museum's library and archives is free, but the hours are limited.

Directions to the Bishop Museum:

The Bishop Museum is located at 1525 Bernice Street between Kalihi Street and Kapalama Avenue, just mauka, or mountain side, of the H-1 freeway at the Kalihi Street exit. Coming from Waikiki, you can also take the Houghtailing Street exit then turn right to Bernice Street and make a left.

11. Pearl Harbor

Native Hawaiians originally named the Pearl Harbor area *Wai Momi,* which meant "Water of Pearl." During the 1800s Pearl Harbor was not considered a suitable port due to a coral bar

34 Foster, *Frommer's Hawai'i 2007,* 194–95.
35 Lee S. Dutton, *Anthropological Resources: A Guide to Archival, Library, and Museum Collections* (New York: Garland Publishing, 1999), 174–75.

USS West Virginia. *Courtesy of U.S. Navy.*

that obstructed the harbor entrance. The harbor teemed with pearl-producing oysters until the late 1800s. In 1887, as part of the Reciprocity Treaty between the United States of America and the Hawaiian Kingdom, the United States obtained exclusive rights to Pearl Harbor as part of the agreement to allow Hawaiian sugar to enter the United States duty free. Though the United States had negotiated the use of Pearl Harbor for use as a coaling station, it could not be developed until the coral bar at the mouth of the harbor was dredged.[36] Dredging an access channel began in 1908, and Pearl Harbor became the home of the U.S. Pacific Fleet in February 1941[37]

Pearl Harbor cemented its place in world history on December 7, 1941, when naval and air forces of the Empire of Japan attacked without warning in an attempt to destroy the U.S. Pacific Fleet, thereby catapulting the United States into World War II.

Losses were great: 2,400 personnel lost their lives in less than two hours. Eighteen warships were sunk and 187 aircraft

---

36 Department of the Air Force, "Hickam Air Force Base," *U.S Air Force Fact Sheet;* http://www.hickam.af.mil/library/factsheets/factsheet_print. asp?fsID=5104&page=1.

37 "Facts," *Commander, US Pacific Fleet,* http://www.cpf.navy.mil/about/facts/.

destroyed. The Japanese had success, but it was not total. Although the U.S. Pacific Fleet was shattered, three aircraft carriers, not in port at the time of the attack, survived, and Pearl Harbor's harbor installations and oil supplies were surprisingly intact. Most important, the American people, previously divided over the issue of U.S. involvement in World War II, rallied with a total commitment to victory over Japan and her Axis partners.[38]

Some Latter-day Saint servicemen lost their lives during the attack on December 7, 1941, though there is no known statistic for those casualties. Navy Captain S. Mervyn Bennion, one of the earliest American Latter-day Saint casualties of the war, was a graduate of the U.S. Naval Academy at Annapolis and captain of the battleship USS *West Virginia* moored in Pearl Harbor. During the attack, Captain Bennion heroically led the defense of the *West Virginia*, even after being fatally wounded. Captain Bennion received the Medal of Honor posthumously. He was married to a daughter of President J. Reuben Clark of the First Presidency of The Church of Jesus Christ of Latter-day Saints.

Capt. Mervyn Bennion. Courtesy of U.S. Navy.

When Rhea Akoi was thirteen years old she remembers coming home on the bus to Damon Tract, where she lived near Hickam Field, on December 7, 1941. Someone on the bus said, "Look! There's a lot of airplanes in the air." What Rhea then saw were hundreds of tiny planes. As she looked down the road to Pearl Harbor, all she could see was dark black smoke. As she got off the bus her aunt ran out on the road and screamed, "Rhea, run! Run quick!" Rhea's family quickly jumped in their car and evacuated to Kamehameha Heights in Honolulu. When they were allowed to come back to the house, Rhea found bullets all over the

38 Gordon W. Prange, *At Dawn We Slept: The Untold Story of Pearl Harbor* (New York: McGraw-Hill, 1981), 4.

yard, in the dirt.[39] Such memories are common among Latter-day Saints who lived on O'ahu in 1941.

Pearl Harbor is still the headquarters of the U.S. Pacific Fleet and is a major part of the military's presence in Hawai'i. The memory of its role in the Pacific War is memorialized by the National Park Service at the *USS Arizona* Memorial. The Memorial is open from 7:00 a.m. to 5:00 p.m. daily, and admission is free.

Also of interest in the area is the battleship *USS Missouri*, anchored next to Ford Island, on whose deck the Japanese surrendered on September 2, 1945. The *Missouri* is open daily for tours and can be accessed by shuttle from the Arizona Memorial. There is a charge for admission.

Directions to Pearl Harbor Memorial:
The entrance to the *Arizona* Memorial is off of Kamehameha Highway (State Highway 99) at the intersection of Kalaloa Street.

12. Pearl City Chapel

The little wooden chapel for the Pearl City Branch sat on a peninsula that jutted out into Pearl Harbor. On December 7, 1941, shrapnel and debris from the attack fell in the neighborhood around the chapel, killing some civilians. The chapel, located

Pearl City Chapel. Courtesy of BYU–Hawaii Archives.

at 912 Lehua Avenue, was recently torn down and replaced by an apartment building.

Directions to the Pearl City Chapel:
From Kamehameha Highway in Pearl City turn south on Lehua Avenue two and a half blocks to 912 on the right.

---

39 Rhea Akoi, interview with Mary Jane Woodger, October 22, 2015, Hilo Hawaii, transcription in author's possession.

13. Kahana Valley

Before Euro-
pean contact,
between 600 and
1,000 people were
living in Kahana
Valley. Afterwards,
great numbers of
natives died of for-
eign diseases and
some migrated from

Kahana Chapel. Courtesy of BYU–Hawaii Archives.

rural Kahna which further lowered the population. Prior to the
mahele of 1846–1855, which offered fee simple titles, all land was
under the stewardship of the king. During this division of the
lands of Hawai'i the *ahupua'a* (ancient Hawaiian land division)
of Kahana was awarded to Annie Keohokalole, mother of King
Kalakaua and Queen Lili'uokalani. In May 1857, Keohokalole then
sold the land to Ah Sing, a Chinese merchant, who in turn sold it
to a few other Chinese merchants, including one named Ah Mee.

In 1874, Mission President Fred A. H. F. Mitchell banned the
growing or drinking of *awa* (kava), a major cash crop of the La'ie
Hawaiians. Angered by Mitchell's ban of growing or drinking of
awa, ninety-five Hawaiian members of The Church of Jesus Christ
of Latter-day Saints formed a *hui* (corporation or company) called
Hui Kuai Aina.[40] On August 1, 1874, Ah Mee negotiated a prom-
issory agreement with Hui Kuai Aina to purchase the 5,000-acre
ahupua'a (land division usually extending from the uplands to the
sea, so called because the boundary was marked by a heap, or *ahu*,
of stones surmounted by an image of a pig, or *pua'a*), for $6,000.[41]
The land was then divided into 115 shares, with most members of
the *hui* getting one share. Each shareholder had his or her own
house lot and an interest in pasture, uplands, freshwater rights,
ocean fishing rights, and the Huilua fishpond. In a short time, a
large branch was functioning in Kahana Valley. The Kahana Saints

---

40 Britsch, *Moramona*, 85–86.
41 Lance D. Chase, "The Hawaiian Mission Crisis of 1874: The 'Awa Rebellion
Story," in *Voyages of Faith: Explorations in Mormon Pacific History*, ed. Grant
Underwood (Provo, UT: Brigham Young University Press, 2000), 59–70.

labored diligently to cultivate taro, fruits, medicinal plants, and other food staples.[42]

For decades the Kahana Branch was one of the largest Latter-day Saint congregations in Hawai'i. Andrew Jenson's *Mission History* says that on September 16, 1878, the Kahana Saints were building a new chapel, which was dedicated by Elder Henry P. Richards, who wrote in his journal dated October 2, 1878:

> The Conference at this place is a gathering for the purpose of dedicating a new meeting House which has just been built by this branch of the church. At 11 am we commenced our services. H P Richards presiding, Kinimakalehua was chosen clerk. The House was full to overflowing and probably as many more outside gathered around the door and window to hear the opening session, the most important of which was the dedication prayer which was offered by myself after singing the first hymn by the choir.[43]

Later on, there was also a separate social hall next to the chapel. Old photos suggest there may have been more than one chapel on this site, as the branch functioned up until 1953. The few members left in the valley were then included in the Hau'ula Second Ward. After 1953, the building was used intermittently for many years until it became unsafe and was eventually torn down in 2009. Many of the early Kahana Latter-day Saints moved to Iosepa, the Hawaiian community in Skull Valley, Utah, beginning in 1889.[44] A cemetery at the chapel site includes the graves

---

42 Britsch, *Unto the Islands*, 134–35.

43 Henry P. Richards Journal, October 2, 1878, Henry P. Richards Papers, 1854–1900, MS 1487, Church History Library, Salt Lake City.

44 For more information on Iosepa, see James Mathew Kester, "Remembering Iosepa: History, Place and Religion in the American West" (PhD diss., University of California, Santa Barbara, 2008) and the publication of his dissertation by Oxford University Press in 2013 by the same name. See also the following articles/book chapters: Hokulani K. Aikau, "Indigeneity in the Diaspora: The Case of Native Hawaiians at Iosepa, Utah," *American Quarterly* 62, no. 3 (September 2010): 477–500; Richard H. Jackson and Mark W. Jackson, "Iosepa: The Hawaiian Experience in Settling the Mormon West," *Utah Historical Quarterly* 76, no. 4 (Fall 2008): 316–37; Tracey E. Panek, "Life at Iosepa, Utah's Polynesian Colony," in *Proclamation to the People: Nineteenth-Century Mormonism and the Pacific Basin Frontier*, ed. Reid L. Neilson and Laurie F. Maffly-Kipp (Salt Lake City: University of Utah Press, 2008), 170–81; Dennis H. Atkin, "Iosepa: A Utah Home for Polynesians," in *Voyages of Faith*, 71–88; Richard H. Jackson, "Joseph: The Hawaiian

of some Church members. The graves of the three Latter-day Saint Kanakanui children drowned in the tidal wave April 1, 1946, are also found here.[45] For many years, the Mormon Pacific Historical Society worked with residents of the valley and with the Hawai'i Department of Land and Natural Resources, as well as the managers of Kahana Valley State Park, to restore the chapel and cemetery, but nothing ever came of the proposal. The chapel disintegrated beyond repair.[46]

During World War II the United States military moved the Japanese families out of Kahana and used the valley to practice jungle warfare, which ruined some of the valley's archeological sites. Pua Ha'aheo, a famous hula instructor, was branch president for many years. Many of Hawai'i's hula masters trace their knowledge of hula back to him.

By the 1960s, the State of Hawai'i became interested in Kahana and eventually bought the valley and made the area into a state park.

Located on the windward side of Oahu, the Kahana State Park is "owned by and for all residents of Hawai'i." Kahana Valley contains all the resources ancient Hawaiians used for survival: wetlands for taro production; dryland areas for fruits such as mango, breadfruit, and coconut; and land compatible with Hawaiian bamboo, ti leaves, and kukui, hala trees; as well as the Huilua fishpond. Kahana is also unique because of its "living park" arrangement: the descendants of lessees (including many with Latter-day Saint backgrounds) live on the land and serve as the stewards of the land and interpreters of Kahana's rural culture.[47]

Directions to Kahana Valley:

Kahana Valley is seven miles south of La'ie. On the Kane'ohe side of the valley about 200 yards up Trout Farm

Experience in Settling the Mormon West," *Utah Historical Quarterly* 76, no. 4 (Fall 2008): 316–37.

45 Jimmy Kaanaana, "Historical Highlights of Kahana," *Mormon Pacific Historical Society, Proceedings* (May 21, 1987), 10.

46 Kenneth Baldridge, "The Restoration of the Kahana Chapel," *Mormon Pacific Historical Society, Proceedings* (1991), 1; for more information on Kahana Valley, see Robert H. Stauffer, *Kahana: How the Land Was Lost* (Honolulu: University of Hawai'i Press, 2004).

47 Ibid, 8; John J. Fox to Hawai'i Senators, February 2, 2009, Kaneohe, HI.

Road is the chapel site and the cemetery—part of which sits behind the chapel with the other part several yards up the hill behind the chapel.

14. Nanakuli Chapel

The dry west side of O'ahu attracted few residents except a few Hawaiians and the Waianae sugar plantation laborers. The Hawaiian Homestead Act of 1922 opened up land on the west side for Hawaiians to settle on. A lawyer from La'ie, George P. K. Kekauoha, who had unsuccessfully opposed the sale of the La'ie beach lots in 1928, decided to move out to Nanakuli and take up some homestead land. The Church members out that way needed a chapel to meet in, and George decided to donate some land on which to build a chapel. The chapel was built and dedicated on April 28, 1929, by Mission President William M. Waddoups. This little wooden chapel was later replaced by a large brick chapel in 1963 in Waianae, built by labor missionaries. This little chapel still stands and is used by the Hawaiian organization Alu Like.

Directions to the former Nanakuli Chapel:
Drive out Farrington Highway to Nanakuli and turn left on Nanakuli Avenue a half block to 89-117 on the right.

Nanakuli Chapel. Courtesy of BYU–Hawaii Archives.

15. Wahiawa Chapel

Wahiawa, up in the central plateau of O'ahu, began with the cultivation of pineapple by James Dole in 1901 and as the civilian

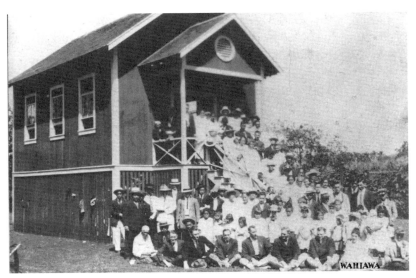

Wahiawa Chapel. Courtesy of BYU–Hawaii Archives.

community next to the U.S. Army's Schofield Barracks, which was established in 1908. The first chapel was a small wooden building built up high on stilts so that classes could be held underneath. It was dedicated on February 8, 1920 by Mission President E. Wesley Smith, son of Joseph F. Smith. With the influx of military during World War II and after a larger building was needed, the little wooden chapel was torn down in June, 1950, and a larger brick chapel built in 1952 and dedicated by Elder Henry D. Moyle on May 16. A new chapel has recently been built in upper Wahiawa; the old chapel was to be sold, but because of growth in the area it has been retained.

> *Directions to the former Wahiawa Chapel:*
> The World War II–era chapel can be seen at 538 Avocado Street, the first right after exiting the H-2 Freeway and crossing the bridge over the lake. The little wooden chapel was on the west side of the church lot behind the pawn shop.

16. Waialua Chapel

Missionary work began in the Waialua district in 1851 by Elders William Farrer and Henry Bigler, nineteen years after the first Protestant missionaries, John and Ursula Emerson, started a church and school there. The early LDS missionaries had several confrontations with Rev. Emerson, but over time, two branches developed, one at Waialua and one at Kawaihapai at what is now the Dillingham Airfield. Both branches were quite "lively," according to Elder Henry P. Richards, who held conferences there in the late 1870s.

Waialua Chapel. Courtesy of BYU–Hawaii Archives.

The current Waialua Chapel, a product of the labor missionary program in 1963, replaced an older wooden chapel that had been built about 1890 and was dedicated by Elder Ward E. Pack in March of 1895. This chapel eventually included a cemetery on land donated by a Sister Kahalekihao (1833–1922). This little cemetery behind the chapel was all but forgotten until two Boy Scouts of the Waialua Ward decided to clean it up as their Eagle Scout project in 1989.

Directions to Waialua Chapel:

The Waialua Ward Chapel is located at 66-847 Kaukonahua Road (Highway 930) about 400 yards south of Weed Circle at the south end of Haleiwa town. The cemetery is behind the chapel.

La'ie

The *ahupua'a*, or land division, of La'ie has been inhabited for at least a thousand years. It encompasses over six thousand acres and extends along the coast for over four miles, then follows the boundaries of watersheds back to the summit ridge of the Ko'olau mountain range. This gave its inhabitants access to the natural resources of the various ecological zones, including the near-shore ocean resources. These varied resources provided sustenance for perhaps a thousand people in ancient days. La'ie was also one of the most famous taro lands on O'ahu. The taro patches were mostly located in the valley behind where the Latter-day Saint Temple now stands. In 1796 Kamehameha I gave La'ie to his half brother Kalaimamahu, who gave La'ie to his daughter Kekauluohi. More than fifty years later the *mahele* of 1848 awarded La'ie to a young chief, William Charles Lunalilo, son of Kekauluohi, under the stewardship of his father, Charles Kanaina. However, William Lunalilo sold La'ie to pay off some debts, and the LDS Church ended up buying it from American Vice Consul Thomas T. Dougherty on January 26, 1865.[1]

Latter-day Saints in La'ie

"In October 1864, President Brigham Young called Francis A. Hammond and George Nebeker as co-presidents of the [Hawaiian] mission," asking them to find a place for the Saints to gather following the loss of Palawai on the island of Lana'i. Brigham Young instructed these men that their mission was to show the Hawaiian Saints "how to labor and how to live the principles of the gospel."[2]

---

1 Riley M. Moffat, Fred E. Woods, and Jeffery Walker, *Gathering to La'ie* (La'ie: Jonathan Napela Institute of Hawaiian and Pacific Islands Studies, 2011), 10.
2 Brigham Young to King Kamehameha V, March 24, 1865, Outgoing Correspondence of Brigham Young, 1843–1877, CR 1234 1, Church History Library.

On March 1865, President Young wrote to King Kamehameha V that Hammond and Nebeker were traveling to Hawai'i as

> religious teachers, but . . . they will not confine their labors to spiritual matters only. According to the precepts of our religion, the spiritual and temporal are so intimately blended that we view no salvation or system of salvation as being complete, which does not provide means for the welfare and preservation of the body as well as the salvation of the Spirit. . . . Mr. Hammond, and my other friends . . . will therefore endeavor to teach your Majesty's subjects . . . practical salvation.[3]

Leaving Salt Lake City on November 10, Hammond and Nebeker were met in San Francisco by returning Mission President Joseph F. Smith, and Elders William W. Cluff, and John R. Young, who were returning home from the islands and learned about conditions in the Islands, which were in a state of flux following the Civil War and decline of the whaling industry. After arriving in Honolulu on December 23, Hammond and Nebeker began searching for a new gathering place for the Hawaiian Saints. They investigated properties on Hawai'i at Papa'ikou, on Maui at Hana, and on Kaua'i at Lumahai.

Thomas T. Dougherty, U.S. vice consul, owned over six thousand acres in northeast Oahu called "Laie." The plantation seemed promising to Hammond when he and Dougherty met on January 20, 1865, and Dougherty described it to Hammond. The decision to purchase La'ie was made after Elder Hammond had a dream that Brigham Young and Heber C. Kimball came to him and reviewed the many desirable features of La'ie. At the same time, another missionary, William W. Cluff, was visiting La'ie and saw Brigham Young in a vision, who told him, "This is the place to gather the native Saints to."[4] Over the next five days, Hammond "rode over the crop land, investigated the mountain part of the property, [and] looked over the buildings." After returning to Honolulu, on January 26, 1865, Hammond discussed his desire to

---

3 Ibid.
4 Moffat et al., *Gathering to La'ie*, 23–24.

buy Dougherty's plantation.[5] Hammond wrote of the negotiations and purchase in his journal,

> Called on Mr. T. T. Dougherty and offered him 12,000 dollars for "Laie" with all the stock, horses and improvements thereon—he would not take less than 14,000 dollars. I finally after a little consideration consented to give it. I agreed to send him a draft for 3000 dollars in ten weeks from date and pay 5000 dollars more by the 1st of July/65—6000 dollars in two years from date bearing at 12 per cent per annum—giving a mortgage on the place for security. I take possession immediately.[6]

La'ie was to become a school "in hard work, in virtue, and in morality," a place where Hawaiian Latter-day Saints could find "refuge from the world" and live as Christians. "The haoles were to be the teachers, the Hawaiians the students."[7] As historian R. Lanier Britsch explains, "It was paternalism, although altruistic in intention."[8] Brigham Young had basically one purpose—to elevate the Hawaiian Saints." He also hoped that both cotton and sugar could be produced in Hawai'i and shipped to Utah. Previously, cotton and sugar grown in southern Utah's Dixie proved only marginally successful.

After taking possession of the plantation Hammond immediately set about organizing the local Hawaiians in putting up fencing, ploughing, and planting. An October 1866 reference says that "about two hundred Hawaiians were living on the land, 'mostly members.'"[9] This was far fewer Hawaiians than probably lived in La'ie in ancient times, western diseases and out-migration having taken their toll. A branch of the Church had existed in La'ie since 1851, and it was considered the best place on O'ahu for new missionaries to learn the language.

Following the advice of early converts Jonathan Napela and George Raymond, the missionaries in 1868 settled on sugarcane as

5 Ibid., 73.
6 Francis A. Hammond, "Journal 1864–1867," January 26, 1865, MS 1430, Church History Library.
7 Brigham Young to William King, March 29, 1865; Brigham Young to Hammond and Nebeker, December 29, 1864, Letterbooks, Church History Library; and Francis Hammond, Journal, March 9, 1865, Church History Library.
8 Britsch, *Mormona*, 75.
9 Jenson, Manuscript History, October 14, 1866.

the plantation's cash crop. They bought a small mule-powered mill to grind the cane, and on November 12, 1868, after seven months of preparation, the mill was put into operation. "The first cane crop was exceptionally heavy," a total product of around a hundred tons of sugar. However, the next year, a dry one, produced a far less promising yield. Overall, "sugar production over the years was disappointing almost as often as it was satisfactory."[10]

During his third mission to Hawaiʻi, from 1885 to 1887, Joseph F. Smith made a prophecy about Laʻie which has become an important part of the faith among Laʻie Saints.[11] The prophecy grew out of discouragement about the plantation and a blight that was affecting the Hawaiians' main food crop, taro. When some brought their complaints to President Smith, he prophesied:

Joseph F. Smith. Courtesy of BYU–Hawaii Archives.

> Dear brothers and sisters, do not leave this land, for it is the land chosen by God as a gathering place for the Saints in the Church of Jesus Christ of Latter-day Saints in Hawaiian Islands as well as the islands of the sea.
>
> Do not complain because of the many trials which come to you, because of the barrenness of the land, the lack of water, the scarcity of food to which you are accustomed, and the poverty as well.
>
> Be patient, for the day is coming when this land will become a most beautiful land. Water shall spring forth in abundance, and upon the barren land you now see, the Saints will build homes, taro will be planted, and there will be plenty to eat and drink. Many trees will be planted and this place will become verdant, the fragrance of flowers will fill the air, and trees which are now seen growing on the mountains will be moved by the

---

10 Britsch, *Moramona*, 83.
11 Moffat et al., *Gathering to Laʻie*, 40–46.

Saints and will grow in this place near the sea, and because of the great beauty of the land, inland birds will come here and sing their songs.

And upon this place the glory of the Lord will rest, to bless the Saints who believe in Him and His commandments. And there are some in this house who will live to see all these things fulfilled, which I have spoken from the Lord.

Therefore, do not waver, work with patience, continue on, stand firm, keep the commandments and also the laws of the gathering, and you will receive greater blessings, both spiritual and temporal, than you now enjoy or have enjoyed in the past.[12]

After this prophecy was given, developments came that greatly helped the struggling Saints. Britsch explains:

Most serious was an insufficient water supply. This problem was overcome in the early 1880s when a flume more than two miles long was constructed to bring water from the mountains, and an artesian well was drilled. A consistent sales outlet for the sugar had to be arranged. [In 1869] Nebeker, acting on the suggestions of Brigham Young, tried to establish marketing relationships with Salt Lake City merchants, but without success. Over the years most of the sugar produced on the Laie plantation was sold to Waterhouse and Company in Honolulu, who in turn shipped it to San Francisco.[13]

A new agreement between Laie plantation and the newly formed Kahuku Plantation Company . . . was arranged in 1892 to have the Kahuku mill cut, haul, and process Laie's cane crop for half the end product. This was a great boon because the mill built in 1882 was totally out of commission and the Laie plantation could not afford to construct a new one. Because the Kahuku mill was so efficient, the gross production per acre was higher than ever before. This arrangement with the Kahuku plantation was modified almost yearly, but the broad terms of the agreement remained.[14]

Another source of income for the plantation was the leasing of some swampy land to a Chinese *Hui* to grow rice.

---

12 Ibid.,44.
13 Britsch, *Unto the Islands*, 132.
14 Britsch, *Moramona*, 110.

One of the most important men to serve the Church in Hawaiʻi was Samuel Edwin Woolley (1859–1925). Called as mission president and plantation manager in 1895, Woolley remained in Hawaiʻi until 1921, and was an important influence in shaping the destiny of the Hawaiian mission and the Laʻie community, making significant contributions to the modernization and institutionalization of the mission and plantation.[15]

Samuel E. Woolley family. Courtesy of BYU–Hawaii Archives.

When the Koolau Agricultural Company properties were put up for sale in 1918, President Woolley acted as agent for the Laʻie plantation in buying the property. This added 800 acres of sugarcane land stretching from Laʻie to Kahana, "purportedly valued at a half million dollars, almost double the sugarcane acreage of Laʻie plantation."[16] It included the narrow-gage Koolau Railroad from Kahuku to Kahana Bay, which brought the cut cane to the mill for refining. Also around this time Japanese farmers leased 250–300 acres on the hillsides above the sugarcane to grow pineapples.

> The production of sugarcane at Laie continued to increase steadily over the years. Under President Samuel Woolley's watchful eye and skillful leadership, the small-time farming enterprise of the nineteenth century grew into a major twentieth-century operation. The sugar crop of 1894–1895 was

---

15 Samuel E. Woolley Journals, Church History Library; and Jenson, Manuscript History, November 9, 1895. For more information on the life and contributions of Samuel E. Woolley, see Lance D. Chase, "Samuel Edwin Woolley: An Appreciation," in *Temple, Town Tradition: The Collected Historical Essays of Lance D. Chase*, ed. Dale Robertson, Zach Chase, and Lavina Fielding Anderson (Salt Lake City: Publishers Press, 2000), 57–70. See also Samuel Edwin Woolley: A Valet's Hero," *Mormon Pacific Historical Society, Proceedings* (May 25, 1991), 20–34.

16 Britsch, *Unto the Islands*, 149; and Jenson, Manuscript History, August 22, 1918.

339 tons. The best crop was 3,103 tons of sugar, an almost ten-fold increase, produced in 1917–1918 during World War I.[17]

In 1921, Antoine R. Ivins was called to manage the Church's sugar plantation in the Hawaiian Islands. As plantation manager he supervised the many different nationalities, including Chinese, Japanese, and Filipinos. During the 1920s, the plantation was having a difficult time competing in the world sugar market, and by 1927 it was falling into debt.[18] Acting on behalf of the Church, Ivins sold some agriculturally useless beach front property in Laʻie to help relieve the plantation of some of its debt.

Some of Laʻie's residents did not believe that any property could be sold without their approval, and Ivin's actions angered them. These Laʻie citizens felt that the land belonged to the people who had answered the call to gather with the Saints in Laʻie. Subsequently, in a court case brought before the land court by these residents, the Church's right to sell the land was upheld on February 28, 1928.[19] Now that once useless beach-front property is worth a fortune.

In 1921, Laʻie was held up as an example of what could be done to preserve the Hawaiian people at a time when it was feared they would become extinct as a people. Laʻie's example helped Hawaiʻi's delegate to Congress, Prince Jonah Kuhio Kalanianole, get Congress to pass the Hawaiian Homes Act in 1920, which provided approximately 220,000 acres to native Hawaiians for homesteading.[20]

Another prophecy concerning Laʻie came in a prayer at the groundbreaking of the Church College of Hawaii, later to be known as Brigham Young University–Hawaii, by President David O. McKay on February 12, 1955: "We dedicate our actions in this service unto thee and unto thy glory and to the salvation

17 Britsch, *Unto the Islands*, 149.
18 Florence Ivins Hyde, "Antoine Ridgeway Ivins of the First Council of the Seventy," *Improvement Era* 57 (July 1954): 496–99, 521.
19 Jenson, Manuscript History, February 28, 1928; and Cynthia Woolley Compton, "The Making of the Ahupuaʻa of Laʻie into a Gathering Place and Plantation" (PhD diss., Brigham Young University, 2005), 2.
20 Jenson, Manuscript History, February 28, 1928; and Cynthia Woolley Compton, "The Making of Ahupuaʻa of Laʻie into a Gathering Place and Plantation" (PhD diss., Brigham Young University, 2005), 2.

of the children of men, that this college, and the temple, and the town of Laie may become a missionary factor, influencing not thousands, not tens of thousands, but millions of people who will come seeking to know what this town and its significance are."[21] This refers to an experience he had in La'ie while watching a flag-raising ceremony at the La'ie mission school on February 8, 1921. As the years have gone by, these prophecies are being fulfilled: La'ie has become a sacred place for members of The Church of Jesus Christ of Latter-day Saints, and millions of visitors have come to the Polynesian Cultural Center.

Latter-day Saint Historic Sites in La'ie

1. First La'ie Chapel

The first La'ie chapel was part of the original mission compound that had been part of Thomas Dougherty's ranching operation. Construction of a chapel in La'ie was a top priority for the Saints, and they began building one at the same time that they constructed their homes. The 1866 chapel was small, 24 by 36 feet, but it served as an improvement over the bowery they used before, or the crowded Mansion House, which was sometimes used for church meetings. Separate church meetings were held for Hawaiians and *haoles* because of language differences until the missionaries learned the language.[22] The exact site of this chapel has not been determined, but it was part of the plantation buildings at the head of Lanihuli Street.

21 Reuben D. Law, *The Founding and Early Development of the Church College of Hawai'i* (St. George, UT: Dixie College Press, 1972), 69.

22 Jenson, Manuscript History, October 7, 1866.

I Hemolele, 1887. Courtesy of BYU–Hawaii Archives.

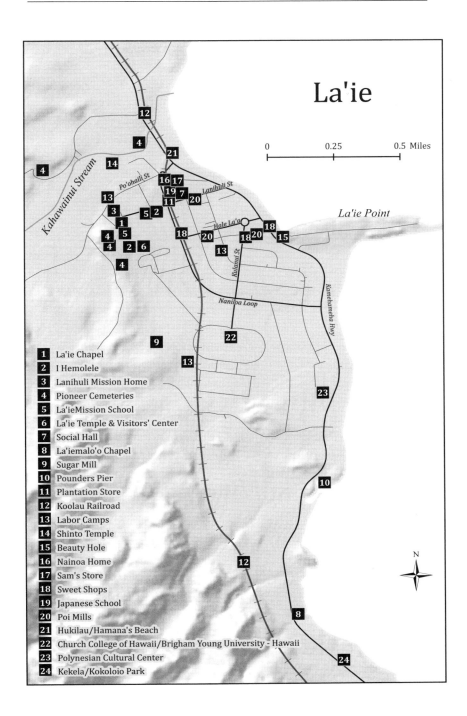

La'ie

0   0.25   0.5 Miles

La'ie Point

Po'ohaili St

Lanihuli St

Hale La'a

Kalanui St

Naniloa Loop

Kamehameha Hwy

Kahawainui Stream

1 La'ie Chapel
2 I Hemolele
3 Lanihuli Mission Home
4 Pioneer Cemeteries
5 La'ieMission School
6 La'ie Temple & Visitors' Center
7 Social Hall
8 La'iemalo'o Chapel
9 Sugar Mill
10 Pounders Pier
11 Plantation Store
12 Koolau Railroad
13 Labor Camps
14 Shinto Temple
15 Beauty Hole
16 Nainoa Home
17 Sam's Store
18 Sweet Shops
19 Japanese School
20 Poi Mills
21 Hukilau/Hamana's Beach
22 Church College of Hawaii/Brigham Young University - Hawaii
23 Polynesian Cultural Center
24 Kekela/Kokoloio Park

N

I Hemolele interior, 1887. Courtesy of BYU–Hawaii Archives.

2. I Hemolele

In 1881, because of the increase of members in La'ie, it became necessary to construct a new building in which the Saints could meet. I Hemolele, built just south of the mission compound where the Laie Temple now stands, was planned and built to endure. King Kalakaua and Queen Kapiolani attended the corner-stone-laying ceremony on April 6, 1882 and donated $100 towards the construction fund. On October 6, 1883, Mission President Edward Partridge Jr. dedicated the building, which dedication King Kalakaua also attended. Afterwards, King Kalakaua gave a short speech, saying that the LDS people "were his best subjects in 'fulfilling the laws and keeping the peace of the kingdom.'"[23]

The chapel was 35 feet wide and 65 feet long, with a 19-foot ceiling, a raised stand and pulpit, a choir loft in back, and a belfry that housed a 250-pound bell. The building cost about $8,000 to build.[24] It was said to seat 500 people for the semi-annual mission conferences.

King Kalakaua and his wife, Queen Kapiolani, paid many visits to La'ie, and Kapiolani applied what she learned from the Relief

23 *Hawaiian Mission Manuscript History*, 1881–83.
24 Britsch, *Moramona*, 97–98.

Society organization to set up her own kingdom-wide benevolent organization to assist the kingdom's poor.

When it was determined a temple would be built where I Hemolele stood, the chapel was lifted off its foundation and

I Hemolele, 1922. Courtesy of BYU–Hawaii Archives.

rolled down the hill on logs to a new site on Lanihuli Street in January 1916 so that construction could begin on the temple.

I Hemolele burned down on July 10, 1940. Workers using a blowtorch to scorch off old paint prior to repainting may have started the fire. No fire trucks were stationed anywhere nearby at the time, and the flames were seen for miles. The Laie Ward then used the Social Hall (see site 7) as their chapel until 1950.[25]

Directions to I Hemolele:

I Hemolele was originally located on the hill where the temple now stands, and then later moved to the space between the Laie North Stake Center and the back chapel. The site will be on the left between the two churches on Lanihuli Street.

3. Lanihuli Home

The mission acquired Thomas Dougherty's ranch buildings in 1865. Andrew Jenson, an Assistant Latter-day Saint Church Historian, records the missionaries complaining about the poor, cramped living conditions. In April 1892, permission came from the First Presidency to build a new mission home. Having been a carpenter in previous years, Mission President Matthew Noall designed the plans. The cornerstone was laid that August; the new mission home was completed and dedicated on October 6,

---

25 Steve Fidel, "A Legacy of Laie," *Deseret News*, Mormon Times section, October 31, 2009, 9.

1894. This impressive Victorian mansion, called Lanihuli, became the headquarters of the Hawai'i Mission. The Lanihuli Home site can now be located a couple of lots north of the temple president's

Lanihuli Mission Home 1910. Courtesy of BYU–Hawaii Archives.

home, where there is also a historic marker. Until the Laie Hawai'i Temple was completed in 1919, the Lanihuli mission home, along with I Hemolele, visually represented the Church in Hawai'i.

A "building modern in all its designs," Lanihuli mixed mainland and Hawaiian styles. The Lanihuli Home included lanais and a small octagonal tower facing the ocean, as well as a kitchen, a dining room, and six bedrooms. In addition, one room was designated for prayer and meetings. A second story with balconies was added a few years later. During conferences in La'ie, a tradition was established: the sisters of the Relief Society would dress in white, gather at the mission home, and then proceed, in pairs, to the chapel. This procession of sisters was described by one observer as "a beautiful, striking sight."[26]

After the temple was built and the mission headquarters were moved to Honolulu in 1921, members from out of town and from the outer islands would stay in the Lanihuli Home after an evening temple session. During World War II, the Lanihuli Home was used by the military as a rest and relaxation center. Then, "from 1955 to 1958, it served as a girls' dormitory for the Church College of Hawai'i when the college was temporarily located on the site of the Laie North Stake Center."[27] In 1960, the termite-ridden Lanihuli Home was torn down to make room for new faculty housing.[28]

---

26 Britsch, *Moramona*, 110–11.
27 Riley M. Moffat, *Historical Sites Around La'ie* (Laie, HI: BYUH Press & Design Center, 1997), 5.
28 Britsch, *Moramona*, 110.

Directions to the Lanihuli Home site:
The house was located at 55-648/652 Lanihuli Place. Follow Lanihuli St. until reaching Lanihuli Place, and then go right and look for the marker.[29]

4. Pioneer Cemeteries

Three "portions of an old cemetery existed on the hill behind the old chapel known as "I Hemolele,'" where the temple now stands. These cemeteries were used until about 1918, when dynamite, used to blast holes in the coral rock for graves, shook the temple. These cemeteries became forgotten and overgrown until Hawai'i Temple President D. Arthur Haycock organized their restoration in 1989. About 350 graves have been identified on the hill behind the temple. The area north of the gazebo seems to be mostly for Hawaiian Saints, the area south of the gazebo for plantation workers, including some missionary children, and another group south of the fence that was just rediscovered in 2007 for Hawaiian Saints. Other old cemeteries exist across Kahawainui Stream (Mokoiki) and along the road to the egg farm (Pa'akea).[30]

Directions to the Pioneer Cemeteries:
The main pioneer cemeteries are located on the hill behind the current temple site. The Mokoiki cemetery is located a hundred yards behind the egg farm shop next to Kahawainui Stream, and the Pa'akea cemetery is almost a mile up the Egg Farm Road on the right.

5. La'ie Mission School

Mildred E. Randall, a sister missionary, opened two schools in La'ie on October 20, 1865, one school for the Hawaiian children and another for the missionary children, though English was primarily used in both. Sister Randall continued running the schools until her release in November 1866. She returned home

29 For information on the erecting of the marker, see Eric R. Beaver, "Remembering Where La'ie Gathered: The Dedication of the Lanihuli Home and Social Hall Historical Markers," *Mormon Historical Studies* 8, nos. 1–2 (Spring/Fall 2007): 159–63.
30 Mike Foley, "Explores Old La'ie Cemeteries," *Kaleo: Koolauloa News*, December 2007, 2.

to Utah, and the remaining missionaries shared the teaching responsibilities in her absence. The school was taught in the small chapel in La'ie. In 1873, Sister Randall returned to Hawai'i by herself on a second mission to supervise the La'ie schools.

La'ie School, 1900. Courtesy of BYU–Hawaii Archives.

By 1883, the school was large enough that it required the full-time attention of at least one missionary. In 1885, fifty students, between ages six and eighteen, were enrolled in the school. Several missionaries handled the responsibility of teaching at the school between 1883 and 1887. In 1887, Elder Fred Beesley petitioned for and received financial aid from the Hawaiian government for the school. Up until 1915 the mission school was located where the current temple president's house is located.[31] When the temple was under construction, the school building was used as the workshop for artisans working on the temple. A new school with individual classroom buildings was then constructed where the back chapel is located on Lanihuli Street.

La'ie School flag-raising ceremony. Courtesy of BYU–Hawaii Archives.

31 Moffat, *Historical Sites*, 6.

The mission school, though not large, served to educate the expanding population of La'ie, members and nonmembers alike. After the turn of the century, the Church, seeing the importance of the school, invested in the school by maintaining professional teachers who were able to stay at the school for several years. It was at this mission school where Elder David O. McKay, during his world tour of LDS missions and schools, witnessed a flag-raising ceremony on February 8, 1921. President McKay was "stirred by the sight of children of many races united by the common bond of citizenship as they saluted their national emblem and sharply aware of the greater bond of the Gospel which linked them together." President McKay wrote of the impression that occasion had on him:

> As I looked at that motley group of youngsters, and realized how far apart their parents are in hopes, aspirations, and ideals, and then thought of these boys and girls, the first generation of their children, all throng into what Israel Zangwell has aptly called the "Melting Pot" and coming out Americans, my bosom swelled with emotion and tears came to my eyes, and I felt like bowing in prayer and thanksgiving for the glorious country which is doing so much for all these nationalities. But more than that, when I realize these same boys and girls have the opportunity of participating in all the blessings of the Gospel which will transform the American into a real citizen of the Kingdom of God, I feel to praise His name for the glorious privileges vouchsafed to this generation. We held short services in the school room in which all—American, Hawaiian, Japanese, Chinese, Filipino—participated as though they had belonged to one nation, one county, one tongue.
>
> America and the Church of Christ will truly make of all nations one blood. May God hasten the day when this is accomplished."[32]

The impression left by this experience prompted Elder David O. McKay (a member of the Quorum of the Twelve at that time) to be mindful of the need for greater educational opportunities for the youth of Hawai'i and the Pacific.

---

32 David W. Cummings, *Mighty Missionary in the Pacific: The Building Program of the Church* (Salt Lake City: Bookcraft, 1961), 257–58; and Owen J. Cook, "Church Colleges of Hawaii," *Ensign*, May 1971, 42.

"The Hawai'i Mission organized and maintained the mission school in La'ie until 1927," when the territory had sufficient money to pay for the cost of educating La'ie's children. One of the last missionary teachers was Sister Flora Amussen, who later married Ezra Taft Benson. Another, Sister Billie Hollingshead, returned years later as an education professor at the Church College of Hawai'i. Most "buildings were moved to the present [Laie Elementary] school site and taken over by the Territory."[33] Some of the mission school classrooms that were moved were still in use up until 1989.

Directions to the La'ie Mission School:
The 1883 school was located near the current temple president home, near the address of 55-180 Lanihuli St. The 1915–1927 campus was on on Lanihuli Street, where the back chapel is located. Look for the historical plaque.[34]

6. Laie Hawai'i Temple and Visitors' Center

The Hawai'i Temple was built from 1916 to 1918 on the original site of the large wooden chapel named I Hemolele. The temple was originally surrounded by open fields. At first there was a small Bureau of Information at the bottom of the pools, as seen in early photographs. Missionaries were assigned to greet visitors during the day and officiate in the temple in the evenings.

On December 22, 1900, in the Laie Branch Sunday School, President George Q. Cannon expressed his opinion that Hawaiians needed the sealing blessings available in a temple. After Cannon's observation, temple work was discussed frequently in mission conferences, and President Samuel Woolley encouraged his people to live worthy to enter the temple someday. In the mission conference on April 1915, Woolley told Hawaiian Saints: "Have we searched out our genealogies? Are we prepared for a temple to be built? . . . Who knows but what the Lord wants to build a temple in this land? I tell you that there are people here today who, if they continue in the work of the Lord, shall enter into the temple

---

33 Moffat, *Historical Sites*, 5–6.
34 This plaque was funded by the Mormon Historic Sites Foundation and the Mormon Pacific Historical Society, Hawai'i Reserves Inc., and the Laie Community Association.

or other temples; and the time will come, in my judgment, that a temple will be built here."[35] Woolley's admonition was prophetic. Two months later, on June 1, while President Joseph F. Smith was visiting the Islands, he selected a temple site and dedicated it to the Lord. President Smith confided to his companions, Elder Reed Smoot of the Quorum of the Twelve and Presiding Bishop Charles Nibley, that the idea of a La'ie temple had not yet been discussed with the Quorum of the Twelve and the First Presidency. Elder Reed Smoot, of the Quorum of the Twelve, recorded the sacred occasion of the temple grounds dedication in Laie.

> President Smith came to me and said, "Reed, I want you to take a walk with me." And as we went out the door, he said to Bishop Nibley, "I wish you would accompany us." I never saw a more perfect night in all my life; the surroundings were perfect. You who have been to Laie know the surroundings; all nature smiles. We walked toward the meetinghouse. Nothing was said of what we were going for until we stood at the back of the meetinghouse, and President Smith then said: "Brethren, this is the birthday of President Brigham Young, June 1, 1915. I feel impressed to dedicate this ground for the erection of a Temple to God, for a place where the peoples of the Pacific Isles can come and do their temple work. I have not presented this to the Council of the Twelve or to my counselors; but, if you think there would be no objection to it, I think now is the time—to dedicate the ground." I have heard President Smith pray hundreds of times. He has thrilled my soul many times with his wonderful spirit of prayer and his supplications to our Heavenly Father. But never in all my life did I hear such a prayer. The very ground seemed to be sacred, and he seemed as if he were talking face to face with the Father. I cannot and never will forget it if I live a thousand years.[36]

President Smith announced the construction of the Laie temple in October that year at general conference. He explained to the Church why the temple was being built in La'ie: "So that the good people of these islands may reach the blessings of the House

---

35 General Minutes, Hawaiian Mission, Conference, April 3, 1915, folder 5, Church History Library.
36 Joseph Fielding Smith, *The Life of Joseph F. Smith* (Salt Lake City: Deseret News Press, 1938), 421.

of God within their own borders, and that the people from New Zealand, if they do not become strong enough to require a house to be built there also, by and by, can come to Laie, where they can get their blessings and return home and live in peace, having fulfilled all the requirements of the Gospel the same as we have the privilege of doing here."[37] "When the plans for the temple were announced, Polynesian Church members all over the Pacific began making preparations to attend the temple."[38]

The architectural firm of Hyrum E. Pope and Harold W. Burton was chosen to design the Laie temple, the same firm that designed the temple in Alberta, Canada, already under construction at the time. Ralph E. Woolley, son of Hawaiian Mission President Samuel E. Woolley and just twenty-nine years old at the time, was the construction supervisor. In the summer of 1917, Leo, age twenty-eight, and Avard Fairbanks, only eighteen years old, came as sculptors; and Hawaiian missionary LeConte Stewart was chosen to paint scenes in various rooms. After surveying the available building materials in Hawai'i, Pope and Burton decided the building should be made from concrete and steel. Building with reinforced concrete was new to the islands, and only one firm, Spalding Construction, was prepared to do it. The Spalding company gave the Church a big discount because of the nature of the project. It was decided that the "abundant supply of lava rock could be ground into aggregate for use in the concrete."[39]

The construction process was slow. First the wooden chapel, I Hemolele, had to be moved down off the hill starting on January 12, 1916. To crush the lava for use in concrete, a rock plant needed to be built, and then a foundation had to be carved in the soil and coral, in some places fifteen feet deep. Following the construction of the crushing plant and the digging of the foundation, the work proceeded smoothly until the building was built.

Then finishing work began. The high humidity and lack of air conditioning caused a fungus to grow on the interior of the temple. Three rooms were completed, and then had to be refinished

37 In Conference Report, October 1915, 8–9.
38 Britsch, *Moramona*, 122.
39 Riley M. Moffat, "The Spalding Construction Company," *Mormon Pacific Historical Society, Proceedings* (2011).

Laie Hawai'i Temple dedication 1919. Courtesy of BYU–Hawaii Archives.

after an antifungus finish was applied. This fungus problem slowed the completion of the interior of temple, and the importation of most of the building materials because of World War I also caused delays. The interior was finally completed by April 18, 1918, and the landscaping around the temple was finished a year later. The worldwide influenza pandemic prohibiting public meetings contributed to the delay. There was a positive side to the many delays in construction: the Hawaiian Saints had more time to prepare themselves for temple worship, and they were granted more time to raise their portion of the $250,000 temple construction costs.[40]

The finished temple, declared by newspapers to be the "Taj Mahal of Hawaii," was dedicated on November 27, 1919, Thanksgiving Day. Church President Heber J. Grant presided at the services, accompanied by his counselors, Anthon H. Lund and Rudger Clawson. President Grant "expressed his deep personal regrets that President Joseph F. Smith could not be there to conduct the services." President Grant offered a prayer, thanking the Lord for his care of the Saints, the restoration of the gospel, and the labors of George Q. Cannon, Joseph F. Smith, and Jonathan H. Napela. He thanked the Lord "that thousands and tens of thousands of the descendants of Lehi, in this favored land, have come to knowledge of the gospel." He also asked the Lord to provide a way for Hawaiians and other Pacific Islanders to attend "this holy house and become saviors unto their ancestors."[41] Baptismal work began in the temple on December 2, 1919, and soon thereafter the temple was fully functioning. Temple President William Waddoups wrote in his journal: "Tuesday, Dec 2nd 1919. This morning

40 Ibid., 136.
41 Heber J. Grant, "Dedicatory Prayer in the Hawaiian Temple," *Honolulu Star-Bulletin*, December 6, 1919.

at 8 a.m. we opened the doors of the Temple the first time for the baptisms for the dead. . . . We had some trouble with the heater and the water was cold, . . . but we got along very well. I did the baptisms. We baptized 279. I was tired but happy."[42]

One of the first patrons of the temple was Ma Manuhiʻi, who had cared for President Joseph F. Smith as a fifteen-year-old elder on Molokaʻi when he fell ill during his first mission to Hawaiʻi in 1854. Whenever Smith returned to the

Ma Manuhiʻi. Courtesy of BYU–Hawaii Archives.

Islands, he would show his concern for her. Ma Manuhiʻi was present at one of the five dedication services at the temple. Blind and unable to walk, she had to be carried to and from the service. The week following the dedication, she received her own endowments. Being very feeble, she had to be carried from room to room by missionaries during the temple session. While in the temple she testified she heard President Joseph F. Smith say "aloha" ("love to you") to her, and it caused her to weep for joy.

The next week she returned to her home in Honolulu and shortly after became ill. She called for Joseph F. Smith's son, Mission President E. Wesley Smith, to come and see her. On his entering of the room, she sat up in bed and said, "*Auhea ke keiki*" (meaning "Where is the boy?" the son of President Joseph F. Smith). President Smith took hold of her hand. She clasped it to her breast, kissed it, and wept. Then she said in her own tongue, "It is enough, I am satisfied and ready to go now." She had been to the temple, an event for which she had lived, and she had now felt the hand of the son of the man she loved so much. She was ready to return to her Maker.[43]

---

42 William M. Waddoups, "Journal," William M. Waddoups Papers, 1883–1969, MS 15040, December 2, 1919, Church History Library.
43 Jenson, Manuscript History, December 11, 1919.

Bureau of Information, 1919. Courtesy of BYU–Hawaii Archives.

Ma Manuhiʻi passed away the next morning, December 11, 1919. With her passing and the completion of the temple, an era passed in the history of the Church in Hawaiʻi.[44] "President Joseph F. Smith, who represented the first generation of missionaries, was now gone. At this time President Samuel E. Woolley, who had worked so diligently to create a beautiful and productive Laʻie, was released as mission president but stayed on for two more years as plantation manager. The mission headquarters were moved from Laʻie to Honolulu, and a different kind of administration was about to begin."[45]

A visual highlight of the Laie Hawaiʻi Temple is the friezes that band the top of the temple, which were created by the Fairbanks brothers, J. Leo and Avard. They depict 130 historic figures from the Old Testament, New Testament, Book of Mormon, and Latter-day Saint history. Other scuptures on the temple grounds by the Fairbanks include *Maternity* and *Lehi Blessing Joseph*.

From 1919 to 1963, there was a small Bureau of Information at the bottom of the stepped pools, staffed by missionaries during the day; they then officiated in the temple in the evenings. A new

44 Joseph F. Smith, "Editor's Table," *Improvement Era* 19 (November 1915): 79–80; J. A. Hendrickson, "Why a Temple in Hawaii," *Improvement Era* 29 (January 1926): 258–62.
45 Britsch, *Unto the Islands*, 156.

and enlarged Visitors' Center was constructed by labor missionaries in 1963.

An inspirational incident of divine protection over the Laie temple during World War II has circulated among Latter-day Saints. According to Brigham Young University–Hawaiʻi Professor Lance D. Chase's research on the subject, the story is as follows:

A Japanese pilot returning from Pearl Harbor with a bomb still undelivered spotted the Hawaiʻi Temple. Determined to destroy the building, a target of opportunity, before it became necessary to jettison his bomb harmlessly into the nearby sea, he dived on the temple. His bomb would not release. He then decided to dive again and strafe, but his guns would not fire. It is unclear whether he made three or more passes, but on what may have been a third pass his controls failed to work even as he contemplated a suicide dive.

Fearful of expending his fuel before reaching his ship, he headed out to sea now. He worked his bomb release mechanism and the bomb fell now. His guns responded. Feeling disgraced but encouraged by his now properly functioning plane, he decided to try a last strafing run at the building. A final time his controls refused to respond, and he was forced to continue back to his ship.

This information is from the journal of Robert Thomas Stout, who had learned of it when tracting as a missionary. Stout reported that on Sept. 9, 1957, he had been in Matsumoto City [Japan] and met a middle-aged man who had been a Japanese pilot in the Pearl Harbor attack. As Stout was talking to him about the Church, he showed him a postcard aerial view of the Hawaiian temple. When the pilot saw this picture, he "turned pale and was shocked" and then told his story. He said he had tried to bomb that temple the morning of the Pearl Harbor attack, but his controls froze and the bomb would not release.

On his last attempt he felt "a strange power protected that white building with its blue pools." He felt a powerful influence and felt he had angered God. He did not even look back, so great was his fear. The elders told him about the temple to which the man replied, "it has giant magic. . . . You two missionaries make me feel those feelings again. You must leave me again and not torment my mind and heart."

Robert Stout returned to Japan more than 50 times, including once as a mission president from 1977–80. In 1983 Stout and his wife, Kay, visited the Hawai'i Temple on their 25th wedding anniversary and told the story to temple President Bob Finlayson. Later Stout sent his journal to the Hawai'i Temple for their archives.[46]

On Sunday morning, December 7, 1941, as most people in La'ie were getting ready for Church in the social hall, they noticed many loud planes flying overhead toward Kane'ohe. Some thought the planes were part of U.S. maneuvers, but when the people heard of the Japanese attack on Pearl Harbor, most wisely stayed inside their houses. The few who were outdoors claimed they saw a plane attempt to drop a bomb, without success, on the temple. Robert KaHawai'i notarized his recollection. William Kanahele and Charles Barenaba believed they also saw this incident. Tom Nakayama said he saw the plane but did not see the bomb. This story reinforced the belief that the temple and La'ie were divinely protected. The La'ie boys in the Territorial Guard were called to their stations along the coast that day in anticipation of an invasion.[47]

In 1963, Church building missionaries involved with the construction of the Church College of Hawai'i and the Polynesian Cultural Center replaced the old Bureau of Information building located adjacent to the Laie Hawai'i Temple with two structures on either side of an open court with reflecting pools and covered colonnaded walks. These buildings are now the Visitors' Center on one side, the Family History Center and Beehive Clothing outlet on the other side. The building missionaries also made additions to the temple from the plans drawn up by Church architect Harold W. Burton.[48]

---

46 Mark Albright, "Is This Story True? Pearl Harbor Pilot Couldn't Bomb Hawai'i Temple," *Meridian Magazine*, August 30, 2015, http://ldsmag.com/is-this-story-true-pearl-harbor-pilot-couldnt-bomb-hawaii-temple/

47 For more information on this story, see Alf Pratte, "Not Quite 'Purported,'" *Mormon Pacific Historical Society, Proceedings* (2005), 60–78; Ken Baldridge, "In Search of a Tale," *Mormon Pacific Historical Society, Proceedings* (1988), 50–58; Lance D. Chase, *Temple, Town, Tradition* (La'ie: Institute for Polynesian Studies, 2000), 99–112.

48 Alice C. Pack, ed., *Building Missionaries in Hawaii, 1960–1963* (La'ie: Church College of Hawaii, 1963), 36.

In 1978, the temple was renovated and rededicated. The First Presidency attended the dedication, and President Spencer W. Kimball presided—making the dedication a historic event in Hawai'i.[49] In 2009 and 2010 the temple experienced another refurbishing and was rededicated on November 21, 2010 by President Thomas S. Monson.

Directions to the Laie Hawaii Temple:
The Laie Hawaii Temple and Visitors' Center are at the head of Hale La'a Boulevard.

7. Social Hall

The Social Hall, built in 1913 for $4,500 and dedicated on September 30, was used for movies, dances, *luaus,* and then church services after I Hemolele burned

Social Hall. Courtesy of BYU–Hawaii Archives.

in 1940 and until the "Back Chapel" was built in 1950. There were two basement classrooms, and the benches in the Hall could be arranged for classes, funerals, weddings, dances, movies, etc. There was a stage at one end and a kitchen in back. The Social Hall was also used as an industrial arts classroom and for college activities during the early years of Church College of Hawai'i. It was demolished in 1960.[50]

Directions to the Laie Social Hall site:
From Kamehameha Highway go right on Lanihuli Street, and left on Loala Street. The Social Hall was located at 55-647/49 Loala Street. Look for the marker.[51]

---

49 Ibid., 190.
50 Moffat, *Historical Sites*, 6–7.
51 For information on the erecting of the marker, see Eric R. Beaver, "Remembering Where La'ie Gathered: The Dedication of the Lanihuli Home and Social Hall Historical Markers," *Mormon Historical Studies* 8, nos. 1–2 (Spring/Fall 2007): 159–63. This marker was funded by the Mormon Historic Sites Foundation and the Mormon Pacific Historical Society, Hawai'i Reserves Inc., and the Laie Community Association.

8. La'iemalo'o Branch Chapel

A small LDS branch was established in the 1920s at 55-105 Kamehameha Highway to serve the members living on *kuleana* or cultivated garden plots in the La'iemalo'o area. The La'iemalo'o branch chapel was located a few lots down the beach from the Castle family's beach house, which is now the Kokoloio Beach Park. The La'iemalo'o branch combined with Laie Ward when the Oahu Stake was formed in 1935. The chapel was later sold and moved to the Sacred Falls area and can still be seen there.[52] Cultural expert Cy Bridges contends

La'iemalo'o Chapel. Courtesy of BYU–Hawaii Archives.

that this chapel was moved to the site of the Hau'ula makai chapel, but the photo of the old Hau'ula chapel torn down in 1963 does not match the photos of the La'iemalo'o chapel.[53] The Sacred Falls Park area has been closed since a rockslide on Mothers Day 1999 claimed ten lives.

Directions to Kokoloio Beach Park (Kakela Beach) and La'iemalo'o Chapel:

The La'iemalo'o Chapel was located at 55-105 Kamehameha Highway about a mile south of La'ie. The former chapel, which can be seen at 53-840 Kamehameha Highway, is now called the Kamalamalama O Keao church.

9. Sugar Mills

The Hawaiian Mission plantation operated two sugar mills on a hillside overlooking a swampy area of taro patches called Waieli. The original mill built in 1868 was small and inexpensive,

---

52 Moffat, *Historical Sites*, 5.
53 Pack, *Building Missionaries*, 122.

La'ie Sugar Mill, 1887. Courtesy of BYU–Hawaii Archives.

and was operated by mule power. Within a few years the equipment became rusty, broken, and dilapidated. Lack of working capital for upkeep was the most persistent problem. When Elder George Nebeker was released from his mission in 1873, the mill was in poor condition; during the next year or two it almost fell apart. The sugar produced was of low quality and the amount of waste high.

"When Harvey H. Cluff took over in 1879 as mission president . . . he soon recognized that it would be necessary either to ship the cane to another mill or to build a new one. He decided on the latter course because it would keep the local Saints employed."[54] The mill was rebuilt with steam power in 1882, and continued in working order for the next few years.[55]

By 1890 the steam-powered mill had broken down just as the new sugar mill at the Kahuku plantation came online. The La'ie plantation negotiated with the Kahuku mill to process its sugarcane and split the profits. In 1931, the Church turned over all its sugar operations to the Kahuku Plantation. This arrangement continued until the Kahuku mill and plantation shut down in 1971.

Dr. Dale Berge, an archaeologist from BYU in Provo, excavated part of the foundations of the first two sugar mills in 1984 and reburied the site for preservation, so there is nothing to see of the site.[56] In order to visit this site you will need permission from Hawai'i Reserves Inc. (808–293–9201).

54 Britsch, *Moramona*, 83.
55 Moffat, *Historical Sites*, 3–4.
56 See Dale L. Berge, "Laie Plantation Sugar Mill (1868–1900): Archeaology and History," *Mormon Pacific Historical Society, Proceedings* (1986), 41–52.

Directions to the Sugar Mill:

The sugar mill site is 200 yards behind the BYU–Hawaii Ceramic Studio. It is covered up and overgrown and there is nothing to see.

10. Pier at Pounders Beach

Built in 1887, the pier and warehouse at Pounders Beach were "used to load sugar and molasses from the Laʻie sugar mill and later the Kahuku mill onto small steamers and schooners," along with rice from the Chinese rice farmers.[57] The raw sugar was taken to Honolulu to be trans-

Pier at Pounders Beach. Courtesy of BYU–Hawaii Archives.

shipped to the C&H refinery in California. Before this pier was built, missionary journals say the raw sugar was carted to landings at Hauʻula or Punaluʻu, where it was rowed out to waiting coastal schooners or steamers. Other times equipment and people were landed through the surf on the beach here. The Laʻie mill shut down for good about 1890 and the sugarcane was sent to Kahuku for processing. When the Oahu Railroad reached Kahuku in 1899 and the Koolau Railroad reached Laʻie in 1907, sugar and other produce were exported around the island the other way, so the pier may not have functioned for very long. Some of the pier's pilings are still visible but are rusting away. Traditionally, Hawaiians called this beach Laʻielohelohe. As the name indicates, Pounders Beach is an excellent place to bodysurf.

---

57 Ibid.

Directions to pier at Pounders Beach:

The pier was located just north of Pounders Beach Park, which is on Kamahameha Highway just south of the Polynesian Cultural Center. Look for the pilings.

11. Laʻie Plantation Store, also known as Goo's Store

The Laʻie Plantation always operated a store to serve the needs of the workers. Originally the store was located in one of the plantation buildings at the head of Lanihuli Street and operated out of a single room until a separate building was constructed in 1892. When the Koolau Railroad was laid through Laʻie, a new store was built in 1907 on the corner where the railroad crossed Lanihuli Street. This new Plantation Store was built on a raised platform along the railroad track so that passengers could step out of the train and onto the porch around the store. In 1955, Charles K. C. Goo from Honolulu was asked to come to Laʻie to manage the store when the temporary campus of the Church College of Hawaiʻi was set up across the street. The Plantation Store was a lifesaver for many local families, because they could sometimes buy on credit. This harkened back to the days when plantation workers were paid in script that could be redeemed at the plantation store. An icehouse and later a laundromat and beauty shop were also attached on the Naniloa Loop side. On the Lanihuli Street side was a barber shop. Next door to the Plantation Store, on the *makai* (seaward) side, were the plantation office of Zion's

La ʻie Plantation Store, ca. 1910. Courtesy of BYU–Hawaii Archives.

Goo's Store, ca. 1960. Courtesy of BYU–Hawaii Archives.

Securities and post office. This building was later used as a bank. The store was closed in 1986 when Goo retired and was then torn down a couple of years later.[58]

> *Directions to the Plantation Store Site:*
> The plantation store was located at 55-075 Lanihuli Street on the corner of Lanihuli Street and Naniloa Loop. Look for the marker.[59]

12. Koolau Railroad

The Oahu Railroad around Pearl Harbor, Wai'anae, Kaena Point, and Hale'iwa to Kahuku was completed in 1899. It was used to service the sugar plantations around the coast and bring a few tourists out to the Haleiwa Hotel on weekends. Before the Koolau Railroad was built, the cut cane was brought to the mill on ox-carts or later by a little steam engine on temporary tracks that were laid down and taken up in sections

Koolau Railroad. Courtesy of BYU–Hawaii Archives.

---

58 Ibid., 8.
59 This marker was funded by the Mormon Historic Sites Foundation, the Mormon Pacific Historical Society, Hawai'i Reserves Inc., and the Laie Community Association.

wherever they were needed. The narrow-gage Koolau Railroad was built from Kahuku through La'ie to Kahana Valley from 1906 to 1908 by James B. Castle to haul sugarcane to the Kahuku Mill. Mr. Castle threatened to cease hauling the La'ie Plantation's cane to his Kahuku mill unless the Church sold the La'ie Plantation to him. Samuel Woolley was able to stall him until Mr. Castle died in 1918 and it was the Church that bought Koolau Railroad.[60] It also took passengers and operated until 1946 when the tidal wave of April 1 washed out portions of the railroad bed, and cane hauling was switched to trucks. Approaching La'ie, the railroad ran along the ocean side of Kamehameha Highway from Kahuku and crossed Kahawainui Stream just *makai* (seaward) of the present highway bridge, then followed the *makai* (ocean) side of Naniloa Loop until it reached the Temple View Apartments, then continued straight through the Brigham Young University–Hawai'i Library and boys' dorms toward Hau'ula. There was a spur line along Po'ohaili Street to the valley behind the Laie Hawaii Temple and a spur heading *mauka* (inland) from the Hale 2 area.[61]

Directions to the Koolau Railroad:
The Koolau Railroad came along Kamehameha Highway from Kahuku on the *makai,* or ocean side of the road. At the hukilau area it turned up Naniloa Loop and went along the *makai* side of Naniloa Loop in front of the temple, then headed across the BYU–Hawaii campus at the School of Education building and right through the Library and the *mauka* dorms. The right-of-way and railbed can still be seen heading south from the road to the quarry.

13. Plantation Labor Camps

After the Kahuku plantation took over the milling of La'ie's cane in 1891, and especially after Kahuku took over all the sugarcane operations in 1931, the Kahuku plantation built small groups of workers' housing out among the fields to minimize commuting time for the workers, since the Kahuku plantation cane fields stretched from Sunset Beach to Kahana Valley. Groups of

60 Riley Moffat, et al. *Gathering to La'ie*, pp. 84–85.
61 Ibid., 7–8.

plantation houses in the Iosepa Street area south of Pu'uahi Street in La'ie comprised one section of housing for families and another group for single workers; another was against the hill behind BYU–Hawaii's General Classroom Building called Mauka Camp, and another behind the current cemetery. These Kahuku plantation laborers, from the Phillipines, Portugal, Puerto Rico, and Japan, were considered part of the community; they attended the mission school and participated in community events. Some families of Japanese in the Po'ohaili Street area also leased land from the plantation to grow pineapples on the hillsides above the sugarcane from about 1910 to 1925.

> *Directions to the labor camps:*
> The camps were located just south of the General Classroom Building of BYU–Hawaii. Other camps were also behind the new cemetery, and there was one for the Japanese pineapple farmers at the end of Po'ohaili Street. The largest group was along Iosepa Street just south of Pu'uahi Street.

14. Shinto Temple and Torii

"A few Japanese families lived behind what was then the 'new' cemetery," in La'ie. "One of the men, Totaro Nakayama, an ordained Shinto minister, built a shrine for the Japanese plantation workers" to worship at. The shrine was torn down after he died in 1949, but a concrete *torii*, or ceremonial arch, was left as a memorial until it was accidentally knocked down in 1995."[62] An interview by LDS Pacific historian Kenneth Baldridge in 1989 with Tom Nakayama, son of Totaro Nakayama, gives us interesting details about the relationship between the Shinto and Mormon congregations:

> Ken Baldridge: I assume most of the Japanese were Shinto, members of your father's congregation.
> Tom Nakayama: That's right. This is why, you know, in the later years, I think back I say, "Gee, it's a wonder the Mormon people had tolerated that and had my father stay there". This is something that, you know, you would think, well, this is a

---

62 Moffat et al., *Gathering to La'ie*, 136–37.

Mormon town; maybe we should have only the Mormon religion, but freedom of religion, so I guess it worked out all right.

Ken: Was there any problem that you were aware of?

Tom: None whatsoever, none whatsoever. Even in school, during my school days, nothing—no such thing as "You are a Shinto and I'm a Mormon." No segregation of that sort. We all worked together, pitch in together and did our work together.[63]

Directions to the Shinto Shrine Site:

From the traffic circle where Naniloa Loop meets Po'ohaili Street go north on Wahinepe'e Street beside the cemetery and cross over Kahawainui Stream. The site is on your right in the bushes.

15. Beauty Hole

The Beauty Hole was located across from the present Foodland grocery store in La'ie. "Also called Lua Laniloa, this 'bottomless' pond was connected underground to the ocean and rose and fell with the tides." Discovered in 1912 by Lyons Baldwin Nainoa and Hamana Kalili, who were excavating the end of La'ie Point as a county gravel pit, it became the popular swimming hole at La'ie. "There was a diving board and changing shed." The Tanoai's snack shop nearby "was washed into the Beauty Hole during the tsunami of April 1, 1946." Children used to dive here for coins tossed by tourists. This pool was

Beauty Hole. Courtesy of BYU–Hawaii Archives.

Beauty Hole. Courtesy of BYU–Hawaii Archives.

63 Tom Nakayama, "Kenneth Baldridge Oral History Interview" (1989), box 111, 11, BYU–Hawaii Archives.

where village children learned to swim. When they could swim around the Beauty Hole, they were then considered ready to swim on their own in the ocean. "The Beauty Hole was filled in about 1969."[64]

Directions to the Beauty Hole:

The Beauty Hole was located across Kamehameha Highway from Foodland at 55-539/543 Kamehameha Highway.

16. The Nainoa Home

The Nainoa home is possibly the oldest home in Laʻie. It was built by District Judge Lyons Baldwin Nainoa (ca. 1842–1918) about 1913.[65] Judge Nainoa was one of the first to gather to Laʻie from the Kohala district on the Big Island in 1865. He would hold sessions of court in Hawaiian on his front porch. He was one of the last to be buried in the cemetery behind the temple in 1918. It is still occupied by his descendents.

Directions to the Nainoa Home:

The Nainoa Home is on the corner of Wahinepeʻe Street and Loala Street across from the Hukilau Cafe at 55-680 Wahinepeʻe Street.

17. Sam's Store

Known earlier as the "Pake Store," or the "Do Drop Inn," during World War II, Sam's Store was built in the 1920s by the Pang family. In the 1950s, the store was operated by the Kawahigashi family, and then by Sam Choy from 1960 to 1992. No matter the name, the sweet shop/snack bar/restaurant/store has always been a part of the community.[66] The store and café are still in business. The restaurant was formerly run by Sam Choy's son, named also Sam Choy, who became a famous chef. It is now run by a greatgrandson of Judge Nainoa.

Other little mom-and-pop stores were operated by the Tashiro family across Kahawainui Stream behind the egg-farm store and

---

64 Moffat, *Historical Sites*, 7. Moffat et al., *Gathering to Laʻie*, 146–47.
65 Ibid., 9.
66 Ibid., 8.

La'ie Sweet Shop. Courtesy of BYU–Hawaii Archives.

the Nakayama family store and blacksmith shop on the Kahuku side of Wahinepe'e Street near the Hukilau Café.

> *Directions to Sam's Store:*
>
> The store is on the right, at the intersection with Wahinepe'e Street and Loala Street. The restaurant is now the award-winning "Hukilau Café."

18. Sweet Shops

Old La'ie had several little family-run "sweet shops" where local kids and occasionally tourists could buy snacks. "Logan's Cool Spot (also known as Laie Curios or Laie Sweet Shop) was popular in the 1940s, selling snacks and curios, especially *lauhala* weaving, and featuring local live entertainment by the Logan family. It was located near where Pu'uahi Street came off Kamehameha Highway. Pu'uahi Street was one of the main roads coming into La'ie and was near the Beauty Hole. Another sweet shop, operated by the Hyun family from the 1930s to the 1950s, also catered to the tourists visiting the Laie Hawai'i Temple." The Hyuns' shop "used sections of coconut logs for stools and showed outdoor movies on Friday and Saturday nights for the children. Masepa Tanoai had a snackshop on Kamehameha Highway at the Beauty Hole in the

1930s and 1940s."[67] The April 1, 1946, tsunami washed it into the Beauty Hole.

Directions to the Sweet Shops:
Logan's Cool Spot was located at 55-132 Pu'uahi Street. The one operated by the Hyun family was at 55-601 Naniloa Loop at the intersection of Naniloa Loop across from the Temple. Tanoai's snack shop was located at 55-545 Kamehameha Highway across from Foodland.

19. Japanese Language School

A Japanese language school was formed during the 1920s and 1930s in La'ie to serve the children of the Japanese plantation workers after their regular school. Laie Plantation manager and Mission President Samuel Woolley donated to its construction. It was shut down when the United States went to war with Japan. It was then used as a classroom when the Laie Ward met in the Social Hall across the street from 1940 to 1950.

Directions to the Japanese Language School:
The address was 55-650 Loala Street.

20. Poi Mills

Poi pounding. Courtesy of BYU–Hawaii Archives.

The importance of taro in the lives of traditional Hawaiians cannot be overemphasized. It was their staff of life. Grown in wet land paddies, the corm, or root, was pounded or crushed into a paste called poi. Each family traditionally made their own, but later La'ie went into commercial production or used machinery for communal production. The machinery mashed the taro instead of having to pound it by hand. "The famous taro lands

---

67 Ibid., 9.

of La'ie supported at least three poi factories. One was started in the 1920s by Keau Makahanohano and was later sold to Peter Enos. He turned it over to the Church during World War II, at the request of Bishop Po'i Kekauoha, to supply poi to Honolulu as a building fund-raiser. It was later operated by Kalehua Makanoe Kekauoha until her death in 1951. Another poi factory was owned and operated by Hamana Kalili (originator of the *shaka* sign) from the 1920s to the 1950s. A third poi factory was operated by William and Mary Keli'i from the early 1930s until about 1956.[68]

Directions to the poi factories:

The Makahanohano/Enos/Kekauoha poi mill was at 55-044 Lanihuli Street where the telephone building and tower is located. Kalili's poi mill was at 55-167 Pu'uahi Street, and the Keli'i poi mill at 55-122 Pu'uahi Street.

21. Hukilau Beach (Hamana's Beach)

Before the Church's *hukilau* fund-raiser activity, the area was called Hamana's Beach, named after Hamana Kalili (1882–1958), Laie's chief fishing master during the first half of the twentieth century. The term *hukilau*

Hukilau with Hamana Kalili, 1923. Courtesy of BYU–Hawaii Archives.

derives from the Hawaiian form of fishing in which a long net is let out from a boat to surround a school of fish; then people on the beach pull (*huki*) the net, with ti leaves (*lau*) attached to it, up to the beach. Fund-raising *hukilaus* began in 1948. "The Hukilau was an expansive *luau* organized by members of the Laie Ward . . . as a way for raising money to rebuild their chapel, which burned to the ground in 1940."[69]

---

68 Ibid., 9.
69 Steve Fidel, "A Legacy of Laie," *Mormon Times, Deseret News*, October 31, 2009, 1.

Hukilau grounds, 1950. Courtesy of BYU–Hawaii Archives.

In 1947, Bishop Poʻi Kekauoha and his Relief Society President Viola Kawahigashi organized the Laʻie *hukilau* as a stake welfare and building fund-raiser to build a new chapel for Laie, which was dedicated by Elder Matthew Cowley of the Quorum of the Twelve on May 5, 1950. Tickets were printed and left with tour groups in Honolulu to lure them to the windward side of the island, and dancers danced by the side of the highway to persuade people passing by to stop. The first *hukilau* was a great success, with more than a thousand participants. The Relief Society cooked; the priesthood was responsible for the *imu*, or underground oven, used to cook the pig and other foods as well. The youth served the guests. The Relief Society sisters also made and sold handicrafts. The Laʻie Hawaiian and Samoan communities entertained with dancing and music. The Laʻie *hukilau* became a grand luau, put on about twice a month.[70] "The Laʻie wards continued the *hukilau* until 1969. Busloads of tourists would come out from Honolulu to enjoy a traditional Hawaiian luau, as well as entertainment by the Laʻie Saints. A large shed was built to serve the luau, which was cooked outside in the *imus*. In the early 1960s, the building missionaries added bleachers, a stage, and a restroom."[71]

---

70 Ibid.
71 Pack, *Building Missionaries*, 103.

Jack Owens, a popular songwriter of the day, visited the event and wrote the "Hukilau Song" in 1948. It became popular on the mainland. Probably millions of people have learned some basic hula from this song:

> What a beautiful day for fishing,
> The Old Hawaiian way,
> And the huklau nets were swishing
> Down at old Laie Bay.
> Oh, we're going to a hukilau.
> The huki, huki, huki, hukilau.
> Everybody loves the hukilau
> Where the laulau is the kaukau at the big luau.
> We throw our nets
> Out into the sea
> And all the 'ama'ama
> Come swimming to me.
> Oh, we're going, to a hukilau
> A huki, huki, huki
> Huki, huki, huki hukilau.[72]

Hamana Kalili, a counselor to Bishop Po'i Kekauoha, portrayed Hawaiian King Kamehameha in the early *hukilau* royal court. Brother Kalili had lost his three middle fingers on his right hand in an accident, so when he waved, it was only with a thumb

Hukilau Court, 1950. Courtesy of BYU–Hawaii Archives.

72 Ibid.

and little finger. His wave has became known worldwide as the Hawaiian "shaka" wave.[73] It was popularized by Honolulu mayor Frank Fasi as his political symbol.

The *hukilau* continued long after the La'ie chapel was rebuilt, and thereafter proceeds were used for the ward budget. The *hukilau* idea, along with the talent and organization of La'ie residents, was transferred into what was to become the Polynesian Cultural Center.

It was from Hukilau Beach that BYU–Hawaii's voyaging canoe, *Iosepa*, was launched on November 3, 2001. Thousands of people gathered on the beach for the launching, and Elder M. Russell Ballard of the Quorum of the Twelve, and a descendent of Joseph F. Smith, offered the blessing.[74] The *Iosepa* is now on display at the Polynesian Cultural Center.

Directions to the Hukilau Beach:
At the north end of La'ie on Kamehameha Highway before crossing Kahawainui Stream there is a parking lot and plaque on the right, open to the ocean.

22. Brigham Young University–Hawaii/Church College of Hawai'i

During the last sixty years, some of the most important developments for the Church in Hawai'i have been in education. Brigham Young University–Hawaii, formerly known as the Church College of Hawai'i (CCH), is the result of these developments.

President David O. McKay envisioned a Church-run institution of higher learning in La'ie in 1921 when he visited the La'ie mission school. His dream became a reality when he became President of the Church. On July 21, 1954, the establishment of a Church college in Hawai'i was officially announced by the First Presidency.

The unusual "purposes and goals [of CCH] were made clear by President McKay when he dedicated the land" on which BYU–Hawaii now stands. A year after he announced plans to build a college, "he journeyed to La'ie to preside at the ground-breaking

---

73 Ibid.
74 Mike Foley, "Iosepa Completes Maiden Voyage," *Brigham Young University-Hawai'i Magazine*, Fall 2004, 6.

ceremonies of CCH. During the service . . . he spoke not only of the role Laʻie and the school were to play in the lives of the Hawaiian [people], but also of the influence the college would have on the peoples of the South Pacific and Asia. He praised God that Laʻie had been dedicated ʻas a gathering place for the Hawaiians and other races on these cherished islands.ʼ"[75] He then declared that every teacher at the CCH ought to "have in his or her heart an assurance, not a mere belief, an assurance, that God has had a hand over this entire valley, that that dedication offered years ago was inspired, that this land is a choice land. Itʼs part of America, part of Zion."[76] Then, in a spirit of prophecy, President McKay spoke of CCHʼs destiny.

> From this school, Iʼll tell you, will go men and women whose influence will be felt for good towards the establishment of peace internationally. Four hundred and fifty million people waiting to hear the message over in China, a noble race. Iʼve met them. I donʼt know how many million over in Japan. You prepare to go and carry that message. Three hundred and fifty million down in India. We have scarcely touched these great nations, and theyʼre calling us today.[77]

When he announced plans to build the college in 1954, President McKay was informed that the Church College of Hawaiʻi would open in September 1956. He expressed his desire that the CCH open a year earlier than planned. Stake President Edward L. Clissold remembers that in an effort to fulfill President McKayʼs desire, "There was a feverish several months of labor." [78] A temporary campus of war surplus buildings was set up in Moke Hiramʼs watermelon patch next to the Laie Ward chapel at the intersection of Naniloa Loop and Lanihuli Street near where President McKay had witnessed a flag-raising ceremony thirty-two years earlier. Ground was broken south of the village in a cane field for the permanent campus of the new institution of higher learning to be called the Church College of Hawaii (now called Brigham Young University–Hawaii or simply BYU–Hawaii), on February 12, 1955.

---

75 Britsch, *Moramona*, 178–79.
76 Law, *Founding and Early Development*, 67.
77 Ibid.
78 Britsch, *Mormona*, 180.

Temporary CCH campus, 1957. Courtesy of BYU–Hawaii Archives.

President McKay was concerned about budgeting for the new school. When he learned what the construction price would be, he requested that building missionaries be used to cut construction costs.

The building missionary system of the LDS Church was first conceived in Tonga as an emergency measure to build the Liahona High School in 1950. It was later used in Samoa and New Zealand before coming to La'ie and then going worldwide and taught hundreds of young men valuable trade skills. Credit for the method belongs to many people, but it was chiefly Wendell B. Mendenhall, appointed as chairman of the Church Building Committee in 1955, who developed the system into a Pacific, and then a worldwide, program for the Church. Building missionaries used to construct CCH were called by the Church to serve for two or more years at a time.[79]

Joseph E. Wilson was called to be the general building supervisor of the CCH, and the project began in December 1955. At times during the construction, more than fifty experienced construction missionaries from the mainland and their wives worked on the project, along with approximately seventy-five missionaries from the Hawai'i and many local Saints. The wives of the builders cleaned windows, offered moral support, and laid down 174,000 square feet of floor tile.[80] The final cost estimate of the completed buildings came to about twelve dollars per square foot (far below the usual price for similar construction projects in the islands) and around four million dollars total. The completed structures

79 Cummings, *Mighty Missionary of the Pacific*, 263.
80 Britsch, *Moramona*, 181.

Church College of Hawaii, 1959. Courtesy of BYU–Hawaii Archives.

accommodated the needs of between one thousand and twelve hundred students.

Dedication services for the initial college buildings were held on December 17, 1958. In the dedicatory prayer, President McKay again laid out the purpose of the CCH:

> Thou hast emphasized the responsibility which rests upon thy people to carry the message of the restoration of the gospel to all nations. Thus doth thou emphasize the fact that it is not sufficient merely to testify to the world of the restoration, but to present the principles of the gospel in an intelligent manner that the honest in heart may be convinced of the truth, and may be led from paths of error into the way of righteousness. To this general and glorious purpose, therefore, our Father, we unitedly assemble and authoritatively dedicate the Church College of Hawai'i.[81]

"Dignitaries from Hawai'i and the mainland were in attendance, and many other important people from government, education, and religious groups sent notes of congratulation."[82]

81 David Oman McKay, *Dedicatory Prayer: An Address by President David O. McKay at the Dedication of The Church College of Hawai'i* (Laie, December 17, 1958).
82 Britsch, *Moramona*, 181.

The first day of class in 1955 at the temporary campus began with 153 students, and twenty faculty and administrators.[83] The administrative organization and curriculum of the CCH was quite broad for a new two-year school. In addition to academics, the new school also provided a full slate of athletic and recreational activities. Some college activities were held in the Laie Ward chapel and the social hall until the present campus was built.[84] CCH was accredited as a two-year college in October 1959.[85] In 1961, the Western Association of Schools and Colleges granted full four-year accreditation to CCH. On June 3 of the same year the college awarded its first bachelor degrees to seventy-six graduates.[86]

Since 1958, more dormitories have been completed, along with the Joseph F. Smith Library, the Aloha Center, the George Q. Cannon Activities Center (the third largest indoor seating facility in Hawai'i), the Lorenzo Snow Administration Building, and a student stake center. In addition, an annex to the cafeteria, tennis courts, curbing, and paved walks were added.[87] The original administrative and classroom building was renamed the David O. McKay Building in 1980. Beginning in 2012, a major expansion aimed at doubling the size of the student body commenced, with more new dorms and remodeled old dorms and the Heber J. Grant combination stake center and School of Business Building.

From 1969 to 1975 the campus hosted the Asia/Pacific Language Training Mission in one of the dorms behind the library. Thousands of missionaries heading for missions in Asia and the Pacific picked up basic language and cultural skills here.

In 1974, CCH became BYU–Hawaii, a branch of Brigham Young University in Provo, Utah.[88] The newly named BYU–Hawaii grew quickly and now hosts over 2,500 students from more than 70 countries and has the highest percentage of international students in the United States. This eclectic student body is instructed by over 120 faculty members. On May 16, 2003, Elder Henry B.

83 Ibid., 180.
84 Moffat, *Historical Sites*, 6–7.
85 Britsch, *Unto the Islands*, 183.
86 Britsch, *Moramona*, 183.
87 Pack, *Building Missionaries*, 83.
88 Britsch, *Unto the Islands*, 185.

Eyring, Church Commissioner of Education, announced to the BYU–Hawaii administration that the university would, from then on, report directly to the Board of Trustees, instead of to BYU in Provo.[89]

Directions to BYU–Hawaii/Church College of Hawaii:
    Coming from Kaneʻohe on Kamehameha Highway turn left on to Naniloa Loop two blocks to the entrance of the University on the left.

23. Polynesian Cultural Center (PCC)

The Polynesian Cultural Center is a nonprofit organization of The Church of Jesus Christ of Latter-day Saints. Its principal purposes are to provide employment for students at BYU–Hawaii, to generate money to help support that institution, and to give large numbers of people favorable contact with the Church. It also provides the part-time student workers from the Pacific Islands an opportunity to share their culture while being paid and to learn more about their culture from full-time cultural experts.

Polynesian Cultural Center, 1964. Courtesy of BYU–Hawaii Archives.

89 "Fifty Golden Moments for Fifty Golden Years," *Brigham Young University–Hawaiʻi Magazine*, Spring 2005, 8. See also Alf Pratte and Eric B. Shumway, *BYU–Hawaii: Prophetic Destiny* (Laie: Brigham Young University–Hawaii, 2015).

About seven hundred students are currently employed part-time at the PCC. Since its opening in 1963, about eighteen thousand students have worked at the center. The PCC provides many different opportunities for employees to learn and polish their English-speaking skills through their interaction with thousands of visitors daily. The talent of the students who work at the PCC has attracted millions of visitors, and the center has produced over $150 million for BYU–Hawaii and its students.[90]

Since opening, the PCC has become Hawai'i's most successful paid-admission visitor attraction. When the PCC opened in October 1963, the total annual visitor count to Hawai'i was 110,000. Now over eight million tourists visit Hawai'i each year.[91] September 1–8, 2013, PCC celebrated its 50th anniversary. To date, over 40 million visitors have come to the PCC. For over five decades the PCC has proven the authenticity of its cultural activities by hosting many Pacific island leaders in the correct ceremonial ways. "Some of the leaders who have honored both the Church and the PCC by making official visits include Her Majesty Te Atairangikaahu, the Maori Queen of New Zealand; Ratu Sir Kamisese Mara, Prime Minister of Fiji; Their Majesties Taufa'ahau Tupou IV and Halaevalu Mata'aho, King and Queen of the Kingdom of Tonga; His Highness Malietoa Tanumafili II, head of state of Western Samoa," and Premier Zhao Ziyang of China.[92]

The PCC had its beginnings in 1951. Elder Matthew Cowley of the Quorum of the Twelve and Edward L. Clissold, a member of the Pacific Board of Education, discussed ways to offset the expenses required of the Maori Saints when they came to La'ie from New Zealand to attend the temple. Elder Cowley

Matthew Cowley and Edward Clissold. Courtesy of BYU–Hawaii Archives.

---

90 "PCC Updates Cumulative Totals," *Polynesian Cultural Center Newsletter,* Spring 2006. See also Laura F. Willes, *Miracle in the Pacific: The Polynesian Cultural Center* (Salt Lake City: Deseret Book, 2012).

91 Ibid.

92 Ibid.

suggested that "the Maoris build a large Maori house, a communal dwelling, where they could live inexpensively while at La'ie. Also, he thought these people might do some entertaining, attract some tourists, and thus make a little money to sustain themselves. But nothing immediately came of their discussion."[93] (Cowley and Clissold had begun talking about this idea in the late 1930s, but it was not publicly mentioned until 1951.) Later, as President Clissold and college leaders contemplated "the needs of the students and their abilities as dancers, singers, and living representatives of Polynesian cultures, they conceived a plan to create a living center of Polynesian culture and entertainment. The students, according to the plan, would provide a large part of the employees for the center, and thus their financial needs could be met."[94]

President Clissold and Wendell Mendenhall approached the First Presidency with the idea of a Polynesian cultural center associated with CCH, and the Church approved the idea in November 1959.[95] Construction of the Polynesian Cultural Center did not get underway by labor missionaries until early 1962, because the chosen construction site was moved to a location closer to the Kamehameha Highway from the original site between the temple and the college. A group of students began entertaining in Waikiki under the direction of Professor Wylie Swapp, and by March of 1960, the student cast of the Polynesian Panorama received rave reviews for their performance in the Kaiser Dome at the Hilton Hawaiian Village in Waikiki.[96]

Building missionaries from the islands and local volunteers from La'ie constructed the PCC. Cultural experts were brought in from the islands of Fiji, Tahiti, Tonga, and New Zealand to supervise the construction of the various villages. The center covered sixteen acres, with huts and a lagoon. Six different villages represented the Center: Hawaiian, Samoan, Tongan, Fijian, Maori, and Tahitian. So they would be portrayed more accurately, the buildings were built by people from the different island groups; everything was as true to the native style as possible. On October 12,

---

93 Pack, *Building Missionaries*, 132.
94 Britsch, *Unto the Islands*, 186.
95 Cummings, *Mighty Missionary of the Pacific*, 293.
96 Laura E. Willes, *Miracle in the Pacific: The Polynesian Cultural Center* (Salt Lake City: Deseret Book, 2012).

1963, President Hugh B. Brown dedicated the Polynesian Cultural Center, with over one thousand people attending the dedication.[97] President Brown prayed, "May all who come here see in this center an effort to bring people of different nations and races together in a better exemplification of true brotherhood."[98]

Although the directors of the undertaking, Clissold and Mendenhall in particular, were sure the PCC would be successful, many skeptics in the Honolulu tourist industry and elsewhere "prophesied doom" for the Center. They argued, "An eighty-mile round-trip journey from Honolulu to Laie and back is too far," and "tourists don't really want an authentic cultural experience, particularly if the dancers are dressed modestly." The subsequent success of the PCC proved its critics wrong, and the center was soon declared a success by Honolulu newspapers and leaders in the tourist industry as the "flop that flipped."[99] By 1975, about half of the visitors to the islands went through the PCC. By 1984, the PCC was hosting over one million visitors a year and was the most popular paid attraction in Hawaiʻi.[100]

Since 1976, an expansion was undertaken that covered forty-two acres and included a 2,500-seat theater, a dining pavilion the size of a football field, and a number of cultural attractions. Popular attractions at the PCC include replica villages representing Fiji, Hawaiʻi, Marquesas, New Zealand, Samoa, Tonga, Tahiti, Samoa and an exhibit from Rapa Nui (Easter Island). There are shows and demonstrations at each village throughout the day. A *luau* dinner show, canoe rides, and an IMAX film are also highlights of a visit to the PCC. There is, of course, a fee to enjoy the cultures of the Pacific at the PCC.

A missionary tool, conceived and developed by Norm Nielsen and Steven Bennett, formerly of the PCC staff, is a free guided tour of Laʻie, the BYU–Hawaii campus, and the temple grounds. Trams take visitors on the tour while they listen to a monologue about the history of the Laʻie plantation, the purposes of the college, and

97 Britsch, *Unto the Islands*, 187.
98 "Polynesian Cultural Center Dedicatory Prayer and Address," in *Something Special: Brigham Young University–Hawaiʻi Foundational Speeches* (Laie: BYU–Hawaii, 2012), 34.
99 Britsch, *Unto the Islands*, 187.
100 Ibid., 187–88.

the temple. The final stop on the tour is at the Temple Visitors' Center.[101]

In 2015, the PCC added the Hukilau Marketplace in front, and the old Laniloa Lodge was replaced by the Marriott Courtyard Oahu North Shore.

Directions to the Polynesian Cultural Center:
The Polynesian Cultural Center is located on Kamehameha Highway next to the BYU–Hawaii campus.

24. Kokoloio Beach Park (Kakela Beach)

James Castle, who owned the Kahuku plantation, developed the Koolau Agricultural Co., which included all the sugarcane lands between La'ie and Kahana and the narrow gauge Koolau Railroad from Kahuku to Kahana. When Castle died in 1918 the La'ie plantation bought the Koolau Agriculture Co. and the Koolau Railroad. In the 1920s the La'ie plantation sold beach lots here to Julia Castle and Maude Cooke, and the Castle family built a fancy beach house with gardens and statuary.

In the early 1950s when Edward Clissold was manager of Zions Securities, the Church bought back the Castle property and brought in WWII surplus Quonset huts that served as boys' dorms and the labor missionaries' quarters while the permanent campus was being built. In the 1950s the Oahu Stake also had a piggery in Kokoloio Gulch. This beach property was also famous as the location of Church ward camps from the 1970s to 1990s. Each ward would set up camp for a week at a time, bring generators, and have TVs, refrigerators, *luaus,* and movies. It was the highlight of the year in each ward.[102]

Directions to Kokoloio Beach Park (Kakela Beach)
The park is about one mile south of La'ie on Kamehameha Highway behind a low rock wall. The *ahupua'a* of La'ie extends to the south end of the park.

---

101 Ibid., 188.
102 Riley Moffat, "Kakela/Kokoloio." 2008. Copy in possession of author.

Maui

Maui, named for the Hawaiian god Maui, is the second largest of the Hawaiian Islands (727 square miles) and is formed by two large shield volcanos, Haleakala, or House of the Sun, 10,032 feet high; and Halemahina, or House of the Moon, also known as Pu'u Kukui or the West Maui Mountains, 5,788 feet high. Between the two mountains is a low, fertile isthmus. From this feature comes Maui's nickname, the "Valley Isle." The West Maui Mountains are older and have eroded into deep valleys, while the slopes of Haleakala on east Maui are smoother, except on the windward side, where the crater of Haleakala is very recognizable. Haleakala is still considered an active volcano, and an eruption low on its southwest flank occurred as recently as the 1790s.

Many powerful chiefs or kings have ruled on Maui, and many legends recount its history and lore. Maui was the first island Kamehameha I conquered in 1791 after he consolidated his control of the island of Hawai'i.

Lahaina, on west Maui, was the capital of the Kingdom of Hawai'i from the 1820s to 1845. Even before the death of Kamehameha I in 1819, Lahaina began to receive frequent visits from explorers, and the first Christian missionaries arrived at Lahaina by invitation of Queen Keopuolani in 1823. Lahaina is by far the best place to see the heritage and impact of whaling in Hawai'i that occurred between the 1820s and 1860s before Lahaina became a sugar plantation town. In 1823, the main thoroughfare was Alanui Mo'i (King's Road), which is called Front Street today. It was a simple dirt road lined by numerous residences, shops, and the royal enclosure at Moku'ula. From the early 1820s to the 1860s, Lahaina Roads was the anchorage for most whaling ships, trading, and commercial shipping to Hawai'i before it was eclipsed by Honolulu. Now Kahului on the north shore is the main port of Maui and the location of the airport.

As the whaling industry declined, the sugar industry grew, especially after water was captured in the wet north slopes of Haleakala and brought to the thirsty sugarcane growing on the isthmus. There were also pineapple plantations higher up on the slopes above the sugarcane. The sugar industry has declined and there is only one active plantation left in Hawai'i at Pu'unene. Now the tourism industry has taken off, centered around the sunny seashores from Lahaina to Kapalua and from Kihei to Makena.

Latter-day Saints on Maui

Three LDS missionaries from the original ten sent to Hawai'i were assigned to Maui: George Q. Cannon, James Keeler, and Henry W. Bigler. Upon arriving at the whaling port of Lahaina on December 19, 1850, they found lodgings for $4.00 a week in a "native house" made of grass (which Elder Cannon thought looked like a haystack). The rent soon exhausted their funds. "At the end of three weeks the Maui missionaries were almost destitute and found it necessary to leave the small native house" and split up. The missionaries decided to go in different directions, because they thought strangers would be more likely to help them individually than in a group, but just as they were parting, a kind elderly Hawaiian woman named Nalimanui, who had done their laundry, offered her own room to them, allowing the missionaries to stay together.[1]

The missionaries began their missions teaching only English-speaking residents, but they had little success. They soon realized that "if [they] were to confine [their] labors to the whites, [their] mission to those islands would be a short one."[2]

On January 24, 1851, the missionaries received a letter from Mission President Hiram Clark, which said that some of the missionaries were discouraged and planned to return to the United States. George Q. Cannon did not like the thought of leaving, because "matters had been moving in a positive direction in Maui," and he refused to entertain such an idea. He was adamant that

1 Adrian W. Cannon, Richard E. Turley Jr., and Chad M. Orton, eds., *The Journals of George Q. Cannon: Hawaiian Mission, 1850–1854* (Salt Lake City: Deseret Book, 2014), 33, 43; Min et al., *Stewards of the Promise*, 5–7.
2 Cannon, *My First Mission*, 127.

he could not go home "without feeling condemned." Feeling that the Lord would hold him accountable for not doing his duty and that in some future day the Hawaiians "might rise up in judgment" against him "for not having given them the privilege of hearing the truth," Cannon suggested that just because they had not found whites that would receive them, they should not "turn around and go home, and leave a whole nation to welter in ignorance, because it did not happen to tell us that we were to preach to them in their own tongue."[3] Upon hearing Cannon's determination, four of the other missionaries decided to stay in Hawai'i.

Troubled, Cannon went to Nalimanui's garden to pray and ask what the Lord would have him do. This prayer was answered in a very direct way. Cannon later related that during his prayer, "he talked with the Lord, heard his voice and felt His holy presence."[4] The Lord told him that he was to stay in the Sandwich Islands.[5] When Clark saw that Cannon and the other four missionaries were determined to stay in Hawai'i, he agreed to let them stay until they were satisfied they had warned the people. Clark then left alone for the Marquesas Islands.[6]

On August 10, 1851, more missionaries arrived in Maui, including Philip B. Lewis, who became the mission president.[7] In 1854, fifteen-year-old Joseph F. Smith arrived in Hawai'i to begin his mission. Among other challenges, Smith found that to be an effective missionary, he must learn the language, and he felt obligated and determined to do so: "I felt resolved to stay there, master the language and warn the people of those islands, if I had to do it alone; for I felt that I could not do otherwise and be free from condemnation; the spirit of it was upon me." Young Smith felt it a duty to teach everyone on the isles, regardless of their skin color or their language. Consequently, he exercised great faith in the Lord, and in one hundred days he was able to conduct meetings, perform ordinances, and speak "with greater ease then he could

3 Ibid., 133–34.
4 Bryant S. Hinckley, *The Faith of Our Pioneer Fathers* (Salt Lake City: Deseret Book, 1956), 165.
5 Cannon, *My First Mission*, 127.
6 Jenson, Manuscript History.
7 *Unto Every Nation: Gospel Light Reaches Every Land*, ed. Donald Q. Cannon and Richard O. Cowan (Salt Lake City: Deseret Book, 2003), 152.

when he spoke English." By the time Smith was only sixteen, he was called to preside over the Saints on Maui.[8]

In a revelation that George Q. Cannon received at Lahaina, Maui, the Lord told him that the Hawaiians were of the House of Israel. "From the time of Cannon's revelation forward LDS missionaries began to preach that the Hawaiian people were an offshoot branch of Israel through the posterity of Lehi, a Book of Mormon prophet."[9] As this doctrine spread that the Hawaiian people and all other Polynesians are heirs to the blessings promised to the posterity of Abraham, the work began to grow, and converts joined the Church in unprecedented numbers.

By the October 1853 semiannual mission conference, there were more than eight hundred members on Maui out of a population of eighteen thousand, and the idea of gathering the Saints was being discussed. The place chosen for this gathering was the island of Lana'i. With the Saints then gathering to Lana'i, its later abandonment, and then the purchase of La'ie on O'ahu for a new gathering place, growth on Maui was very limited for the next thirty years.[10] For the first twenty or thirty years of the Latter-day Saints church in Hawai'i (1850s to 1870s), Church membership on Maui, both in gross numbers and percentage, was higher than on any other island.

After the mission was reopened in 1864, proselytizing was less successful, and some members were also choosing to gather in La'ie. The April 1886 conference reported 474 members. The work slowly grew the remainder of the nineteenth century. In 1895, Andrew Jenson listed fifteen branches, many with their own little chapels, and 869 members. In December 1900 the Jubilee Celebration brought President George Q. Cannon back to the islands. During the celebration Elder Cannon met some of the children of his first converts. The new century also brought an increase in convert baptisms.

By 1921 when Elder David O. McKay of the Quorum of the Twelve visited Maui on his world tour of Latter-day Saint missions and schools, he found three conferences (districts) organized on

8 Ibid., 154.
9 Britsch, *Moramona*, 15.
10 Min et al., *Stewards of the Promise*, 17.

Maui with eighteen branches and thirteen chapels. On November 9, 1975, Elder Thomas S. Monson of the Quorum of the Twelve organized the Kahului Hawai'i Stake, consisting of approximately two thousand Saints on Maui, Moloka'i, and Lana'i. The forty-two branches with one thousand members in the stake area in 1855 had been consolidated into five wards and four branches. Commenting upon the occasion, Elder Monson remarked, "We are very proud of the Church in this area and particularly with the fact they have shown the growth and leadership that enables them to take this step."[11] The establishment of this stake and its continued growth remain promising for future generations of LDS who will join the Church and make their own sacred sites on the islands of Maui, Moloka'i, and Lana'i, or in Maui County. The growth of the Church continues on Maui; the Kahului West Stake was organized on May 4, 2014.

Maui was where it really all began for The Church of Jesus Christ of Latter-day Saints in Hawai'i. In the early days as many as half the members of the Church were from Maui, and the core of the early mission's local leadership were Maui men, usually educated at Lahainaluna.

LDS Historic Sites in Maui

1. Nalimanui's Hale

The first missionaries in Lahaina "went up into the mountain behind Lahaina, Maui and fasted and prayed all day that the Lord would aid them in learning the language and would help them to touch the hearts of the natives with the gospel message."[12] Following these labors in prayer, Elder George Q. Cannon received a great blessing:

George Q. Cannon. Courtesy of BYU–Hawaii Archives.

---

11 *Maui News*, November 18, 1975.
12 M. C. Josephson, "A Glance at Hawaii: Hawaiian Mission History," *Improvement Era* 53 (August 1950): 620.

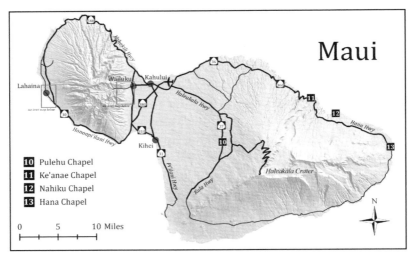

My desire to learn to speak was very strong; it was present with me night and day and I never permitted an opportunity of talking with natives to pass without improving it. I also tried to exercise faith before the Lord to obtain the gift of talking and understanding the language. One evening, while sitting on the mats conversing with some neighbors who had dropped in, I felt an uncommonly great desire to understand what they said. All at once I felt a peculiar sensation in my ears, I jumped to my feet, with my hands at the sides of my head, and exclaimed to Elders Bigler and Keeler, who sat at the table, that I believed I had received the gift of interpretation! And it was so. From that time forward I had but little, if any, difficulty in understanding what the people said. I might not be able at once to separate every word which they spoke from every other word in the sentence; but I could tell the general meaning of the whole. This was a great aid to me in learning to speak the language, and I felt very thankful for this gift from the Lord.[13]

It was at Waikapu, Maui, where the LDS doctrine that the island peoples are descendants of Abraham through Lehi and are heirs to all the blessings of Abraham and his posterity was revealed by President Cannon. This doctrine has been accepted

---

13 Cannon, *My First Mission*, 23.

by Latter-day Saints ever since, but the fact that it had its inception through him was not known until Cannon explained this to the Saints at Waikapu on December 28, 1900. President Samuel Woolley recorded that President Cannon "told them they were of the seed of Abraham, he knew it because the Lord told him so at Lahaina."[14]

When President George Q. Cannon returned to Lahaina during the Hawaiian Mission's golden anniversary, he searched for the place he stayed in 1851.

> I started out this morning to find if possible the place where Nalimanui lived when she gave us shelter. I wanted to find the site of this house and the garden where I sought the Lord in secret prayer and where He condescended to commune with me, for I heard His voice more than once as one man speaks with another, encouraging me and showing me the work which should be done among this people if I would follow the dictates of His Spirit. Glory to God in the highest that He has permitted me to live to behold the fulfillment of His words.
>
> I found the place that I thought must have been the site but great changes have been made. I made inquiries about Nalimanui and Kealakai Monua. Discovered that the house where we stopped was the house of her grand-son. His father was Chilean and his mother a daughter of Nalimanui. We all felt that this was an extraordinary coincidence and the natives called it Kupaianaha. Before leaving, a number of folks assembled and I addressed them. The spirit of God was poured out upon us.[15]

Behind the site of the old Lahaina chapel is believed to be the location where the *pili* grass *hale* was offered to Elder George Q. Cannon by Nalimanui, an elderly lady related to King Kamehameha the Great and also the early convert William H. Uaua.[16]

Nalimanui Hale site. Courtesy of Riley Moffat.

14 Samuel E. Woolley, Journal, December 28, 1900, Church History Library.

15 Cannon, *My First Mission*, December 17, 1900.

16 Spurrier, interview by Shannon Kanekoa, Maui, 2011, 98–99, transcription in authors' possession.

On December 17, 1900, Cannon revisited the site where he said the Lord had spoken to him.

Directions to the Nalimanui's Hale site:
From Waine'e Street turn makai/west behind Hale Pa'ahao prison on the little dead end lane marked Waianae Place at the north end of the prison to the end of the prison wall.

2. Lorenzo Snow Drowning Site

A visitor's walk around Lahaina town should include going behind the library at the north end of the small boat harbor on the seawall near the site of Kamehameha I's little brick "palace."

Lahaina beachfront. Courtesy of Riley Moffat.

There one can look past the surf on the north end of the harbor and see the place where Lorenzo Snow almost drowned in 1864. Consider setting out from here in a rowboat or small sailboat for Manele Bay on Lana'i across the channel, just as early missionaries did when they were building the City of Joseph in the Palawai Basin, which became the first gathering place for the Latter-day Saints in Hawai'i. On April 31, 1864 the Church authorities coming to investigate Walter Murray Gibson's activities on Lana'i arrived at Lahaina Roads. Passengers and goods were off-loaded into whale boats to be rowed ashore. Apparently a large south swell that was running created high surf along the reef offshore of Lahaina. The boats had to negotiate a narrow channel to reach the beach. The boat carrying Elder Snow was flipped in its attempt to get through the narrow channel, and all aboard were thrown into the surf. An account of this dramatic event was recorded in the journal of one of the returning missionaries, William Wallace Cluff:

> On the 29th of March (1864) we sailed for Lahaina, on the schooner *Nettie Merrill*, Captain Fisher, for the island of Maui, a

distance of about ninety miles from Honolulu. On the morning of the 31st of March, we came to anchor about one mile from the mouth of the little harbor of Lahaina.

Apostles Ezra T. Benson, Lorenzo Snow, Brother Alma L. Smith, and myself, got into the small boat to go on shore! Brother Joseph F. Smith, as he afterwards stated, had some misgivings about going in that boat, but the manifestation was not sufficiently strong to indicate any general accident. He preferred to remain on board the vessel until the boat returned. (Joseph would not allow them to take any of their bags with them, but made them leave them on the boat.) The boat started for the shore. It contained some barrels and boxes, the captain, a white man, two or three native passengers, and the boat's crew, who were also natives.

The entrance to the harbor is a very narrow passage between coral reefs, and when the sea, is rough, it is very dangerous, on account of the breakers. Where the vessel lay, the sea was not rough, but only presented the appearance of heavy swells rolling to the shore.

As we approached the reef it was evident to me that the surf was running higher than we anticipated. I called the captain's attention to the fact. We were running diagonal to the waves, and I suggested that we change our course so as to run at right angles with them. He replied that he did not think he was in any danger, and our course was not changed. We went but little farther, when a heavy swell struck the boat and carried us before it about fifty yards. When the swell passed, it left us in a trough between two huge waves. It was too late to retrieve our error, and we must run our chances. When the second swell struck the boat, it raised the stern so high that the steersman's oar was out of the water, and he lost control of the boat. It rode on the swell a short distance and swung around just as the wave began to break up. We were almost instantly capsized into the dashing, foaming sea.

I felt no concern for myself about drowning, for while on my former mission I had learned to swim and sport in the surf of those shores. The last I remember of Brother Snow, as the boat was going over, I saw him seize the upper edge of it with both hands. Fearing that the upper edge of the boat, or the barrels, might hit and injure me as the boat was going over, I plunged head foremost into the water. After swimming a short distance, I came to the surface without being strangled or injured.

The boat was bottom upwards, and barrels, hats and umbrellas were floating in every direction. I swam to the boat and as there was nothing to cling to on the bottom, I reached under and seized the edge of it.

About the same time Brother Benson came up near me and readily got hold of the boat. Brother Alma L. Smith came up on the opposite side of the boat from Brother Benson and myself. He was considerably strangled, but succeeded in securing a hold on the boat. A short time afterwards the captain was discovered, about fifty yards from us. Two sailors, one on each side, succeeded in keeping him on the surface, although life was apparently extinct.

Nothing yet had been seen of Brother Snow, although the natives had been swimming and diving in every direction in search of him. We were only about one-fourth of a mile from shore. The people, as soon as they discovered our circumstances, manned a life boat and hurried to the rescue. We were taken into the boat, when the crew wanted to row for the shore, and pick up the captain by the way. We told them that one of our friends was yet missing, and we did not want to leave. We discovered that a second boat had left the shore and could reach the captain as soon as the one we were in. Seeing this, the crew of our boat consented to remain and assist us.

The captain was taken ashore, and by working over him sometime was brought to life. Probably his life would not have been much endangered but for a sack of four or five hundred silver dollars which he held in his hand, the weight of which took him at once to the bottom. The natives dove and brought him up, still clinging to the sack. When his vitality was restored, the first thing he inquired about was the money; intimating to the natives, with peculiar emphasis, that it would not have been healthy for them to have lost it.

Brother Snow had not yet been discovered, and the anxiety was intense. The natives were, evidently, doing all in their power.

Finally, one of them, in edging himself around the capsized boat, must have felt Brother Snow with his feet and pulled him, at least, partly from under it, as the first I saw of Brother Snow was his hair floating upon the water around one end of the capsized boat. As soon as we got him into our boat, we told the boatmen to pull for the shore with all possible speed. His body was stiff, and life apparently extinct.

Brother A. L. Smith and I were sitting side by side. We laid Brother Snow across our laps, and, on the way to shore, we quietly administered to him and asked the Lord to spare his life, that he might return to his family and home.

On reaching the shore, we carried him a little way to some large empty barrels that were lying on the sandy beach. We laid him face downwards on one of them, and rolled him back and forth until we succeeded in getting the water he had swallowed out of him.

During this time a number of persons came down from the town; among them was Mr. E. P. Adams, a merchant. All were willing to do what they could. We washed Brother Snow's face with camphor, furnished by Mr. Adams. We did not only what was customary in such cases, but also what the Spirit seemed to whisper to us.

After working over him for some time, without any indications of returning life, the by-standers said that nothing more could be done for him. But we did not feel like giving him up, and still prayed and worked over him, with an assurance that the Lord would hear and answer our prayers.

Finally we were impressed to place our mouth over his and make an effort to inflate his lungs, alternately blowing in and drawing out the air, imitating, as far as possible, the natural process of breathing. This we persevered in until we succeeded in inflating his lungs. After a little, we perceived very faint indications of returning life. A slight wink of the eye, which, until then, had been open and death-like, and a very faint rattle in the throat were the first symptoms of returning vitality. These grew more and more distinct, until consciousness was fully restored.

When this result was reached, it must have been fully one hour after the upsetting of the boat. A Portuguese man, living in Lahaina, who, from the first, rendered us much assistance, invited us to take Brother Snow to his house. There being no Saints in the place, we gladly accepted his kind offer. Every possible attention was given for Brother Snow's comfort.

We will here append Brother Snow's account of the upsetting of the boat, and what he can recollect of the sensations of a man drowning and afterwards coming to life.

As we were moving along, probably more than a quarter of a mile from where we expected to land, my attention was suddenly arrested by Captain Fisher calling to the oarsmen in a

voice which denoted some alarm, "Hurry up, hurry up!" I immediately discovered the cause of alarm. A short distance behind
us, I saw an immense surf, thirty or forty feet high, rushing
towards us swifter than a race horse. We had scarcely a moment
for reflection before the huge mass was upon us. In an instant
our boat, with its contents, as though it were a feather, was
hurled into a gulf of briny waters, and all was under this rolling,
seething mountain wave. It took me by surprise. I think, however, that I comprehended the situation in the midst of turbulent
waves a quarter of a mile from the shore, without much proba-
bility of human aid.

I felt confident, however, there would be some way of
escape; that the Lord would provide the means, for it was not
possible that my life and mission were thus to terminate. This
reliance on the Lord banished fear, and inspired me up to the
last moment of consciousness. In such extreme cases of excite-
ment, we seem to live hours in a minute, and a volume of
thoughts crowd themselves into one single moment. It was so
with me in that perilous scene.

Having been somewhat subject to faint, I think that after
a few moments in the water I must have fainted, as, I did not
suffer the pain common in the experience of drowning persons.
I had been in the water only a few moments, until I lost consciousness. The first I knew afterwards, I was on shore, receiving
the kind and tender attentions of my brethren. The first recollection I have of returning consciousness, was that of a very
small light the smallest imaginable. This soon disappeared, and I
was again in total darkness. Again it appeared much larger than
before, then sank away and left me, as before, in forgetfulness.
Thus it continued to come and go, until, finally, I recognized,
as I thought, persons whispering, and soon after, I asked in a
feeble whisper, "What is the matter?" I immediately recognized
the voice of Elder Cluff, as he replied, "You have been drowned;
the boat upset in the surf." Quick as lightning the scene of our
disaster dashed upon my mind. I immediately asked, "Are you
brethren all safe?" The emotion that was awakened in my bosom
by the answer of Elder Cluff, will remain with me as long as life
continues: "Brother Snow, we are all safe." I rapidly recovered,
and very soon was able to walk and accompany the brethren to
our lodgings.

Brother Cluff resumes the narrative:

As soon as Brother Snow was out of danger, it occurred to me that I had better return to the vessel. As I reached the deck by the rope ladder over its side, I saw at a glance that Brother Smith was under great anxiety of mind. We were both under an intensity of feeling which men usually experience only a few times in their lives. Brother Smith had been informed by a native that the captain and an elderly white man were drowned. The latter he supposed to be Brother Benson, hence his great anxiety. My own nervous system was strung up to an extreme tension by the events of the past two hours. When I told Brother Smith that all were safe, the sudden revulsion of feeling almost overcame him. We rejoiced together that through a merciful Providence, and the faith that had been bestowed upon us, we were all alive.[17]

Directions to the Lorenzo Snow drowning site:

From Front Street turn west/*makai* on Hotel Street, turn right in front of Pioneer Inn to Lahaina Banyan Court behind Lahaina Public Library. The drowning occurred 200 to 300 yards offshore at the boat channel entrance. It was from here that boats going back and forth to Lana'i came and went. It is also site of Kamehameha I's small brick palace built about 1798.

3. George Q. Cannon Missionary Sites

A few historical sites in Lahaina date from the days of George Q. Cannon's missionary days. The Lahaina Restoration Foundation has been active in preserving and documenting many of these sites. Sites contemporary with the early years of the Hawaiian Mission include the home of the Rev. Dwight Baldwin on Front Street, dating from 1834; and the Hale Pa'ahao prison at the corner of Prison Street and Waine'e Street, which was built in 1852. Near its northwest corner is believed to be the site of Nalimanui's little grass *hale* where Elder Cannon communed with the

---

17 Fred G. Beebe, *The Cluff Missionaries in the Hawaiian Islands* (n.p.: self-published, 1987), 52–53. See also other versions in Francis Gibbons, *Joseph F. Smith: Patriarch and Preacher, Prophet of God* (Salt Lake City: Deseret Book, 1984), 71–72; and Joseph Fielding Smith, *The Life of Joseph F. Smith* (Salt Lake City: Deseret News Press, 1938), 212–16.

Lord. The Waiola Church at 535 Waine'e Street was established as the Waine'e Church, the Protestant missionaries' church in 1826. The present chapel is probably the fifth at the site. In the adjacent graveyard are buried many individuals important to Hawaiian history. Between Waiola Church and Front Street is a park which is the site of Moku'ula, the royal enclosure of Kamehameha III when Lahaina was the seat of government of Hawai'i from the 1820s to 1845, before it was moved permanently to Honolulu.[18]

4. Lahaina Chapel

The first mention of a Latter-day Saint chapel in Lahaina is of a meeting house completed on August 15, 1888, and remodeled in 1935. A 1919 map shows it at 622 Luakini Street, which is now the site of Blackie's Boat Yard.[19] A new Lahaina chapel was dedicated on July 28, 1965 by Elder Howard W. Hunter. The other small branches in West Maui at Honokohau and at Olowalu merged with the Lahaina Branch when the new chapel was built.

Lahaina Chapel. Courtesy of BYU–Hawaii Archives.

Directions to Lahaina Chapel:

Luakini Street is just one short block in from Front Street. The chapel site is just north of the intersection of Luakini Street and Prison Street.

---

18 For more on historical sites in Lahaina see Maui Historical Society, *Lahaina Historical Guide*. (Honolulu: Star Bulletin, 1961, Inez Ashdown; *Stories of Old Lahaina*. (Honolulu: Hawaiian Service, 1947); Roy Nickerson, *Lahaina: Royal Capital of Hawai'i* (Honolulu: Hawaiian Service, 1978,); and Christiaan Klieger, *Moku'ula: Maui's Sacred Island* (Honolulu: Bishop Museum Press, 1998).

19 Moikeha, Jubilee H. "Chapels on the Island of Maui," *Mormon Pacific Historical Society, Proceedings* (1989), 84–89; Dwayne Wada to Mary Jane Woodger, e-mail, October 16, 2009, in author's possession.

5. Lahainaluna High School and Hale Paʻi

Hale Paʻi Lahainaluna. Courtesy of Fred E. Woods.

Lahainaluna High School sits on the mountainside above Lahaina town. The school, founded by Protestant missionaries in 1831, is the oldest high school west of the Rocky Mountains. The best and brightest young men of Hawaiʻi were selected to attend, including early Hawaiian historians David Malo and Samuel Kamakau. Many of the early stalwarts of the Latter-day Saint Church in Hawaiʻi were also educated here: Jonathan Napela, W. H. Uaua, J. W. H. Kauahi, George Raymond, Keau Kalawaiʻa, J. H. Keanu, J. W. H. Kou, and J. W. Kaleohano.

The first headmaster, Lorrin Andrews, was also a printer. He helped translate the Bible into Hawaiian and established a printing press in the Hale Paʻi to publish over one million pages of educational materials in Hawaiian for use in schools throughout the islands. The Lahainaluna press was the first one west of the Rocky Mountains. There is a beautiful view from the school overlooking Lahaina town and across Lahaina Roadstead to Lanai. From this vantage point you can picture in your mind's eye scores of whale ships anchored in the roadstead and missionaries sailing or rowing small boats over to Manele Bay on the south end of Lanaʻi to get to the City of Joseph, the first gathering place of the Saints in the 1850s.[20] A museum is in the Hale Paʻi, the old press building, which is on the Lahainaluna school grounds. Lahainaluna became a public high school in 1923, but continues to offer boarding to students from remote areas.

Directions to Lahainaluna School:

Lahainaluna High School is located one mile up Lahainaluna Road past the old sugar mill. The school is up the hill at the end of the road. The Hale Paʻi is on the west side of the parking lot.

---

20 Min et al., *Stewards of the Promise*, 9; and *Maui News*, December 1, 1926.

6. Waikapu Chapel

This village was where George Q. Cannon, in a meeting on December 28, 1900, elaborated on his understanding that Hawaiians were descendents of Lehi, as has been revealed to him in Lahaina in 1851. It is also where mission leaders reinforced the need for a Church school in Hawai'i to Elder David O. McKay on February 8, 1921.[21] In the early twentieth century, Church leaders were often hosted here by the Enos family.

Directions to the Waikapu site:
   From Honoapi'ilani Highway turn west on West Waiko Road about ⅓ mile to where the road bends right to 239, which is now Nohoana Farm.

7. Ka'ahumanu Church

On March 4, 1851, Cannon left his companions in Lahaina and made his way in bad weather to Wailuku. On his way, he felt that "he was to meet someone who would be interested in his message and who would be willing to care for his needs."[22]

Ka'ahumanu Church. Courtesy of Fred E. Woods.

On Sunday, March 30, 1851, Cannon listened to Reverend Daniel T. Conde preach against the Latter-day Saints in the Congregationalist meetinghouse in Wailuku. Cannon records that in his sermon, Conde said that

> Joseph Smith had pretended to see angels . . . and claimed that an angel had taken away the plates from which the Book of

---

21 Law, *Founding and Early Development*, 29.
22 Ibid., March 30, 1851, 143.

Mormon was translated, which, if genuine, should have been left for all the world to see. . . . [He] called Joseph Smith "a notoriously bad character," a thief, a lawbreaker, a dissolute rake with "many wives or concubines"—in short, "a very wicked man." If Joseph Smith had truly seen angels, . . . why did they not deliver him from death?

Miraculously, Cannon understood what Conde had said in Hawaiian, even though he did not feel as if he were fluent enough to respond to Condie's charges in Hawaiian. Cannon wrote in his journal,

My feelings while sitting listening to this tirade, can be better imagined than described. I felt as though if I had owned the world I should have given it to have been able to have talked the Native. I thought of standing up after meeting and contradicting but I thought he had the pulpit & could out-talk me.

After the meeting, Cannon went to Conde and asked if he could "inform him better in regard to the things he had told this people" so that Conde could "disabuse the people of the lies he had told them."

Conde brushed aside the implication that he had spread lies, and Cannon challenged him to prove Mormonism wrong from the scriptures. Cannon declared, "I could prove before this whole people that he did not agree with the scriptures and that he did not preach the gospel of Jesus Christ."[23] The conversation between Conde and Cannon was not cordial, but it had the effect of rousing the congregation's interest in Cannon's purpose there.

Among the congregation was a Hawaiian judge named Jonathan H. Napela, a man of considerable influence in the area, of chiefly rank, descending from Maui royalty. His wife, Kitty Richardson, was also of chiefly blood. Napela was well

Jonathan Napela. Courtesy of BYU–Hawaii Archives.

---

23 Cannon, Turley, and Orton, *Journals of George Q. Cannon*, 71.

educated at Lahainaluna, owned land in several areas of Maui, and was a circuit court judge when Cannon met him. Cannon stayed with Napela for several days and spoke to him and several of his friends about the restored gospel. These men were interested in the differences between Protestantism and Mormonism. Despite persecution, Napela endured, and out of interest in the message of Mormonism he persisted in his study with Cannon. Conde threatened to take away Napela's judgeship if Napela continued with his study. While Napela was not worried about Conde's threats, Cannon did not want to jeopardize Napela's station among his own people, so he left Wailuku to stay with some of Napela's friends up in Kula on the hillside of Mount Haleakala.

Several months passed before the elders resumed the work in Wailuku.[24] On January 5, 1852, George Q. Cannon baptized Jonathan Napela. It is assumed that Kitty Napela was also baptized on this occasion, though there is no documentation of her baptism. Jonathan's brother Kanahunahupu of Waihe'e and William H. Uaua were also baptized soon after. Uaua was prominent in the area and eventually was elected to the House of Representatives of the Kingdom. Jonathan Napela would later become the first Hawaiian to receive his endowment on August 2, 1869, at the Endowment House in Salt Lake City.[25]

Approximately one year after meeting Cannon, Napela composed the following letter to Brigham Young.

> To the person justified, Brigham Young; Great love to thee.
> The thought springeth up in me to tell thee concerning the things of the Kingdom of the Everlasting God.
> In the year 1851, in the month of March, the 8th day, George Cannon came into my house at Wailuku, the Island of Maui, of the Hawaiian group. He was afterwards persecuted by our former teacher, D. T. Conde; therefore, George Cannon went to my house in Kula, upon this Island. He afterwards established a branch of the church of the Lord there; and when the last month of that year arrived, George Cannon and [Elder Francis]

---

24 Britsch, *Moramona*, 18; and Min et al., *Stewards of the Promise*, 9–10. For more information on Napela's trip to Utah, see Fred E. Woods, "An Islander's View of a Desert Kingdom: Jonathan Napela Recounts his 1869 Visit to Salt Lake City," *BYU Studies* 45, no. 1 (2006): 23–34.

25 Min et al., *Stewards of the Promise*, 15, 22.

Hammond established a Branch of the church of the Lord at Wailuku, and when the year 1852 arrived, it had increased, and it is constantly increasing at this time: and it is very plain to us that this is the church of God, and that it is the gospel which is preached by the white men from the Rocky Mountains; and there are many upon these islands who have obtained strong faith by the grace of God, through Jesus Christ the Lord, that we might receive the Holy Ghost: Amen.

May the true love of the Lord be with you, worlds without end: Amen.

My desire is great to see you, ye Fathers of the gospel of Jesus Christ; and my thoughts are buoyant to go to your place, when the proper time arrives.

Yours with admiration,

J.H. Napela

Wailuku, April 8, 1852.[26]

On the back of this letter to President Young, Elder Cannon added: "He (Bro. Napela) is the most influential man that has joined the Church; he has come out and embraced the work in the face of all the opposition of the majority of his friends and relatives; and his whole heart seems to be engaged in the work and its progress here."[27]

The stone church where Cannon encountered Conde was the fourth church on that site. It was replaced by the present church in 1876, which is quite imposing with its tall steeple.

Driving directions to the Ka'ahumanu Church:

Coming up Main Street (Highway 32) into Wailuku to Honoapi'ilani Highway (Highway 30), turn left at the county buildings and the church will be on the right.

8. Jonathan Napela's House

When Cannon first arrived in Hawai'i, an initial lack of success among the foreigners and his inability to understand

---

26 This first of four letters written to Brigham Young by Napela was included in a letter written by George Q. Cannon to Brigham Young. This letter appeared in "Foreign Correspondence," *Deseret News* 3, no. 1 (November 27, 1852), 4, in both the Hawaiian language, followed by the English translation which George Q. Cannon provided.

27 Ibid.

the Hawaiian language afforded him extra time with the scriptures. He later recalled that it was during this time that he developed a real love for the Book of Mormon.

Jonathan Napela's house. Courtesy of BYU–Hawaii Archives.

> If I felt inclined to be lonely, to be low spirited, or homesick, I had only to turn to [the Book of Mormon] to receive consolation, new strength and a rich outpouring of the Spirit. Scarcely a page that did not contain encouragement for such as I was.[28]

In January 1852, Cannon's love of the Book of Mormon led him to commence the book's translation into Hawaiian. Jonathan H. Napela, a very intelligent man who knew the Hawaiian language exceptionally well, and was arguably the most prominent and influential Hawaiian convert of the nineteenth century, effectively served as a collaborator in the translation. Cannon later explained, "I would then read the translation to him, . . . going carefully over every word and sentence, and learning from him the impression the language used conveyed to his mind. In this way I was able to correct any obscure expression which might be used, and secure the Hawaiian idiom."[29] Napela gave "the exact meaning of words." Use of the proper idiom was vital to the correct translation of the book. Other Hawaiian men of experience and education also listened and gave advice for the necessary revisions. In this way Cannon and his Hawaiian associates adjusted the language of the translation to fit local cultural requirements and meanings. Fortunately there was but one native language in the Sandwich Islands. One translation of the Book of Mormon was enough.

The First Presidency of the Church was aware of Cannon's efforts, and some alternative methods of translation were discussed, but "since Cannon had started the project and obviously

28 Cannon, *My First Mission*, 58.
29 Ibid., 181–3.

had the spirit to finish the work, it was decided that he should be set apart to complete it by himself."[30]

The first draft of the Hawaiian translation was completed by July 1853, but it was necessary to check and revise the work carefully. Cannon went to Kaua'i to obtain the aid of Elder Farrer and some Hawaiian Saints there, particularly Elder Kauwahi. By the Hawaiian October conference of 1853, the translation was nearly finished, and some action was needed regarding its publication. A committee of three men—George Q. Cannon, Philip B. Lewis, and Benjamin F. Johnson—were appointed to raise the funds required to purchase a press, and Cannon was released from his calling as president of the Maui conference and charged to travel throughout the islands to collect the money.[31]

Cannon asked the Saints to purchase their copies of the Book of Mormon in advance, so that they could purchase a press with the advanced funds. However, many of the Saints were poor, and so they could give very little. The missionaries appreciated the sacrifices made by the Saints to donate funds, and the project received large donations from unexpected sources. Elder Dennis, a convert to the Church in Hawai'i and a man of considerable means and great generosity, promised to loan the mission one thousand dollars.[32] In January 1854, Levi Ha'alelea, a Hawaiian chief, also helped fund the press by loaning the mission $500 for the project, and the first Hawaiian edition of the Book of Mormon was published.[33]

"On 31 December 1854, there were thirty-one foreign missionaries in Hawai'i. The number of Hawaiian missionaries is not known. Foreign elders held all the mission and conference (district) offices, but the majority of the branches was presided over by local Saints. By this time there were seventy-five branches. . . . *Haole* missionaries could not lead each flock." Local converts to

---

30 Conference Minutes of the Sandwich Islands Mission, October 6, 1852, CR 3695 11, box 1, folder 1, Church History Library.

31 Woodbury, Journal, July 25, 1853; and Farrer, "Biographical Sketch, December 2, 1853.

32 Farrer, January 17, 1854.

33 Ibid., November 6, 1853; and Henry W. Bigler Journal, January 5, 1854, Church History Library. For more information on the translation of the Book of Mormon into the Hawaiian language, see "The Western Standard: A Momento of Other Days," *Juvenile Instructor* 36 (September 15, 1901): 547–50.

the Church were quickly involved in the work and leadership of the Church. When branches were formed, local brethren were given the priesthood and asked to minister to the people. Not much time passed before Hawaiian men were ordained elders and sent on missions throughout the Hawaiian Islands. As one missionary journal described it, "Hawaiian members of the Church were not left as passive onlookers but were involved in responsible ways from the beginning."[34]

Napela, as a member of the Maui Conference presidency, established the first language training school for missionaries in the Pacific area. On April 16, 1853, Napela began his school at his own home by teaching newly arrived missionaries the Hawaiian language in the Bible.[35] He also deserves credit for having first suggested the idea of a Latter-day Saint mission training center. Missionary Reddick Allred explained that "Napela wanted to keep us [Utah elders] in school 2 months & then we might go, for he thought we would begin to talk [in Hawaiian] in that time to get our places of appointment." These plans were implemented immediately in Napela's home and are the same regimen currently used at LDS missionary centers worldwide to train missionaries learning a new language. Further, the Jonathan Napela Center for Hawaiian and Pacific Islands Studies, named after Napela, is now an integral part of the BYU–Hawaii campus in Laʻie, Hawaiʻi.[36]

Apparently the sounds emerging from the newly arrived elders were less than encouraging. In the evening Napela made the missionaries practice reading from the Bible again. Two days later, Elder Ephraim Green wrote: "I have all ways [been] a hard working man all the days of my life but this is the [hardest] work I ever [done] to set and study all day our teacher is very attentive [some] of the [Brethren] have got so they can read quite well but cant [sic] tell the meaning of what they read."[37] The missionaries did not stay

34 Britsch, *Moramona*, 28.
35 Woodbury, Journal, April 9, 1853.
36 See Fred E. Woods, "A Most Influential Mormon Islander: Jonathan Hawaiʻi Napela," *Hawaiian Journal of History* 42 (2008): 140.
37 Ephraim Green, Diary, April 18, 1853, typescript in L. Tom Perry Special Collections, Harold B. Lee Library, Brigham Young University, Provo, Utah.

long under Napela's tutelage, but the language training did boost their attempts to learn Hawaiian.[38]

A plat map of Wailuku drawn in 1882 by Marcus D. Monsarrat shows several properties of Napela awarded during the *mahele*. One is just across the street from the Ka'ahumanu Church. Monsarrat labels it Apana 12 of Land Commission Award 406. This location best matches Cannon's description of where he encountered Jonathan Napela and his friends.

It was in the Wailuku area where Elder Cannon labored at translating the Book of Mormon into the Hawaiian language for two and a half years. Cannon says he stayed at Napela's house during that time.[39] The location was pointed out to Elder David O. McKay and President Hugh J. Cannon during their visit in 1921, but the place where the translation was done was not in the house and cannot be identified today.

Directions to Jonathan Napela's House:
    The site of Napela's house is located at 2246 Main Street in Wailuku across from the Ka'ahumanu Church.

9. Wailuku Chapel

Located on the corner of Vineyard and Muliwai Streets, this large concrete chapel was built in 1926 for $17,000 and dedicated by Mission President William M. Waddoups on November 27. It was the second or third chapel built in Wailuku, hometown of Jonathan Napela and some other important early pioneers of the Church. It served as the headquarters of the Maui District until the stake center was built in Kahului in 1969. It had a seating capacity of 500 and included a separate cultural hall across Vineyard Street, which still stands. District conferences would fill it to overflowing, especially when General Authorities visited.[40] It was situated on the west side of the lot. An earlier wooden chapel built in 1913 for $1,500 existed across the river to the north at 2141 Mokuhau Road.

---

38 Britsch, *Moramona*, 28–29.
39 Cannon, *My First Mission*, 59–61.
40 Jubilee H. Moikeha, "Chapels on the Island of Maui," *Mormon Pacific Historical Society*, *Proceedings* (1989), 84–89, and *Maui News*, December 1, 1926.

Wailuku Chapel. Courtesy of BYU–Hawaii Archives.

Directions to Wailuku Chapel:

Approaching Wailuku from the east on Main Street, turn right on High Street one block to Vineyard Street, then turn left on Vineyard Street. The address is 2244 Vineyard. The site is now a parking lot.

10. Iao Valley

Anciently, Iao Valley was the site of a major battle fought in 1790 between the chiefs of Maui and Hawai'i to establish Kamehameha I's rule over the Islands. Tradition has it that the river ran red with blood, and the bodies of the dead dammed the stream after the Battle of Kepaniwai. The first Church conference in Hawai'i was held in the valley in 1852. It was also here that Elder Spencer W. Kimball sought seclusion to pray

Iao Valley with David O. McKay, Hugh J. Cannon, and E. Wesley Smith, 1921. Courtesy of BYU–Hawaii Archives.

on one of the anniversaries of his call to the the Quorum of the Tweve.[41]

Directions to Iao Valley:

Follow Main Street through Wailuku, past the Bailey House Museum and Maui Historical Society (which dates from 1833), and bear right on Iao Valley Road up the valley for about three miles to a park at the deadend, where the Iao Needle can be seen.

11. Pulehu Chapel

After persecution mounted from in Wailuku, Napela advised Cannon to go to the Kula District, which means "the country near the base of a mountain." The mountain, in this case, is Haleakala. Napela recommended the area because he had friends there. At a place near modern Pulehu, Cannon stayed with a man by the name of Akuna Pake, who was in charge of Napela's interests there. The Kula District was especially important to Hawai'i's economy at this time, because Irish potatoes were grown there and exported to

Pulehu Chapel, 1912. Courtesy of BYU–Hawaii Archives.

41 Min et al., *Stewards of the Promise*, 36.

California for sale to gold miners cheaper than potatoes shipped from the Eastern States.

Cannon worked diligently to spread the gospel in and around Kula. About a month after Cannon's arrival in Kula, friends of Napela completed the construction of a Hawaiian-style hut that Cannon was able to use as a regular meetinghouse nearby at Kealahou.[42] The following week, he was joined at Kula by Elder Keeler, whom he had not seen for two months. Among the new converts was a man named Kaleohano, a relative who was Cannon's host; and Pake and Maiola, who had been friends since Cannon's first arrival.

On August 6, 1851, Cannon organized the first branch of the Church in Hawai'i, the Kula Branch, established in the village of Kealahou just to the south of Pulehu. Two teachers and three deacons were ordained, and one of the teachers, Kaleohano, was appointed clerk of the branch.[43]

There is a small wooden chapel in Pulehu. "Although the Pulehu LDS chapel is not an official church historical site, it is the oldest LDS church building still standing in Hawai'i and one of the first permanent structures completed by the Church in Hawai'i."[44] It is about two miles downslope of where some of the first baptisms in Hawai'i took place. "This property came into the hands of the Church when Kiki, the daughter of Ka'ala, through a proclamation dated July 16, 1903, conveyed two acres of a former three acre parcel to the Church 'for . . . the good works and advancement of the gospel of the kingdom of Jesus on this earth' and as 'a place where the chapel would stand for the worshipping of Jehovah, Most High God.'"[45] An earlier structure, a small rectangular building, was built, then replaced in 1912 by the building that now stands. Inside the chapel there is a stand that is elevated two

---

42 Cannon, *My First Mission*, 152; Cannon, Turley, and Orton, *Journals of George Q. Cannon*, 189, 192–93.

43 Jenson, Manuscript History, August 6, 1851; Cannon, Turley, and Orton, *Journals of George Q. Cannon*, 110.

44 http://www.puamanaproperty.com/newsletters/nov2010nl.php (assessed February 6, 2015). For more information on the Pulehu LDS Chapel, see Frank Alan Bruno, "Faith Like the Ancients: The LDS Church in Pulehu and on Maui," in *Where It All Began: Mormon Pacific Historical Society, Proceedings* (July 28–29, 1989), 37–56.

45 Min et al., *Stewards of the Promise*, 23, 32–3, 62.

steps above the floor. There is no microphone nor any need for one. A few rows of pews extend from the stand; there are two windows on each side wall.

The present-day Pulehu chapel holds a curious attraction for many; though

Pulehu Baptismal Pool, 1912. Courtesy of BYU–Hawaii Archives.

not featured in guidebooks, it receives a steady flow of visitors. Prominent Church leaders and members have made it a point to find it and enjoy its peace.[46] This site is considered sacred ground by Hawaiian Saints because of an incident that took place there during Elder David O. McKay's (then in the Quorum of the Twelve) world tour of LDS missions and schools in 1921.[47] On February 8, Elder McKay, his traveling companion, Hugh J. Cannon, the son of President George Q. Cannon, along with Mission President E. Wesley Smith, son of President Joseph F. Smith, and missionaries Elder David Kailimai and Elder Samuel H. Hurst rode out to visit and have dinner with some Church members who lived far up on the side of Haleakala, one of the largest dormant volcanoes in the world. From there, they drove to Pulehu.

As the five sat in a little Ford car in front of the meeting house, President Smith related the story of how President George Q. Cannon delivered a wonderful discourse in a little church which then stood on the ground they were on. At that meeting in 1851, Cannon appeared to be standing in the air, a halo of light around his head. At the same time all but three of the over one hundred present were transfigured before him. He and Jonathan Napela had preached with such power that ninety-seven of the one hundred people who came to hear them were converted, and Cannon

46 Ibid., 31.
47 For more information on the Pulehu LDS Chapel, see Frank Alan Bruno, "Faith Like the Ancients: The LDS Church in Pulehu and on Maui," *Mormon Pacific Historical Society, Proceedings* (1989), 37–56.

baptized his first converts and organized the first branch of the Church in Hawai'i in 1851.[48] Hugh J. Cannon was greatly touched by visiting this site associated with his father, and the grounds of the little chapel at Pulehu.

The five men left the car, walked around the grounds, then gathered under a beautiful pepper tree on the lot where the Church now has a small chapel, built in 1912. Elder McKay then said: "Brethren I feel impressed that we should render our thanks to the Lord for the labors of this great man and his co-laborer Pres. Joseph F. Smith whose sons are presented here today."[49] During that prayer, all five men were deeply stirred spiritually. After the prayer, Elder Kailimai, speaking in Hawaiian to President Smith, said he had seen a vision in which two men were shaking hands. At first he thought the men were Cannon and Hurst, but when he opened his eyes, they were standing apart. After hearing about this vision, Elder McKay said, "I feel certain that President Cannon and President [Joseph F.] Smith are near, for the veil was very thin." Feeling very moved, Hugh J. Cannon added, with tear-filled eyes, "There was no veil."[50] In 1936, this story was retold by President McKay when he visited Hawai'i again. At that time he clarified what Elder Kailimai had seen: "Those hands were the hands of the two fathers, George Q. Cannon and Joseph F. Smith, in the presence of the two sons, Hugh J. Cannon and E. Wesley Smith."[51]

---

48 LDS Church Historian Richard O. Cowan questions this account: "However, no such episode is recorded either in George Q. Cannon's missionary diary or in his later summary of his experiences in Hawaii, entitled *My First Mission*, nor is it corroborated in any other contemporary source. Moreover, Napela was not baptized until months after this episode was said to have taken place." See Richard O. Cowan, "An Apostle in Oceania: Elder David O. McKay's 1921 Trip around the Pacific," in *Pioneers in the Pacific: Memory, History, and Cultural Identity Among the Latter-day Saints*, edited by Grant Underwood (Provo, UT: Religious Studies Center, Brigham Young University, 2005), 191, n. 14 (199). Min et al., *Stewards of the Promise*, 14, states that the first branch was in Kula.

49 Samuel Harris Hurst, Journal, February 8, 1921, photocopy of holograph in possession of Cleo Hurst Bailey; used by permission; as cited in Lavina Fielding Anderson, "Prayer under a Pepper Tree: Sixteen Accounts of a Spiritual Manifestation," *BYU Studies* 33, no. 1 (1993): 56.

50 Mission Financial and Statistical Reports, Hawaiian Mission, 1921; as cited in *Britsch, Moramona*, 149.

51 Reuben D. Law, *The Founding and Early Development of the Church College of Hawai'i* (St. George, UT: Dixie College Press, 1972), 19–21.

Pulehu Monument, 1930. Courtesy of BYU–Hawaii Archives.

Later in the 1920s, a monument was erected to mark the spot where these events had taken place. On October 26, 1930, the Kula monument was dedicated by Temple President William M. Waddoups, under the direction of Mission President Castle H. Murphy. A bronze marker on the granite shaft tells its purpose. Two thousand members gathered here to celebrate the pioneer centennial in 1947 under the direction of Elder Matthew Cowley of the Quorum of the Twelve, who at the time was administering all the missions in the Pacific.

President McKay made later visits to Pulehu, along with other General Authorities who have gathered to Pulehu when visiting Maui, including President Heber J. Grant in (1935); Elder Anthony W. Ivins, and Elder Richard R. Lyman (1924); President J. Rueben Clark (1935); and Elder Matthew Cowley (July 24, 1947). In 1950 President George Albert Smith and Elder Henry D. Moyle held a special outdoor conference at Pulehu, with hundreds in attendance. During his visit on February 9, 1955, President David O. McKay relived his experience of 1921 at Pulehu. And since then, Elders Howard W. Hunter, Mark E. Petersen, Spencer W. Kimball, and other General Authorities have visited this site.[52]

The Pulehu Branch was closed in 1966 when several smaller branches were consolidated into the Haleakala Branch, now the Pukalani Ward. Since then regular Church meetings have not been held there. However, the small chapel is still used for special functions. Visitors to Pulehu are impressed with the serenity at this special place.[53] The hand-laid rock wall around the chapel grounds dates from the 1800s.

---

52 Min et al., *Stewards of the Promise*, 35–36.
53 Ibid.

In 1978, a granite monument with two bronze plaques was erected.

Directions to Pulehu LDS property:
   From Kahului airport head east on Hana Highway #36 for about 1 mile. Then on the right turn on to Haleakala Highway #37 to Pukulani. Continue south on Kula Highway #37 for about 4 miles. About 200 yards past the True Value Hardware Store make a hard left, turning up on to the Lower Kula Road. You will see the parking lot for the chapel on your right.

12. Ke'anae

Elder Keeler ventured around the Island of Maui teaching the gospel. In July 1851, he asked Elder Cannon to come with him to a place called Ke'anae. When they arrived, the people who had been watching for them gathered to meet them. Elder Cannon recorded in *My First Mission*:

> Our arrival in Keanae created great excitement. The people had been watching for us, and seeing us approach from a long distance, had gathered to meet us. Had we been princes they could not have treated us with greater consideration and honor. We obtained the Calvinistic meeting-house the afternoon of our arrival, and there was a large attendance to hear the preaching.
>
> This was on Wednesday, and from that time until Monday we were constantly speaking, baptizing, confirming and counseling the people. During the time there were upwards of one hundred and thirty baptized. The Spirit of the Lord was powerfully poured out, and all rejoiced. I never enjoyed myself so well before in my life.[54]

Within a short time, 130 Hawaiians were baptized. Soon afterwards, branches at Ke'anae, Wailua, Waianu, and Honomanu were created in this area.[55] While in Ke'anae, Cannon enjoyed recreational activities and the pleasure of conversing with the people and learning their customs and systems of family values.

In 1852, Cannon sought permission to construct a Latter-day Saint meetinghouse in Ke'anae, Maui. Generally, construction of

---

54 George Q. Cannon, *My First Mission* (Salt Lake City, Juvenile Instructor Office, 1879), 156.
55 Britsch, *Unto the Islands*, 99–101.

Keʻanae Peninsula. Courtesy of Maui County Visitors' Bureau.

meetinghouses for Latter-day Saints was a complicated process, as some ministers of other religions and others "opposed to the Mormon cause fought the intrusion of such physical evidence of success."[56] In this case, Cannon's trouble was attempts to contact appropriate government officials. When he looked up the agent of the king's lands, the agent had taken the royal yacht to Lahaina. Cannon took passage on another vessel, and five days later he finally caught up with the agent and the king, but the king was reported to be ill and unable to conduct business. The land agent recommended Cannon call on Prince Liholiho, who was heir apparent to the throne. Cannon was able to locate the prince, and after hearing Cannon's proposal, Liholiho declared that the Mormons should not be interfered with and agreed to check into the legality of the construction of a chapel at Keʻanae.[57]

Cannon and Keeler had great success, and by the time they moved back to Wailuku at the end of the year, the branches in Kula and Keʻanae had been strongly built up in the Church.[58]

Hawaiian missionary Elder Adren Bird relates that in early 1948 he was at Keʻanae with President E. Wesley Smith, who told him, "We have a special responsibility to the people of Keanae as

56 Britsch, *Moramona*, 28.
57 Cannon, Turley, and Orton, eds., *Journals of George Q. Cannon*, 136.
58 Britsch, *Moramona*, 23.

this was a favored place of George Q. Cannon as well as other early missionaries and was the first fully organized branch of the Church in the Hawaiian Islands."[59]

Keʻanae Chapel. Courtesy of BYU–Hawaii Archives.

Elder Henry W. Bigler describes the dedication of the first Keʻanae Chapel, which all the original Hawaiian missionaries attended:

> Saturday, Sept. 4, 1852. The best Latter-day Saint meeting house hitherto erected by the Saints on the island of Maui was dedicated at Keanae in the Koolau District. The house was 56 x 21 feet, built in the native style with lauhala. The people were much pleased with it as it was a better building than the one owned by the Calvinists at the same village. Its dedication was celebrated with large and interesting meetings and a grand feast. Of American Elders, Bros. Cannon (who offered the dedicatory prayer), Keeler, Hawkins, Hammond, Bigler, and Farrer were present. These brethren, accompanied by others, arrived in Keanae Aug 31st and left Sept 7th. During their visit in Koolau district, 26 were baptized, a number of brethren ordained to the Priesthood and meetings held in a number of villages.

A later chapel was built south of the peninsula, just before the road down to Wailua, which was used until the time all the members in the area were reassigned to the Hana Branch.

Directions to the Keʻanae Chapel:

From Kahului, drive 30 miles east on Hana Highway 360. After Nuaʻaliua Bay, turn left onto Keʻanae Peninsula Road. This site of this early chapel on the peninsula was near the ocean, but exactly where is not known. The site of the later

---

59 Henry W. Bigler, Journal, (1848) University of Utah J. Willard Marriott Library, http://content.lib.utah.edu/cdm/ref/collection/uu-uhrf/id/3196; and Arden J. Bird, "Koolau District, Maui: The Beginning of a Successful LDS Mission," *Mormon Pacific Historical Society, Proceedings* (1989), 59–60.

chapel is on the Hana Highway a hundred yards past the Ke'anae School in the jungle on the *mauka* side of the road.

13. Nahiku

Although there were many small branches between Kahului and Hana, one that flourished briefly was at Nahiku. Beginning in 1899, Hawaiian Commercial & Sugar and Maui Agricultural Company began planting thousands of rubber trees, and the Nahiku Rubber Plantation, established between 1905 and 1915, attracted hundreds of workers. As the community flourished, a nice

Nahiku Chapel, 1910. Courtesy of BYU–Hawaii Archives.

frame chapel was built, with a cemetery nearby. When the plantation closed, many families drifted away, and the branch languished. Some rubber trees survived, and local prisoners were sent to harvest rubber in 1942 to aid the war effort. The Hawaiian Mission history notes that it was reopened for a period in January 1950. The chapel no longer exists, but the cemetery is still there.

Directions to Nahiku:

From mile marker 25 on the winding Hana Highway turn left down a narrow road 3 miles. Pass through what's left of the village and head toward the beach landing. Just past a one-lane bridge, which is washed out, over Makapipi Stream, the chapel site and cemetery will be immediately on the left up the stream bank on private property. Please do not approach without permission; this site is on private property.

14. Hana

Shortly after the first Latter-day Saint missionaries arrived, the largest congregations of Saints resided in villages along the road to Hana. Many communities along this road are typical of

Hawaiian settlements established in the early 1900s where one can find old-fashioned stores in tiny villages, an old church, and perhaps an ancient Hawaiian *heiau*, or temple, such as the impressive Pi'ilanihale *heiau.*

Hana Chapel. Courtesy of BYU–Hawaii Archives.

Until the mid-1950s, small Latter-day Saint branches existed in just about every village, almost half a dozen between Kahului and Hana because of difficult transportation issues. Branches had to be within walking or horseback-riding distance. Some villages, such as Nahiku, with branches of over one hundred members at one time, are now practically deserted by both Latter-day Saints and other Islanders alike.

The 56-mile road to Hana, finally finished in 1926, winds its way via Highways 36 and 360 from Kahului, the main commercial hub and location of the airport, to Hana, a rain-bathed, old-fashioned community of about one thousand. The last two-thirds of the highway twists through six hundred curves and over sixty bridges, many of which are one lane, but there awaits incredible views of the ocean, waterfalls, and lush greenery. Stretching above is the 10,023-foot Haleakala volcano, the centerpiece of this side of Maui. Hana has always been just a branch because it is so isolated in a small community.

Now all these branches that once existed in East Maui from Ke'anae around to Kaupo have been consolidated into the branch at Hana. Since the 1850s there have been at least four different chapels in Hana. In 1942 there were 250 members in the district; after consolidation there are now about half that many in the Hana branch. With relatively few opportunities after the sugar plantation closed in 1946 in this paradisiacal but isolated district, many young people have moved away. In the 1850s the chapel would have been a *pili* grass *hale pule.* Then on January 1, 1888, Elder Joseph Dean dedicated a new frame chapel which lasted until

1929, when it was replaced with a new chapel. After World War II, Elder Calvin Boren was assigned to Hana from March 1947 to November 1948. He so impressed the owner of the Hana Ranch, Mr. Paul Fagan, that the latter donated $1,500, which was matched by the Church, to build a gym/social hall behind the chapel. It became a center for youth activities for the whole community. Sister Josephine Kanekoa Bird remembers her husband, Elder Adren Bird, and others building the gym. It was dedicated November 26, 1948 by President E. Wesley Smith. Brother Sam Kekauoha of Laʻie taught school there around 1960 and used the gym to develop an award-winning social dance group of both members and non-members. When the 1929 chapel needed replacement, a local architect, Ed Akiona, designed a one-of-kind LDS chapel shaped in the form of a cross, as in an old Romanesque church, with a tall central nave and wings for the chapel and classrooms. The gym is gone but the mission home remains. This new chapel was dedicated on August 29, 1999.

Directions to Hana:

The road to Hana (Highway 36) starts in Kahului and winds its way east. The Hana Branch chapel is located at 4836 Uakea Road. As you approach Hana at the police station and county building, Uakea Road will fork off to the left, and the chapel will be about ¼ of a mile on the right.

Moloka'i

Moloka'i, the fifth largest of the Hawaiian Islands, is only 26 miles from Oahu. Moloka'i is 37 miles long and 10 miles wide and rises to a height of 4,970 feet.[1] Halawa Valley, on the eastern end of the island, is one of the earliest known Hawaiian settlement sites. Along the south shore are many ancient fish ponds, and along the north shore are steep ocean cliffs and abandoned valleys, along with the Kalaupapa peninsula.[2] Depopulation struck Moloka'i particularly hard. The first missionary censuses counted over 6,000 inhabitants, but by 1910 the island's population was less than 2,000, and half of those were at Kalaupapa. Moloka'i's population is now (2016) back up to over 7,000. Perhaps the most Hawaiian of the Hawaiian Islands, it is known as the Friendly Island.[3]

Since the establishment of the Moloka'i Ranch in 1897 on western Moloka'i, the *paniolo*, or cowboy lifestyle, has been important on Moloka'i. Between 1923 and 1985 several thousand acres of western Moloka'i around Mauna Loa were leased to Libby and Del Monte to grow pineapples, which became the island's mainstay. Since then life has mellowed out even more on Moloka'i, where some Hawaiians practice subsistence living through hunting, fishing and gardening.

---

1 http://dlnr.Hawai'i.gov/dofaw/.
2 Harriet Ne, *The Voice of Harriet Ne,* comp. Gloria L. Cronin (Laie, HI: The Institute for Polynesian Studies, 1992), xviii–xix; and Martha Beckwith, *Hawaiian Mythology* (Boston: Yale University Press, 1940), 105 (hereafter *Tales of Molokai*).
3 http://ags.Hawai'i.gov/wp-content/uploads/2012/09/CENSUSFA.pdf; http://themolokainews.com/2011/04/06/molokai-shows-population-decline-over-the-past-decade/.

Latter-day Saints in Moloka'i

During the October 1850 general conference, John S. Woodbury, just twenty-five years old and newly married, was called on a mission to the Sandwich Islands. Leaving his wife, Elvira, in San Francisco, he arrived in Hawai'i on August 9, 1851; she would join him by the end of that year. Originally the Woodburys were assigned to the Big Island, but then they were reassigned to Moloka'i, where they joined another couple, Elder William and Patty Perkins. When work slowed because of a famine on the island, the Perkins, suffering from near starvation, left for Lahaina after just two months. They eventually recovered and brought back with them to Moloka'i a native missionary by the name of Uaua.[4]

The Woodburys had been advancing the work, and at the first meeting the Perkins and Uaua attended after returning to Moloka'i, there were thirty in attendance. As happened repeatedly in the islands, the missionaries incurred great opposition from the Protestant missionaries. At the end of August, due to poor health, Elder and Sister Perkins received permission to return home, along with Sister Woodbury.[5]

At an October 1852 mission conference Elder Woodbury reported forty-seven Saints on Moloka'i. After a testimony meeting at Jonathan Napela's home on Maui, Elder Woodbury spoke in tongues, declaring that "the Hawaiian [people were] a part of the House of Israel, and prophesied of temples in the islands." Elder Woodbury returned to Moloka'i by himself and continued to labor. After a spiritual dream he went to Kalaupapa and received permission to preach at a Calvinist Church. Here he found success, and a branch of the Church was then formed at Kalaupapa.[6] In 1853, Elder Ephraim Green and a Brother Maiola joined Elder Woodbury in the work on Moloka'i. In time they converted a very influential Molokaian, David Kahukauila, who influenced many others to follow him into baptism. Soon another branch was formed and two meetinghouses were built. On March 21, 1854, Elders George Q. Cannon and Francis Hammond came to Moloka'i to hold

---

4 Min et al., *Stewards of the Promise*, 37–38.
5 Ibid., 39.
6 http://contentdm.lib.byu.edu/cdm/compoundobject/collection/MMD/id/623
   /rec/1.

a conference. At this conference Elder Woodbury was called to preside over the 155 members on Molokaʻi, of whom thirty-seven had been ordained to the priesthood. Elder Woodbury served in this position until July 1854, when he was released to return home. Elder John R. Young, who was serving at Hilo, was then assigned to preside over the Molokaʻi conference. Elder Young felt his safe arrival on Molokaʻi was in answer to a blessing he had received when he was set apart for his mission. He later recorded what happened when he first tried to land on Molokaʻi:

> We were carried westward beyond our proper landing, and [as] we neared the shore of Molokai, the surf ran so high that the canoe was capsized, and I was rolled for a quarter mile over the coral reef, and finally reached shore half drowned, but not a bone broken. When Apostle John Taylor set me apart for my mission, he said, "You shall be cast upon the bosom of the sea, but be not afraid, for the hand of God shall be over you, and you shall return in safety to your father's home." Surely, there is a spirit in man that revealeth things that are to come.[7]

Just a few months after Elder Young's miraculous landing, in September 1854, Joseph F. Smith and eight other missionaries set sail for the Hawaiian Islands, arriving in Honolulu on September 27, 1854. Upon their arrival, Joseph F. Smith was assigned to labor on the islands of Molokaʻi and Maui; however, he fell ill with a high fever and was forced to stay in Lahaina.[8] Three years later, Joseph F. Smith was assigned to preside over the Molokaʻi Conference. He wrote to Elias Smith, "I have been appointed to labor in the Molokai conference. This by all accounts is a hard field to labor in although I have no doubts that it could be worse, one thing is certain, I never shall shrink from my duty, as long as I can keep the spirit of Mormonism about me, for I know better."[9] During his time on Molokaʻi, Smith became gravely ill again for three

---

7 John R. Young, *Memoirs of John R. Young: Utah Pioneer* (Salt Lake City, UT: Deseret News, 1920), 79.

8 Min et al., *Stewards of the Promise*, 48; and David M. Whitchurch, "'My Dear Sister': Letters between Joseph F. Smith and His Sister, Martha Ann Smith Harris," in *Mormon Historical Studies* 5, no. 1 (Spring 2004): 199.

9 Joseph F. Smith to Elias Smith, April 14, 1857, Church Archives as cited in Grant Underwood, *Pioneers in the Pacific* (Provo, UT: Religious Studies Center, 2005), 154.

months and was cared for by a young Hawaiian woman named Ma Manuhiʻi and her husband. The three never forgot each other and always greeted one another with deep affection whenever they met in later years.[10]

A number of Hawaiian Latter-day Saints took up homestead land on the Hoʻolehua Hawaiian Homes development in the 1920s on land above the Kalaupapa settlement, and by 1926 they accounted for half of all homesteaders at Hoʻolehua. At first other residents resented Latter-day Saints moving into their area because negative stories related to polygamy were common. However, through a series of miracles, residents began to accept the Saints as their neighbors.[11] One such miracle took place shortly after the the Saints' arrival. The water supply became contaminated, and many babies fell ill and died, but when the elders blessed the water, it became pure again.[12] Another miraculous occurrence happened in 1927 when there was no rain. Under the leadership of a missionary named Clarence Kinney, a group of elders gathered for a special fast at Kalae, and through the power of the priesthood they blessed Molokaʻi with rain. The elders literally "walked the rain clouds back to Hoolehua" and closed their three-day fast on bended knees. As they uttered "amen," the clouds opened up and rain came pouring from the skies, falling steadily for three days and nights. The successful crops that year were evidence of the faith of the early Saints in that area.[13] A similar experience of the members fasting and praying for rain to end a drought occurred on December 20, 1953. In addition, the elders healed the sick and performed miracles through prayer, faith and righteousness. Some of these miracles, such as bringing rain to the parched crops, helped solve problems all the homesteaders faced, giving the Church great stature in the eyes of the people of Molokaʻi. The members, surviving as homesteaders, became

---

10 Min et al., *Stewards of the Promise,* 50.

11 William Kauaiwiʻulaokalani Wallace III, Martha Kalama, William Kaleimomi o Hoʻolehua Wallace Jr., and Betty Jean (BJ) Kamaile o Kaʻala Lee, "Moʻolelo Kahiko o Molokaʻi, or Stories from Molokai's Past," in ed. Grant Underwood *Voyages of Faith: Explorations in Mormon Pacific History* (Provo: Brigham Young University Press, 2000), 363.

12 Ibid., 363.

13 Ibid., 363.

a "tight-knit" body and had a positive influence on their neighbors. By 1956, there were 447 members in the Hoʻolehua Branch.[14] Today the Church still has great credibility among the people of Molokaʻi.[15] For years the members along the southeast coast had a branch and chapel at Kainalu, which was later closed, and these eastside members were assigned to Kaunakakai.

Since those early days the Church has grown steadily on Molokaʻi. There are now two wards on Molokaʻi, at Kaunakakai and Hoʻolehua, along with the dependent Kalaupapa Branch.

Molokaʻi Latter-day Saint Sites

1. Hoʻolehua Chapel

Hoʻolehua Branch in the Hoʻolehua Hawaiian homestead lands was an early stronghold of the LDS Church after the homestead act was passed in 1922; the population of the branch rose to over four hundred members in the 1950s. The Molokaʻi Saints met in different places, first from 1922 to 1928 in the Hawaiian Homes Commission warehouse behind the Hoʻolehua fire station, sometimes at "Aunty Mary Lee's" house and other times at Brother and Sister Makekau's house on Puʻukapele Avenue. A small one-room

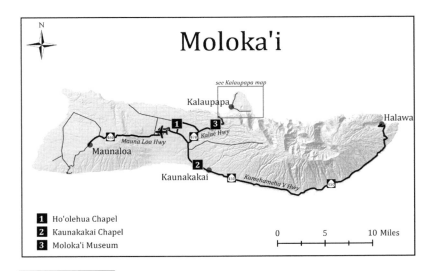

14 Ibid., 357.
15 Ibid., 364.

Hoʻolehua Chapel. Courtesy of BYU–Hawaii Archives.

chapel was built in 1929 near "Mary Lee's homestead," below the Molokaʻi High School. The chapel was dedicated on August 12, 1932. From 1935 to 1938, a newer chapel was built on a hilltop overlooking the village on Puʻupeʻelua Highway; a gym was added in 1953. This chapel had a unique design similar to that of the Kapaʻa chapel on Kauaʻi. In addition to the uniquely designed chapel, the 447 members of the Hoʻolehu Branch in 1953 built on their own separate gymnasium, classrooms, and kitchen. The chapel was dedicated by Elder Alma Sonne. In total, sixty-five branch members donated 11,090 hours of labor. Starting in 1932, members of the branch began traveling by barge to Oahu to spend Thanksgiving week at Laʻie doing temple work.[16] The building still stands and is now the Molokaʻi Baptist Church. The Hoʻolehua Branch raised watermelons right below the chapel for the Church welfare program and farmed taro patches by Molokaʻi High School.[17] The little branch at Mauna Loa that served the pineapple workers merged with Hoʻolehua on July 1, 1962.

Directions to the Hoʻolehua Chapel:

From the Molokaʻi Airport, follow Mauna Loa Highway (Hwy 460) east, then turn left onto Puʻupeʻelua Avenue (Hwy 481). The old Hoʻolehua chapel is about three quarters of a mile north on the hill at 495 Puʻupeʻelu Avenue.

16 "Hawaii Mission President Records," LDS Church Arvchives, LR 3695 21, reel 3, box 1, folder 6.
17 William Kauaiwiʻulaokalani Wallace III, Martha Kalama, William Kaleimomi o Hoʻolehua Wallace Jr., Betty Jean (BJ) Kamaile o Kaʻala Lee," Moʻolelo Kahiko o Molokaʻi, or Stories from Molokaʻi's Past" in Underwood, *Voyages of Faith*, 365.

2. Kaunakakai Chapel

In 1964, a modern chapel was built on the mauka (inland) side of the Mauna Loa Highway by labor missionaries on six acres and dedicated by Elder Gordon B. Hinckley on April 26. It replaced an earlier 1938 wooden chapel that had been dedicated by

Kaunakakai Chapel. Courtesy of BYU–Hawaii Archives.

Elder John A. Widtsoe. The chapel sits across from the Kapuaiwa coconut grove that was planted by King Kamehameha V in the 1860s and was one of his favorite places to visit. The little Kainalu Branch, which had served the members all along east Molokaʻi, had merged with Kaunakakai on August 13, 1961. In 1982, the building was renovated as a stake center and enlarged.[18]

Directions to Kaunakakai Chapel:

The Kaunakakai Chapel is still used today by the Hoʻolehua and Kaunakakai Wards. From Kaunakakai, travel west on Mauna Loa Highway (Hwy 460) for 0.6 miles. Kaunakakai Chapel is located on the left directly across from Kapuaiwa Avenue.

Other Molokaʻi Historical Sites

3. Molokaʻi Museum

In 1849, Rudolph Meyer, an immigrant from Germany, married an *aliʻi* named Kalama. Meyer and his eleven children created a large, self-sufficient plantation and farm at Kalaʻe and managed the land now known as the Molokaʻi Ranch for King Kamehameha V, Princess Ruth Keʻelikolani, and Princess Bernice Pauahi Bishop. Meyer was the Hawaiian government's superintendant of the Kalaupapa settlement on the peninsula. However, while

---

18 Mokihana Davis, "LDS Chapels on Molokai," in the *Mormon Pacific Historical Society, Proceedings* (May 16, 1992), 24.

Napela was there, he served as the on-site superintendant, since he had been the judge at Wailuku, Maui, and was a high ranking *aliʻi*.[19] Meyer also built the Meyer Sugar Mill in 1878. Mule-power and a steam engine were used to crush and process the sugar-cane. The Meyer Sugar Mill, the oldest surviving mill in Hawaiʻi, has been restored to operating condition as an example of what the Laʻie sugar mill would have looked like. The mill and museum photographs show the lives of the plantation workers in the nine-teenth century. Visitors can tour the restored sugar mill and his-torical exhibits. For more information, call 808-567-6436.[20]

> *Directions to the R. W. Meyer Sugar Mill:*
> The sugar mill is located on the left side of the road about half way between Kualapuʻu and the Kalaupapa Lookout.

4. Kalaupapa

According to geologists, Kalaupapa was formed about two million years ago by a small shield volcano that erupted on the north side of Molokaʻi and formed the Kalaupapa peninsula, sep-arated from topside Molokaʻi by some of the highest sea cliffs in the world. Archaeological evidence suggests that Hawaiian people have lived on the peninsula for a thousand years.[21]

The Kalaupapa peninsula is only 2.25 miles across and 2.5 miles long. The 3,500-acre peninsula is flat except for the gen-tly sloping Kauhako volcano in the center. Access to the peninsula is very limited.[22] Visitors can reach the peninsula only by a steep 2.4 mile trail down a 1,600-foot *pali* with twenty-six switchbacks, on foot or mule back, or flying in on a small plane. The penin-sula is divided into three *ahupuaʻa*: Kalawao on the eastern side, Kalaupapa on the western side, and Makanalua in the center. The

---

19 Rhoda Hackler, *R.W. Meyer Sugar Mill Molokai* (Molokai: Molokai Museum and Cultural Center, 1989), 3–9; and Charles S. Meyer, *Meyer and Molokai* (Iowa: Graphic-Agri Business, 1982), 21–115.
20 Foster, *Frommer's Hawaiʻi 2007*, 501.
21 Fred E. Woods, "The Soul of Kalaupapa," *BYU Speeches 2008–2009* (Provo: BYU, 2009), 1, and "Ka ʻOhana O Kalaupapa Position Papers of Recommen-dation for Kalaupapa National Historical Park's General Management Plan," 3, http://kalaupapaohana.org/position.html.
22 Edward K. Noda and Associates, Inc., "Boulder Removal Project, Waihanau Stream, Kalaupap National Historical Park." *Environmental Assessment: State of Hawaiʻi Department of Health* (GK & Associates, 1991), 5.

earliest photos of Kalaupapa show it barren of trees, though the area was probably forested before human occupation, when "slash and burn" or "swidden" agriculture was practiced. Then, after Western contact, sheep, cattle, and goats denuded much of what was left except in the most inaccessible places.

Moloka'i is known as the site of a leprosy settlement, first at Kalawao and later at Kalaupapa. In the mid-1800s, leprosy, or Hansen's disease, thought to have been brought to Hawai'i by Chinese immigrants (hence the name *mai pake*, or "Chinese sickness"), began turning up in Hawai'i. With no known cure, the Hawaiian Board of Health decided to confine to the peninsula those affected. The peninsula was chosen because it was isolated and fairly inaccessible. The south side of the peninsula was cut off from the rest of Moloka'i by a sheer *pali*, or cliff, more than two thousand feet high.[23]

On January 6, 1866, the first group of patients with leprosy, consisting of nine men and three women, were dropped off at the mouth of the Waikolu Valley, the closest accessible point to Kalawao on the east side of the peninsula."[24] Eventually, Kalawao became home to hundreds of leprosy victims moved there from other islands. Later, in 1887, after moving the unaffected Hawaiians on the peninsula "topside," the Hawaiian Board of Health began moving health facilities and patients from Kalawao to the other side of the peninsula at Kalaupapa.[25] During the next decade, the bulk of patients lived at Kalaupapa, and the number of patients increased significantly as the settlement became one of the world's largest settlement for those with Hansen's disease. The Moloka'i settlement reached its peak in population in 1890, with 1,174 patients, which was two percent of the Hawaiian population.[26]

The hardships of the community's early days were unfathomable. At first the government provided very little food. Shelter and

---

23 National Park Service, "Asian-Pacific American Heritage Month: Kalaupapa National Historic Park," *Kalaupapa National Historic Site*, http://www.nps.gov/nr/feature/asia/2005/park.htm (accessed on November 20, 2012).

24 Gerry Avant, "An Uplifting Tableau on Peninsula of Sorrow," *Deseret News Church News*, February 8, 1997, 8.

25 Lance D. Chase and Kuulei Bell, "Faith, Hope, and Hansen's Disease: The Saints at Kalaupapa," in Underwood, *Voyages of Faith*, 374.

26 Ibid., 374–75.

medical care were nonexistent. In 1873, the arrival of Father Damien De Veuster, at age thirty-three, marked the beginning of major improvements for the settlement. A Catholic missionary priest from Belgium, Damien served the leprosy patients at Kalaupapa for sixteen years until he died in 1889 at age forty-nine, after contracting the disease himself.[27] In 2009, Father Damien was declared a saint by Pope Benedict XVI.[28]

Father Damien. Courtesy of BYU–Hawaii Archives.

In 1886, Brother Joseph Dutton, a missionary priest, came to Kalaupapa to help Father Damien. Dutton took on many of the responsibilities Damien was not able to perform as his health declined. Mother Marianne Cope, a Catholic nun, also spent twenty-nine years on the peninsula, serving as an administrator, nurse, and teacher.[29] She was also canonized by the pope, in October 2012.[30]

After Annexation in 1900, the Territorial Board of Health approved a plan to provide better-quality services, facilities, utilities, and medical care for the patients at Kalaupapa. A major construction program began, with individual cottages, dormitories, hospital facilities, and other buildings being constructed. In 1902, Dr. William J. Goodhue became Kaulapapa's resident physician, and John D. McVeigh became the settlement's superintendent. These two men worked to improve the quality of life in the settlement by promoting sports and other activities, improving medical procedures, and treating patients with respect.[31]

---

27 "The Soul of Kalaupapa," 2–4.
28 Mary Vorsino, "Hawaii's Father Damien Canonized," *USA Today*, October 12, 2009. http://usatoday30.usatoday.com/news/religion/2009-10-11-father-damien_N.htm?csp=usat.me.
29 Lance D. Chase, "Mormons and Lepers: The Saints at Kalaupapa," *Mormon Pacific Historical Society, Proceedings* (May 16, 1992), 15.
30 Jen Christensen, "Mother Marianne becomes an American Saint," *CNN*, http://www.cnn.com/2012/10/20/health/saint-marianne-cope/index.html.
31 "Mormons and Lepers: The Saints at Kalaupapa," 20.

By 1938 things had improved dramatically. That year the governor of Hawai'i, Lawrence M. Judd, in an annual report to the Secretary of the Interior, wrote, "Kalaupapa . . . is a settlement where the individuals are permitted to live their lives pretty much as they wish. They maintain their own homes in separate cottages and may have a garden, raise chickens, and live under conditions similar to those elsewhere."[32] Later he became the superintendent of Kalaupapa,[33] following William Waddoups, who had previously served as a missionary in Hawai'i as well as the first La'ie temple president and also Hawai'i Mission president. Brother Waddoups served as superintendent from about 1943 to 1947, during which time he narrowly survived the deadly tsunami of April 1, 1946.

In 1949, sulphone drugs used to arrest the disease brought changes in treatment of Hansen's disease and in attitudes towards its victims. The new medications reduced symptoms and improved the quality of life at Kalaupapa. Before isolation laws were officially abolished in 1969, over eight thousand people had been torn from their families and exiled to the peninsula, where they died and were buried. New drugs reduced the contagiousness of Hansen's disease so much that isolation was no longer necessary. Even with these medical advances, many former victims of Hansen's disease living in Kalaupapa chose to stay there for the rest of their lives.[34]

Today approximately ten former patients are the only residents of Kalaupapa, along with Park Service personnel, while others are at Leahi Hospital in Honolulu at a location known as Hale Mohalu. Some patients are housed at Kalaupapa permanently; others simply visit occasionally for checkups and treatments. Access to the community is strictly regulated by law; control of public access is under the jurisdiction of the State Department of Health. All visitors must be age sixteen or older and receive a permit to enter. Visitors must either be personally invited by one of

---

32 Joseph Poindexter, "Annual Report of the Governor of Hawai'i to the Secretary of the Interior, 1938," *National Park Service*, http://www.nps.gov/kala/historyculture/history4.htm.

33 Fred E. Woods, "A Vow Remembered: Lawrence M. Judd and His Pledge to Kalaupapa," forthcoming in *Hawaiian Journal of History* 50 (2016): 1–31.

34 Landess Kearns, "Kalaupapa, One of Hawaii's Most Fascinating and Haunting Spots, Could Get Easier to Visit," *Huffington Post*, http://www.huffingtonpost.com/2015/05/19/kalaupapa-molokai-leprosy_n_7209568.html.

Kalaupapa's residents or visit as part of an authorized tour group, such as Damien Tours, owned and operated by a Kalaupapa resident (808-567-6171) or Kalaupapa Guided Mule Tour, a National Park Service concession (808-567-6088 or 1-800-567-7550), or by hiking down the trail from the top with its twenty-six switchbacks. A small airstrip at the northern edge of the peninsula brings in supplies and visitors most days; a barge brings supplies from Honolulu a couple of times a year.

Latter-day Saints at Kalaupapa

A branch that was organized on the peninsula by Elder John Stillman Woodbury in 1852, along with Elders James Hawkins and Maiola, one of George Q. Cannon's first baptisms in Kula, lasted for many years. But when the Hansen's disease patients were moved onto the peninsula, the unaffected Hawaiians living there were moved out.

Hawaiian Saints who contracted Hansen's disease were relocated, along with other victims of the disease, to the Kalaupapa Peninsula of Moloka'i. Among the early LDS leprosy patients was Kitty Richardson Napela, the wife of Jonathan Napela, an early convert and leader in the Church. Elder Napela asked for and received permission to go to Kalawao with his wife as her helper or *kokua*. Napela organized the first branch of the Church in 1873 and soon became the resident superintendent, since the government's superintendent lived "topside" and seldom visited down below. Napela eventually contracted leprosy and died six years after his arrival in the settlement. Kitty lived only two weeks after her husband's death.[35]

According to a visiting missionary, "By 1877 meetings were being held in a schoolhouse," though at first they were held "in a grove of trees inside the windward rim of Kauhako Crater."[36] In 1878, Elder Henry P. Richards and Elder Keau Kalawai'a reported branches in Kalawao and Kalaupapa, which consisted of eighty-eight members in a district over which President Napela presided.

35 Fred E. Woods, "A Most Influential Mormon Islander: Jonathan Hawai'i Napela," *Hawaiian Journal of History* 42 (2008): 150.
36 Riley Moffat, "The Church on the Peninsula," *Mormon Pacific Historical Society, Proceedings* (2007), unpaginated.

The visiting elders often stayed with Father Damien and "enjoyed lively conversations."[37] During these years, Damien and Napela became the best of friends.[38]

Elder Henry P. Richards from Utah visited Elder Napela about a year and a half before Napela's death. Richards said that Napela was so disfigured by the disease that he hardly recognized him, but as district president, Napela accompanied Richards to meetings at both of the peninsula's chapels. Richards stated that between the branches, there were seventy-eight Church members.[39] Napela's chiefly rank and former position as a chief judge and magistrate in Wailuku, Maui, qualified him to be resident supervisor of the settlement, though his term of superintendent was short-lived for political reasons.

"After President Napela died in 1879 the elders continued visiting once each year. In 1888, four elders visited to sustain a new branch presidency in Kalawao and to visit Napela's limestone-covered grave on the rim of Kauhako Crater," which can no longer be identified.[40]

By 1894, according to a mission report, the Kalaupapa Branch had 149 members, including the patients and their caregivers, and the Kalawao Branch had 78; these were two of the largest branches of the Church in Hawai'i.[41] "Baptisms were performed in a tidal pool near the Kalawao landing."[42] Over the years, several hundred LDS leprosy patients came to Kalaupapa with the disease.[43]

In 1919, as President William Waddoups waited for the world-wide influenza pandemic to pass so the Hawai'i Temple could be dedicated, he traveled throughout the mission to train the Saints on collecting and preparing names for temple work. He remarked how, even though they would probably never have the opportunity

37 Ibid.
38 Ambrose Hutchison (resident of settlement, 1879–1932), "In Memory of Reverend Father Damien J. De Veuster and Other Priests Who Have Labored in the Leper Settlement of Kalawao, Moloka'i," 19, cited in Fred E. Woods, "The Soul of Kalaupapa," *BYU Speeches, 2008–2009* (Provo, UT: Brigham Young University, 2009), 215–30.
39 Chase and Bell, "Faith, Hope, and Hansen's Disease," 374.
40 Moffat, "The Church on the Peninsula."
41 Chase and Bell, "Faith, Hope, and Hansen's Disease," 374.
42 Moffat, "The Church on the Peninsula."
43 Avant, "An Uplifting Tableau on Peninsula of Sorrow," 12.

to go to the temple, the Kalaupapa Saints were the most enthusi-astic genealogists in the mission. It seems logical that living with death almost daily placed in them a desire to prepare themselves and their loved ones for the next life.[44]

Many General Authorities visited Kalaupapa: the first was Charles A. Callis, followed by Matthew Cowley, Joseph Fielding Smith, Ezra Taft Benson, Mark E. Petersen, and David O. McKay. After visiting Kalaupapa, Matthew Cowley wrote:

> I went there apprehending that I would be depressed. I left knowing that I had been exalted. I had expected that my heart, which is not too strong, would be torn with sympathy, but . . . it had been healed. I went away . . . appreciating my friends, loving my enemies, worshiping God and with a heart purged of all pet-tiness . . . for it, I am indebted to the . . . Saints of Kalaupapa.[45]

Many visitors to the settlement echoed feelings similar to Elder Cowley's.

By 1926, the LDS population on the Kalaupapa Peninsula had dropped to ninety members. Elder John Bright had served as branch president from 1918 to 1926.[46] And by 1949, LDS member-ship was down to twenty-five, due to the deaths of aged patients and the shortage of new patients arriving. Despite the low num-bers of members, "Elder David Hanneman recalls spending the first 6 months of his Hawaiian mission in Kalaupapa in the early 1950s with fond memories."[47] The elders could not proselytize but were put in charge of the Boy Scout troop. After 1949 when the disease was brought under control, LDS missionaries were allowed to live in Kalaupapa but could not proselytize. They did, however, provide service to patients regardless of religion. As of 2015, only about ten patients remain on Kalaupapa; the three remaining LDS Kalaupapa residents have all passed away over the last few years. Many of the Saints living "topside" have fond memories of going

---

44 Moffat, "The Church on the Peninsula."
45 Matthew Cowley, as cited in Chase and Bell, "Faith, Hope, and Hansen's Dis-ease," 378.
46 Moffat, "The Church on the Peninsula."
47 Ibid.

down to Kalaupapa to assist in Sunday services and helping the Saints there.[48]

Latter-day Saint Sites at Kalaupapa

5. Kalaupapa Chapel, Social Hall, and Mission Home

There have been five LDS chapels on the peninsula. A branch had been established at Kalaupapa as early as 1852, and an 1895 map shows a Mormon chapel behind the site of the present chapel. A newer chapel, built in 1901, was dedicated on June 23, 1904 by Elder William Waddoups. The chapel at Kalaupapa just north of the butcher shop took five years to construct and was built by volunteer labor. After the chapels were dedicated, ten people were baptized, and new converts "swelled" Mormon membership to over two hundred people—all patients. The building at Kalaupapa was a small, square chapel with a slanted, peaked roof and a steeple. There were two windows in front and a covered entryway with pillars in front of the door.[49] The Kalaupapa Chapel, which

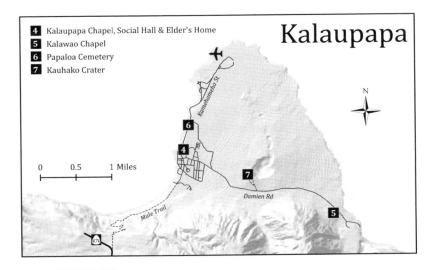

---

48 For more information on Latter-day Saints in Kalaupapa see Fred E. Woods. "The Inspiring Story of Kalaupapa," *LDS Living*, July/August 2015, 30–34, and Fred E. Woods, *Kalaupapa: The Mormon Experience at an Exiled Community* (Provo, UT: Religious Studies Center; Salt Lake City: Deseret Book, forthcoming 2017).
49 Chase and Bell, "Faith, Hope, and Hansen's Disease," 375.

Kalaupapa Chapel. Courtesy of BYU–Hawaii Archives.

seated two hundred people, was "one of the finest buildings in the entire mission," according to Elder Waddoups. There are two pulpits and two bathrooms in the chapel, one for patients and one for visitors. Patients and visitors sat on separate sides of the chapel. "At the time there were 200 members in the two branches. Interviews and recollections highlight the fact that all denominations cooperated and supported each other in addressing the needs of the patients."[50]

Hawaiian Mission President E. Wesley Smith visited in 1920 and was very impressed by the great gospel knowledge of the Saints there. In 1927 the chapel was remodeled and rededicated by then Mission President William Waddoups. David K. Kauhi presided over the Kalaupapa Saints during 1928–1942, and was still leading the branch at the age of eighty-one. In 1935, a modest mission home for visiting elders and Church leaders was built behind the chapel.[51] "A separate cultural hall, no longer in use, was built next to the chapel and dedicated by President David O. McKay on August 21, 1941. With the development of new treatments after World War II that eliminated transference of the disease, missionaries could stay and help with the branch, although they were not allowed to proselyte."[52]

50 Moffat, "The Church on the Peninsula."
51 Chase and Bell, "Faith, Hope, and Hansen's Disease," 377.
52 Moffat, "The Church on the Peninsula."

By the late 1940s, the Kalaupapa Branch population had dropped to thirty-seven. About that time, Jack Sing, a permanent resident, acknowledged greeter, social leader, unofficial mayor, and talented singer, was called to be branch president. On January 24, 1931, Jack Sing had married Mary

Jack Sing and Spencer W. Kimball. Courtesy of BYU–Hawaii Archives.

Kaehukulani, and they converted to The Church of Jesus Christ of Latter-day Saints soon after. Jack Sing was released as an active patient in 1944, and Mary was released in 1947, but they chose to stay in Kalaupapa. They had no children. In 1952, they were sealed in the Hawaiian Temple. Brother Sing became branch president of the Kalaupapa Branch in 1952 and served for thirty years until his death. As the figurative father of the Kalaupapa Branch, he did much good for the branch and the community, including gathering donations for the Kalaupapa Lion's Club annual community Christmas party. Every year, Sing gave out boxes of candy to members and missionaries in Kalaupapa.[53] "Many recall him driving visitors around in his Cadillac."[54] In his calling as branch president, Jack Sing hosted General Authorities of the Church at the Kalaupapa Chapel.[55] "After President Sing died in 1984, Sister Ku‘ulei Bell, until her death in 2009, led the congregation under the direction of priesthood leaders from topside who regularly hiked down to conduct sacrament meetings."[56]

"By 1965, the 1904 chapel had been so damaged by termites and damp weather that it was replaced by the current chapel."[57] The efforts of patients to help construct this new building were amazing. "Members without hands were able to push

53 Chase and Bell "Faith, Hope, and Hansen's Disease," 380–81.
54 Moffat, "The Church on the Peninsula."
55 Chase and Bell, "Faith, Hope, and Hansen's Disease," 377, 379–81.
56 Moffat, "The Church on the Peninsula."
57 Ibid.

wheelbarrows only because the handles were tied to their limbs, which prevented them from releasing their 'hold' on them." When donated labor records for the chapel construction were tallied, members of other faiths were found to have contributed more hours toward construction than members, a figure that illustrates the community togetherness of Kalaupapa. Upon completion, this new chapel was dedicated by Elder Marion D. Hanks of the First Council of the Seventy on December 26, 1965.[58] By 1992, only a handful of Saints remained in Kalaupapa, and priesthood from topside wards were assigned to go down to provide the sacrament on Sundays.

> *Directions to the Kalaupapa Chapel, Mission Home, and Social Hall:*
> The LDS chapel in Kalaupapa is located on the west side of the Kalaupapa Peninsula in the town of Kalaupapa. The Kalaupapa Branch is now dependent on the Hoolehua Ward. A cultural hall built in 1941 is located to the right of the Kalaupapa Chapel, as well as missionary quarters that were built in back in 1935. A monument to Napela stands in the churchyard. The Mormon complex is at the corner of Kamehameha and Damien Streets. The Mormon section of Papaloa cemetery is on the beach area across the road from the Kalaupapa Chapel.

6. Kalawao Chapel

When M. D. Monsarrat's survey of the peninsula for the Hawaiian Government was completed in 1895, the Kalawao Chapel lay just west of the Siloama Protestant church on the north side of the road. Sometime before 1904 it was torn down and a new chapel was built across the road on the south side and about one hundred yards farther west. On June 23, 1904, when Elder William Waddoups dedicated the Kalaupapa chapel, he also dedicated the new chapel in Kalawao.

As the patient facilities moved from Kalawao to Kalaupapa, the Kalawao chapel was no longer needed, though there are indications it may have been used through the 1920s. "Ku‘ulei Bell tells the story that the Church traded the chapel for land on Maui, and

---

58 Min et al., *Stewards of the Promise*, 45.

the new owner used the building materials for a beach house."[59]
Even though most patients moved from Kalawao to Kalaupapa
in the 1890s, the Baldwin Home for Boys, managed by Brother
Joseph Dutton, was built in 1894 across the road from St. Philo-
mena Catholic Church and St. Damien's grave. At the end of the
road where the U.S. Leprosy Investigation Station once existed is
a park with a magnificent view of the 3,000-foot high sea cliffs of
East Moloka'i.

> *Directions to the Kalawao Chapel:*
>
> Kalawao Chapel is located on the eastern side of the
> Kalaupapa Peninsula. Follow Damien Road east until it
> becomes Kalaupapa National Historic Park Road. Continue
> on the road for one-half mile. The 1904 church site is in the
> trees on the *mauka,* or mountain side, of the road across from
> St. Philomena Church.

Other Kalaupapa Historic Sites

7. Papaloa Cemetery

As the headquarters of the settlement moved from Kalawao to
Kalaupapa in the 1890s, a regular cemetery was established along
the beach just past the Mormon chapel. As was common at that
time, sections of the cemetery were designated for various religions, including the Mormons who had their own section. There
are other tombs on the western rim of Kauhako crater. Overall
eight or nine thousand patients have been buried on the peninsula. During the tsunami of April 1, 1946, there was considerable
damage to the Catholic and Protestant sections of the cemetery,
but only minimal damage to the Latter-day Saint section.

> *Directions to Papaloa Cemetery:*
>
> From Kalaupapa, travel north on Kamehameha St. for
> one-half mile. Papaloa Cemetery is north of the Latter-day
> Saint church on the beach side facing the ocean.

---

59 Moffat, "The Church on the Peninsula."

8. Kauhaku Crater

The first Latter-day Saint meetings on the peninsula after Hansen's disease patients were sent there reportedly were held inside the windward, or east side, of Kauhaku Crater. On the leeward side of the crater overlooking Kalaupapa are several graves, and supposedly somewhere on the rim of the crater is the grave of Jonathan Napela. Inside the crater is a small lake that is somehow connected to the ocean. The reported site of the Napela's home is at the top of the saddle of the road that connects Kalaupapa with Kalawao where the short trail heads up the crater rim. It is also the point at which the old trail that went "topside," straight up without switchbacks, started. Another cemetery also lies nearby across the road.

Directions to Kauhaku Crater:

From Kalaupapa head east toward Kalawao on Damien Road about one mile to where a 4wd track heads north about one-half mile up to the western side of the crater overlooking Kalaupapa.

Lana'i

L ana'i, the sixth largest island in the Hawaiian chain, is located right in the center of the archipelago, with Moloka'i and Maui to the north and east. Lana'i, the smallest of the main islands, is thirteen miles wide and eighteen miles long. Its total landmass is just under 140 square miles. From a population of 1,600 in the first missionary census of 1832, it dropped to just 100 by 1896 due to disease and out-migration. This small island became known as the "Pineapple Island" when in 1921 James Dole, the president of the Hawaiian Pineapple Company (later renamed Dole Food Company), bought almost the whole island of Lana'i and developed a large portion of it into the state's largest pineapple plantation; he also built Lana'i City for his workers.

Lana'i is very secluded, being ninety-eight percent privately owned. The only town on the island is Lana'i City, which sits at an elevation of approximately 1,700 feet above sea level. The city was built at the center of the pineapple industry in 1924. In 1985, Castle & Cooke CEO David Murdock transformed Lana'i from a failing agricultural operation into a world-class travel destination when his corporation, Castle & Cooke, terminated pineapple production and built two world-class resorts, one in Koele behind Lana'i City and the other at Manele Bay. The total population of Lana'i today (2016) is a little over 3,100, and there are still no traffic lights. In 2012, Oracle CEO Larry Ellison bought ninety-eight percent of Lana'i from David Murdock.

Latter-day Saints in Lana'i

By 1853, in the Sandwich Islands there were fifty-three Latter-day Saint branches and a total membership of 2,986.[1] Although missionaries were anxious to have these new Hawaiian converts

---

1 Jenson, Manuscript History, October 6, 1853. n.p.

gather with the Church on the mainland, the members simply could not afford to emigrate, and Hawaiian government policy forbade immigration.[2] President Brigham Young therefore counseled the missionaries to find a gathering place in the Islands.[3]

On September 28, 1853, Francis A. Hammond, while traveling on the island of Lana'i, discovered a possible gathering place for the Hawaiian Saints. The spot Hammond chose was the Palawai Basin, which he described as "lying at the foot of the large mountain on the east and extending toward a high ridge on the west, which enclosed completely a large tract of good land, perhaps 5,000 acres of which was in full view." Further, "I have never seen a better tract of land in one body on these islands." Hammond could see only one drawback to the place: its lack of fresh water during the dry season.[4]

Two weeks after Hammond's report, a committee was formed and embarked on a whale boat from Lahaina, Maui, across the eighteen-mile channel to Lana'i to explore the Palawai Basin.[5] At the time, the *ahupua'a* of Palawai was owned by High Chief Levi Ha'alelea. Through the efforts of Jonathan Napela, the influential judge and early convert, the Church was able to lease the land for five years from Ha'alelea for $175.00, to be paid annually.[6] After establishing themselves, the Saints were expected to purchase the land.

Arriving in Lana'i on August 30, 1854, Elders Thomas Karran, Benjamin F. Johnson, Ephraim Green, and Francis A. Hammond took a bath in the sea and then retired to the Palawai Basin, which they called a "sacred place." They dressed themselves "according to the Order of the Priesthood," and Johnson offered a dedicatory

2 Letter of John T. Caine to James Ferguson, April 14, 1855, "Foreign Correspondence," *Latter-day Saints' Millennial Star* 18 (July 14, 1855): 445.
3 Letter of Brigham Young to George Q. Cannon, June 15, 1853, Outgoing Correspondence of Brigham Young, Church Archives 1843–1877, CR 1234 1. It is also quoted in MHHM, August 18, 1853, taken from the journal of George Q. Cannon. Jenson, Manuscript History, October 6, 1853.
4 Francis A. Hammond, Journal, September 28, 1853, Church History Library; and Raymond Clyde Beck, "Palawai Basin: Hawaii's Mormon Zion" (master's thesis, University of Hawaii, 1972), 23–24.
5 Fred E. Woods, "The Palawai Pioneers: The First Hawaiian Latter-day Saint Gathering Place on the Island of Lanai (1854–1864)," *Mormon Historical Studies* 5, no. 2 (Fall 2004): 7.
6 Min et al., *Stewards of the Promise*, 27.

prayer, consecrating the land for the building of a city, which they designated the "City of Joseph" in the "Valley of Ephraim."[7] Returning to the other islands, the missionaries then began gathering people to settle in the newly dedicated land. The Saints that gathered in Palawai Basin for the first eight months or so consisted primarily of men. Since there was not sufficient food on Lana'i, families could not come until the crops of the settlement produced a good yield.[8]

Organizing family life in Palawai took time, but the initial pioneering effort in the fall of 1854 moved quickly. The work accomplished during that year included building a meetinghouse and fifteen homes.[9] On October 16, 1854, a plow struck the Palawai soil for the first time, but almost as soon as the crops were planted, worms began to destroy them.[10] Although the crops were not progressing as the missionaries had hoped, other labors did bear more immediate fruit. In 1855, there were thirty-two men laboring on the farm at Palawai, and pioneers had plastered a cistern to help collect rainwater.[11] The Palawai pioneers, also concerned with education, put Elder Ward E. Pack in charge of a school to teach English to the Hawaiians, and to teach them western farming skills.[12]

The real challenge was determining how much time the Hawaiian Saints would spend working for the Church farm in the Palawai Basin and how much time they would spend on their own homes and gardens. At first, the agreement was that the Hawaiians

---

7 Thomas Karren, Journal, August 31, 1854, Church History Library.
8 For a detailed history of the Lana'i gathering experience, see Fred E. Woods, "The Palawai Pioneers on the Island of Lanai: The First Hawaiian Gathering Place (1854–64)," *Mormon Historical Studies* 5, no. 2 (Fall 2004): 3–35; and Raymond Beck, "Palawai Basin: Hawaii's Mormon Zion" (master's thesis, University of Hawaii, 1972).
9 Ephraim Green, Diary, September 1 and 2, 1854, typescript, Joseph F. Smith Library Archives, BYU-Hawaii, La'ie, Hawai'i (hereafter cited as Green); as cited in Woods, "The Palawai Pioneers," 14–15, and Jenson, Manuscript History, December 30, 1854, Church History Library.
10 Green, November 13 and 19, 1854; as cited in Woods, "The Palawai Pioneers," 15.
11 Eli Bell, Diary, December 9, 1855, typescript, Joseph F. Smith Library Archives, BYU–Hawaii, La'ie, Hawaii; and Green, February 15, 1855; as cited in Woods, "The Palawai Pioneers," 16.
12 Letter from Elder Ward E. Pack, "Correspondence," *Deseret News*, November 14, 1855, 286.

would work full-time for the Church, but some of the Hawaiian pioneers had requested time to work for themselves, so it was decided that they could labor in their own fields after their daily work. Later, it was agreed that the Hawaiians could work two days a week for themselves. This plan was not successful because the Hawaiians worked so hard on their own projects at night that they were too tired during the day to labor for the Church. In addition, the Saints had to deal with fleas, fires, and broken farm tools, and this required a voyage to Lahaina, Maui, for repairs.[13]

Things did not seem to improve in the basin. A ship called the *Lanai* was purchased for transportating Church members to and from Lanaʻi, and the ship that carried produce and livestock to the markets of Honolulu and Lahaina turned out not to be seaworthy.[14] Crops were damaged by worms and dry weather, and the scarcity of water remained an unresolved issue. Though missionaries throughout the Islands preached bold sermons on the need for the people to gather, not many responded as the poor conditions in Lanaʻi became known.[15]

By the time the Sandwich Islands Mission conference was held on October 4, 1857, everyone seemed to feel that due to the failures at Lanaʻi, it would be best to choose other places where the Hawaiian Saints could gather. By April 1858, however, the Utah War influenced President Brigham Young's decision to have the Utah missionaries serving in Hawaiʻi and throughout the world return immediately to the Salt Lake Valley. The departure of the missionaries postponed the selection of a new gathering place. In fact, with missionaries going home, talk was resumed about Hawaiian Saints gathering to Utah. Even a formal request was made for a necessary governmental permit for some Church members to go with the departing Utah missionaries in the fall of 1857, but the government denied the request.[16] "When the mission closed, the Saints on Lanaʻi had one year left in their experimental period. A better gathering place had not yet been found."[17]

---

13 Woods, "The Palawai Pioneers," 18.
14 Beck, "Palawai Basin," 52; Jenson, Manuscript History, March 25, 1855.
15 Woods, "The Palawai Pioneers," 20.
16 Beck, "Palawai Basin," 61.
17 Britsch, *Moramona*, 48.

From the spring of 1858, when the Utah missionaries left, to the summer of 1861, a small group of dedicated members who remained at Lana'i held to their beliefs and looked for deliverance. They were vulnerable for deception. An opportunistic man by the name of Walter Murray Gibson arrived in Hawai'i. Gibson did not turn out to be the leader the Saints were looking for. He had joined the Church in Salt Lake City in 1860 and come to the Palawai Basin the following year with a plan for his own aggrandizement.[18]

Walter Murray Gibson. Courtesy of BYU–Hawaii Archives.

For about three years (1861–1864), Gibson deceived and defrauded the Lana'i Saints, assuring them that the money and properties he had collected from them would be used to buy land for the gathering of the Saints in the Palawai Basin. However, he bought land in the Palawai Basin in his *own* name, intending to use it for his *own* purposes. Gibson's deceptions grew. He sold Church offices[19] and told the Hawaiians that Brigham Young did not have any authority to preside over Church affairs in the Pacific. He also forbade the Palawai Saints to hold meetings, preach the gospel, read the scriptures, or have family prayers.[20] Some of the Saints saw through Gibson's deceptions, observing that Gibson did not conduct his life according to gospel principles as former Utah missionaries had. A few concerned Hawaiian Saints wrote to former missionaries, informing them of Gibson's actions.[21]

18 Jacob Adler and Robert M. Kamins, *The Fantastic Life of Walter Murray Gibson, Hawaii's Minister of Everything* (Honolulu: University of Hawai'i Press, 1986), 46, 57, 64–65.
19 Letter written to Alma L. Smith, July 23, 1863, signed by six Hawaiian Church members: Solomona, Puuanui, Holoa, Hoopiiaina, Kaawa, Mak'uakani "and all the saints," Brigham Young incoming correspondence, Church History Library, as cited in Woods, "The Palawai Pioneers," 25.
20 Letter of Alma L. Smith, April 29, 1864, published in an article titled "Sandwich Islands," *Deseret News* 13:39 (June 22, 1864).
21 Woods, "The Palawai Pioneers," 24–25.

When Gibson's antics came to the attention of President Young, he sent Elders Ezra T. Benson and Lorenzo Snow of the Quorum of the Twelve, and three former missionaries, Joseph F. Smith, Alma L. Smith, and William W. Cluff, in March 1864 to investigate the charges. It was on the way to Lana'i that the elders narrowly avoided tragedy when Elder Snow almost drowned at Lahaina.

The charges against Gibson were found to be true, and a priesthood meeting, including the visiting Church leaders, was held on April 7, 1864, where the excommunication of Gibson was proposed. "Only one Hawaiian elder voted for this proposition; evidently those Church members who had remained on Lana'i were still under Gibson's influence." Returning to Maui, President Young's delegation found Gibson guilty of apostasy, and he was excommunicated.[22] The Bureau of Conveyances lists Levi Ha'alelea selling Palawai to Gibson on February 23, 1863. All told, Gibson had bought eleven parcels on Lana'i, including the *ahupua'a* of Palawai and Kaohai and other *kuleana* between 1863 and 1867.

Gibson refused to turn over title to Palawai to the Church, so the brethren from Utah counseled the Saints at Palawai to return to their former communities. The hope of establishing the City of Joseph on Lana'i was over. In 1865 a new gathering place was chosen and purchased in La'ie on the island of Oahu. A number of faithful Church members who had begun the work at Palawai later gathered to La'ie on the island of O'ahu.[23]

From 1864 to 1946, membership of the Church was sporadic on Lana'i. Elder H. P. Richards found forty-seven members when he visited on February 10, 1878, and dedicated a new chapel; Andrew Jenson recorded thirteen members in the Lana'i branch in 1895. In November 1946, Elders Daniel S. Hess and J. Dale Brown were assigned to labor in Lana'i.[24] Soon after the arrivsal of Brown and Hess, the Dole Pineapple Company donated an old community center to the Church. With the help of local members, the

---

22 *Moramona*, 57; and R. Lanier Britsch, "Lanai Colony: A Hawaiin Extension of the Mormon Colonial Idea," *Hawaiian Journal of History* 12 (1978): 80.

23 Kuykendall, *Hawaiian Kingdom*, 3:104.

24 Daniel Hess, Journal, Nov 19, 1946–Dec. 3. 1947; as cited in Daniel Stewart Hess, "The History of the Reestablishment of the Church of Jesus Christ of Latter-day Saints on Lanai," 2000, 5, typescript in authors' possession.

missionaries renovated the building for use as a chapel, recreation hall, and mission home. Once again, the work of the Church began to grow on Lana'i.

LDS Historic Sites in Lana'i

1. Palawai Valley and the City of Joseph

In 1853, Palawai Valley was selected as a gathering place for the Hawaiian Saints. The Church of Jesus Christ of Latter-day Saints purchased this land, and Hawaiian pioneers called their settlement the Valley of Ephraim and named their city the City of Joseph.

Last house at Palawai. Courtesy of BYU–Hawaii Archives.

The Lana'i pioneers, mainly from the Kula and Wailuku Districts on Maui, were called on missions by Elder Francis Hammond to settle this "barbaric" land. By July 1855, perhaps three hundred members were living in the Palawai Valley. Food was

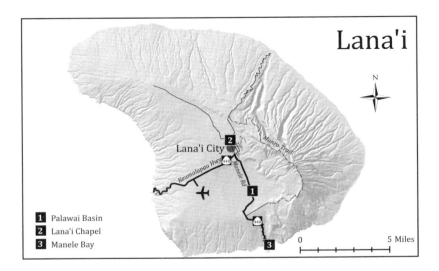

Lana'i

1 Palawai Basin
2 Lana'i Chapel
3 Manele Bay

0   5 Miles

difficult to produce in Lanaʻi, and the only freshwater source for the settlement was located more than a mile away. The low yield produced by the first year of crops made it difficult for the Saints to pay off the debt incurred to buy seeds, and although strong missionaries labored in Hawaiʻi during that time, opposition to their work was also strong.

After the failure of the pioneer settlement, the Palawai Valley had almost become deserted when Walter Murray Gibson was excommunicated. He left his son-in-law, Fred Hayselden, in charge of his ranch and moved to Honolulu to engage in newspaper publishing and politics, later becoming prime minister under King Kalakaua.[25] A handful of Saints remained, but their numbers, as well as the rest of the island, declined over the years. The basin was used for grazing, and after 1922 it eventually became filled with pineapple plants. It is now back to being used primarily for grazing.[26] The Palawai Basin is the crater of the ancient volcano that formed the island.

On October 3, 2004, a monument was placed in the area to commemorate the sacrifices of the early Hawaiian pioneers.[27] The monument consists of a "stone pier of volcanic rock with an anodized aluminum plaque." The monument was dedicated by Lanai Branch President Oscar T. Aguilar. At the dedicatory services, Maui Stake President Arnold Wunder compared the sacrifices of the early Hawaiian Saints with those of pioneers on the mainland called to gather in Ohio, Missouri, Illinois, and finally Utah. "They left their homes like the pioneers on the mainland to answer the call to gather. . . . It is my hope that the memorial on Lanai will

25 Frank W. McGhie, "The Life Intrigues of Water Murray Gibson" (master's thesis, Brigham Young University, 1958), 81; Paul Bailey, *Hawaii's Prime Minister* (New York: Hastings House, 1980), 153–54; Jacob Adler, *The Fantastic Life of Walter Murray Gibson* (Honolulu: University of Hawaiʻi Press, 1986), 86–87; Gwynn Barrett, "Walter Murray Gibson: the Shepherd Saint of Lanai Revisited," *Utah Historical Quarterly* 40 (Spring 1972): 157; R. Lanier Britsch, "Another Visit with Walter Murray Gibson," *Utah Historical Quarterly* 46, no. 1 (Winter 1978): 65–78; and Woods, "The Palawai Pioneers." See also Ralph S. Kuykendall, *A History of Hawaiʻi* (New York: Macmillan, 1926), 215–16, 268–71.
26 David Cheever, *Daytrips to Hawaiʻi* (Fern Park, FL: Hastings House Book Publishers, 2001), 225.
27 Riley Moffat, "Dedication of the Palawai Historical Marker on the Island of Lanai, Hawaiʻi." *Mormon Historical Studies* 5, no. 2 (Fall 2004): 179–83.

remind our members of the sacrifices the early saints were asked to make and were willing to make," President Wunder said.[28] This monument is along the road between Manele Bay and Lana'i City. The actual site of the City of Joseph in the Valley of Ephraim is about a thousand yards east of the monument against the bluff on private land near the remains of a piggery.

Directions to Palawai Basin and Historical Marker:

A ferry operates four daily round trips from the Lahaina boat harbor in front of Pioneer Inn. From the ferry landing on Lana'i, take the Manele Road toward Lana'i City. The road will climb up and enter the Palawai Basin, and about five miles from the harbor you will see the plaque on the right side of the road. For ferry reservations, 1-800-695-2624 or 808-661-3756. Adults $30; children $20 each way.

From the Lana'i Airport, take a right out of the airport on Highway 440 and head toward Lana'i City. Before entering Lana'i City, turn right on Manele Road and go about three miles down into Palawai Basin and look for the plaque on the left side of the road.

2. Lana'i Chapel

In November 1946, Dole Pineapple Company donated an old community center to the Church. Missionaries and members worked hard to renovate the building. Together they built benches and cabinets out of telephone poles, planted a hedge around the building, dug a trench for a sewer line, did the electrical wiring, and installed a bathroom.

Lana'i Chapel. Courtesy of BYU–Hawaii Archives.

28 Julie Dockstader Heaps, "Lanai Legacy Not Forgotten: Monument Honors Early Pioneers' Faith, Sacrifices on Hawaiian Island," *Church News*, October 16, 2004, 11.

On December 12, 1946, the first meeting was held in the renovated community center, now designated for use as a chapel and a mission home. A housewarming party and dedicatory service were held on January 19, 1947.[29] The Latter-day Saint chapel, still in use, includes an apartment for the missionaries when they are on the island.

Activities for Latter-day Saint members on Lana'i have continued to center around this small chapel and family. Given the small island population and the strong influence of other denominations, branch members became very dependent on one another.[30]

In the early 1950s, Elder Gerald R. Walk reported that almost all the auxiliary leaders and teachers were youth between fourteen and eighteen years old who had been converted through activity in MIA and Boy Scouts.

During the summers of the 1970s and 1980s, a number of Latter-day Saint young men, mostly from Utah and Idaho, came to this small island to work in the pineapple fields for the Dole Company in a program called Youth Developmental Enterprises (YDE). These young men conducted their own church services at this small chapel and also performed many community clean-up projects around Lanai City. Almost eighteen thousand boys participated in YDE. One of the goals of the program was to build the character of young men. Most of the boys who worked in this program were Latter-day Saints, though all denominations and religious persuasions were welcome to participate. While in Hawai'i, the young men were expected to live Latter-day Saint Church standards. Hair was kept short, no local girlfriends were allowed, other restrictions were expected, and youth workers were to attend weekly church services (regardless of denomination).

At the end of the season, the boys were taken on a one-week tour of the Hawaiian Islands. The program was discontinued in 1993 when financial difficulties involving the relationship between YDE and Maui Pineapple resulted in cessation of the program.[31]

Steve D. Edwards participated in YDE, picking pineapple in the summer of 1973, then returned as a supervisor in 1979, and

29 Hess, Journal, 5.
30 Min et al., *Stewards of the Promise*, 80–81.
31 Ibid., 98–99.

worked as a YDE counselor in 1980. He remembers that a Latter-day Saint branch was organized on Lana‘i for the boys; a returned missionary supervisor, or *luna*, was called to lead each Aaronic Priesthood age group. A different "gang" of fifteen boys were responsible for the weekly sacrament meeting at the small Lana‘i chapel and performed many community clean-up projects around Lana‘i City.

The YDE young men stayed in barracks along Lana‘i Avenue near 10th Street and held their church servces there.

Steve Edwards recalls his YDE experience:

> My dad and mom knew I needed a change to be away from home. . . . I was just an obnoxious teenager doing what teenagers do. . . . My faith-promoting experience was ten weeks away from home. I had to get on my knees and pray and figure out what life was all about. I realized how important my mom and dad were to me and what they taught me. Your luna, he cared about you, but not like your parents cared about you. For me, that's when I really realized what my parents' love was, and how much they cared about me. Even though I was mad at my dad for making me go to Hawaii, it was wonderful. Trying to prepare a Sunday School lesson as a sixteen-year-old, to teach other guys who could not care less, increased my testimony as nothing had before. . . . I had always been active in the Church, but this was different.
>
> Hawai‘i for me . . . was a faith-promoting experience, where I really grew up. When I came home, my parents said, "You are so different. . . . You left here a lost little boy and you came back more focused on life." I don't know if we can always say where we got our testimonies, but when I came home at age sixteen from Hawai‘i, after being gone for ten weeks, I had a testimony. . . . I quit being rebellious. It did change my life a lot. Shortly after that, for example, I gave up swearing.

Directions to the Lana‘i Chapel:

The Lana‘i Chapel is located at 348 Jacaranda Street between 3rd and 4th Streets in Lana‘i City.

3. Manele Bay

Manele Bay, a Marine Life Conservation District, was once part of an ancient Hawaiian village and is the site of the only public boat harbor on the Island. The bay is located about eight miles south of Lanaʻi City at the end of Manele Road.

Manele Bay is where the missionaries and members landed to go to the City of Joseph. The bay was actually part of the *ahupuaʻa* of Palawai leased by the Church from High Chief Levi Haʻalelea. Today the ferry from Lahaina docks at this same site. To experience what the original missionaries did as they came to Lanaʻi visitors can land in the same spot after crossing over from Lahaina. As of 2015, the ferry makes five round trips a day from Lahaina and takes about forty-five minutes. In the winter months, hundreds of humpback whales congregrate in the waters between Lahaina and Lanaʻi.

Directions to Manele Bay:

There are five sailings a day, with departures from Lahaina in front of the Pioneer Inn and on Lanaʻi at Manele Bay. Call 808-661-3756 for reservations or go to https://www.go-lanai.

The Big Island of Hawai'i

The island of Hawai'i, commonly known as the "Big Island," with 4,029 square miles, is twice as large in land mass as the other seven major Hawaiian Islands combined.[1] Hawai'i continues to grow as new lava flows add hundreds of acres along the southern half of the island. The island of Hawai'i is formed primarily from five volcanic domes: going from north to south and from oldest to youngest, they are Kohala, Mauna Kea, Hualalai, Mauna Loa (the world's largest active volcano), and Kilauea.[2] Another volcanic dome, called Loihi, is forming fifty miles south of Kilauea. It has risen 10,000 feet above the ocean floor, but its summit remains 3,000 feet below the surface of the sea. It may reach the surface in 10,000 years or so to form another island.

Scholars propose that settlement on the Big Island began at least by AD 600 around South Point and Waipio Valley, near fresh-water sources. These coastal settlements continued to expand into the 1200s by their relying on inland fields, as well as marine resources on most of the island and wetland taro patches in the deep valleys of the northeast coast.

Western contact on this island began in 1779 with Captain James Cook's winter stay at Kealakekua Bay. Other explorers and traders followed Cook,[3] introducing Big Island Hawaiians to outside influences, both good and bad—firearms, disease, and alcohol, but also Christianity, reading and writing, cattle, and the introduction of various crops. The diseases began decimating the population since the natives had no immunity.

---

1 Linda Wedel Greene, *A Cultural History of Three Traditional Hawaiian Sites on the West Coast of Hawai'i Island* (United States Department of the Interior: 1993), 3.

2 Jerald Joseph Holland, "Land and Livelihood: The Kona Coast About 1825," (master's thesis, University of Hawaii, 1971), 1.

3 Ibid., 92.

Many of the foundational events in Hawaiian history have occurred on or have seriously affected the Big Island. Sometime between 1753 and 1761, Kamehameha I, which means "the Lonely One," was born on the Kohala coast. Beginning in 1780, he began a series of conquests that eventually gave him control of all the Hawaiian Islands. Under his leadership the islands were united for the first time.

King Kamehameha died in 1819. His son, Liholiho (Kamehameha II), succeeded him and moved his seat of government to Honolulu. In one of his first official acts, he abolished the ancient *kapu* system (Hawaiian for "forbidden" or "taboo"), which allowed for freer association between aristocracy and commoners and also greatly dissolved the existing cultural and social framework. Protestant missionaries from New England, who arrived in Kona in 1820, took immediate advantage of the religious vacuum this action created.

The *mahele* (land division) of 1846–1855 offered Hawaiian families title to the lands they had been farming. Later, extensive sugar plantations developed which required a large, inexpensive labor force. Workers were imported from China, Japan, the Philippines, and other areas, creating a very multiethnic population. These large commercial operations, along with the famous Parker cattle ranch, formed the backbone of the Island's economy until tourism became the major economic engine.

In April 1900, when Congress passed the Organic Act making Hawai'i a United States territory, Prince Jonah Kuhio Kalanianaole became Hawai'i's delegate to Congress and one of its staunchest supporters. Influential and well liked in Washington, D.C., his greatest triumph was helping to pass the Hawaiian Homestead Act in 1922, which provided native Hawaiians with ninety-nine-year leases to thousands of acres of homestead land. Prince Kuhio saw the efforts of the LDS Church to strengthen Hawaiian families as a model for the preservation of the Hawaian people.

This federal act, as well as other previous local homesteading acts, greatly blessed the people of Hawai'i, particularly those living on the Big Island. As many Hawaiians joined the Latter-day Saint Church, they took advantage of these acts and moved onto these lands, forming strong branches in these areas. The sugar plantations are now closed, and the economy revolves around tourism.

Latter-day Saints on the Big Island of Hawai'i

In early 1851, Latter-day Saint missionaries Elders Hiram Blackwell and James Hawkins worked briefly in Hilo. At first they preached the gospel to the few white islanders, then directed their attention to the native population. On Hawai'i, Elder Hawkins experienced indifferent success in South Kohala but made some important contacts who would befriend later missionaries: "The work on Hawai'i from Elder Hawkins' assignment in 1850 through that of Elder Woodbury in 1851 had been slow to take root."[4] There were so few foreigners, or *haoles,* to teach that Blackwell decided he had accomplished all he could in trying to convert them. Although Blackwell made a minimal effort to learn the Hawaiian language, he thought it would take at least a year to speak it, and he doubted that Hawaiians would even accept the gospel. Deciding to leave Hawai'i, Blackwell tried to persuade Hawkins to leave with him, but Hawkins chose to stay until he received other instructions from Church leaders.[5]

On February 1, 1851, Blackwell sailed from Hilo, arriving in Lahaina a day later, where he gave a dismal report of conditions on the Big Island to Elders Cannon and Farrer, saying that the language was impossible to learn. Blackwell then sailed from Lahaina to Honolulu, where he then decided to leave the Hawaiian Islands altogether. Meanwhile, Hawkins stayed alone on the Big Island, while having very little success. Elder John S. Woodbury then joined Elder Hawkins at Keauhou, a village just south of the port at Kailua.[6]

Late in December 1851, Elvira Woodbury reached Keauhou to join her husband, who was supporting himself by cultivating a field of pumpkin to sell and doing missionary work as he could. The Woodburys reported their first Big Island baptisms on April 8, 1852—two young men who were students in a school started by

---

4 Joseph H. Spurrier, *Sandwich Island Saints: Early Mormon Coverts in the Hawaiian Islands*, 17, 128.
5 Farrer, Diary, vol. 1, February 2, 1851, 104–5.
6 Spurrier, *Sandwich Island Saints*, 84.

Sister Woodbury to teach English.[7] A letter from President Lewis a few months later instructed the couple to go to Honolulu, and missionary efforts on the Island ceased for over a year.[8]

Two years later, as the work began showing favorable results on the islands of O'ahu and Maui, the elders decided to reopen the work on the larger islands of Hawai'i and Kaua'i, where earlier attempts to introduce the gospel had been largely unsuccessful.

On May 25, 1853, Hawaiian Elder John W. Kahumoku was assigned with Elders Thomas Karran and Nathan Tanner to reopen missionary work on the Big Island. Even at this early stage of the Church in Hawai'i, local missionaries paired with non-Hawaiians proved an effective team for sharing the restored gospel. Dr. Ralph Kuykendall, the definitive historian on the Hawaiian Kingdom, asserted that the secret of Latter-day Saint success in the Islands was placing local men in offices of leadership as soon as they were competent to serve.[9] Missionaries Nathan Tanner, Thomas Karran, and John W. Kahumoku sailed from Honolulu on June 1, 1853, to reopen the work on the Big Island.[10] After facing rough seas and bouts of seasickness for four days, the missionaries eventually landed at Kawaihae on the Big Island, and then sailed onward toward Hilo. After three aborted attempts at landing because of rough seas, Elder Tanner recorded the following:

> By this time the sails were torn so badly and the rigging so disabled that the captain told us it was impossible to land us at Hilo and asked us what he should do. We were sick, it seemed nigh unto death, and were willing to land anywhere, rather than suffer the horrors incident to the extreme situation any longer; and so we told him [the captain] to run with the wind and land us wherever he could. He then turned and ran back with the wind to Kohala, where we landed; and it soon became apparent to us that it was at Kohala, and not at Hilo, that the Lord wanted us to labor; for we found the people there ready and

7 Woodbury, Journal. See Roy G. Bauer to Mary Jane Woodger, e-mail, October 14, 2009, in possession of author.
8 Spurrier, *Sandwich Island Saints*, 84–85.
9 Ralph S. Kuykendall, "The Hawaiian Kingdom 1778–1854: Foundation and Transformation" (Honolulu: The University of Hawai'i Press, 1957), 344.
10 Dorothy L. Behling, *Love for Ohana Helps Bring the Temple, Mormon Pacific Historical Society, Proceedings* (May 21, 1988), 29; and Hawai'i Temple Visitors' Center, La'ie, Hawaii, 29.

waiting and praying for the elders to come. We landed on the 10th and although we were sick the natives insisted upon hearing us, and according to their desires we held a meeting and Elder Kahumoku addressed them for an hour and a half. The next morning we baptized 25 before we ate our breakfast.[11]

Kohala was one of the strongholds of the Protestant missionaries. In a short time, four branches of the Church were nevertheless organized. There was trouble, and false charges were made against the elders. On June 27, 1853, they were arrested and thrown in jail for allegedly interfering with the school over which the local Protestant minister Elias Bond had charge. Elder Kahumoku, having trained as a lawyer, defended the case in court. More than five hundred spectators turned out to watch the trial. Kahumoku argued that the LDS missionaries were priests, and that they had the same right under the law to organize schools as did any other priests. Kahumoku further argued that the law mandated only fifteen pupils in a school before a group could require the government to build a schoolhouse. The Latter-day Saints already accounted for nineteen of the twenty-five students at the school in question, so the Chuch was legally entitled to the schoolhouse. The defense also suggested that if the Latter-day Saint children contributed toward the erection of the Calvinists' church, then they should jointly own it with the Calvinists. The judge's decision was that the Latter-day Saint children should help build the Calvinist meeting house and be allowed to continue to attend the Protestant school.[12] Although the judge had ruled against the Saints, within a month that same judge, the schoolteacher Kalama, and six of the twenty-five schoolchildren who were not already members had been converted to the Church, and the missionaries assumed operation of the school. The teacher, Kalama, taught during the week and preached on Saturdays and Sundays for The Church of Jesus Christ of Latter-day Saints.[13]

On July 15, 1853, Elder Kahumoku was again arrested, this time for baptizing on a Sunday, but the judge dismissed the case saying that Christ had judged it lawful to do good on His day. Then

---

11 Jenson, Manuscript History, June 10, 1853.
12 Behling, *Love for Ohana*, 30–31.
13 Ibid.

on July 27, 1853, Elder Kahumoku died unexpectedly at the age of twenty-six. Elder Karran testified in his journal that Kahumoku had been called to the world of spirits to preach to his people there.[14]

In April 1854, George Q. Cannon and Jonathan Napela, along with four Hawaiian missionaries, Elders Kaelepulu, Kapono, Ho'opi'iaina, and Pelelu traveled on treacherous seas from the eastern tip of Maui to the Big Island. Arriving at the channel, they built an outrigger canoe and covered it with mats—Elder Cannon said it was like "going to sea on a log." During the trip, the wind stopped blowing, leaving the men stranded. They exercised their priesthood to call up enough wind to fill the sails; Elder Cannon testified that God answered their prayers, allowing them to arrive at their destination safely.[15] They left Maui at eight in the morning and arrived on the Big Island at four in the afternoon the same day.[16] The native elders testified that they had never had so smooth a sea crossing. The group dedicated a meeting house at Pololu, where the Saints held a luau for them. Brother Cannon wrote in his journal that a Hawaiian is never so happy as when he's eating, and he can eat enough to astonish any American.[17]

By 1856, a branch was operating in Waiohinu. Keaukaha also had an organized branch around the same time.[18] In April 1856, Joseph F. Smith was transferred to the Big Island and assigned to preside over the Hilo Conference. In October of that same year, he was assigned to preside over the Kohala Conference until the following summer. He stayed on Hawai'i in this position for the next year.[19] He held a conference in Hilo on April 25, 1858, where there were five elders, three priests, five teachers, and seven deacons, with a total membership of 529 in the Hilo district.[20] That year the

---

14 Thomas Karran, Journals 1853–1855, Microfilm, Joseph F. Smith Library, BYU–Hawaii, La'ie, Hawaii; see also Spurrier, *Sandwich Islands Saints*, 25.

15 Adrian W. Cannon, Richard E. Turley Jr., and Chad M. Orton, eds., *The Journals of George Q. Cannon Hawaiian Mission, 1850–1854* (Salt Lake City: Deseret Book, 2014), 458–59.

16 Ibid., 9.

17 Ibid., 178–79: "the Sandwich Islander is never so happy, so musical, so full of pleasant talk, as when seated at a good meal; and the quantity one eats on such occasions would astonish an American who had never seen them."

18 Ibid.

19 Min et al., *Stewards of the Promise*, 49.

20 Jenson, Manuscript History, April 25, 1858.

elders from Utah returned home, and the Church languished on the Big Island for a decade before being slowly rebuilt.

Of all the islands, work on the Big Island seemed to be the most arduous and difficult, due in part to its larger size and complex terrain. Missionary Edward Clissold remembers that in 1921, when he was called to serve in Kona, no transportation was available, and it was difficult to organize and operate the branches of the three hundred Saints living in that 130-mile-long Kona district. Sister Momi Bell recalled how her uncle, Akui Aina, would travel on horseback with Puna district pioneer Akima Ah Hee to contact members in the vast Hilo and Puna districts.[21]

During the Great Depression, construction of new chapels slowed, but membership continued to grow. It also increased after World War II. In the 1950s and 1960s, given better transportion options, the consolidation of some smaller branches, and the construction of larger chapels by LDS building missionaries, the image of the Church grew.[22]

A milestone was reached with the organization of the Hilo Stake on December 15, 1968, and the Kona Stake on November 24, 1974. This demonstrated that the Latter-day Saints on the Big Island were prepared to handle all their own administrative responsibilities and lead the Church in moving forward.[23] The island was richly blessed with the construction of the Kona Hawaii Temple, which was dedicated on January 23 and 24, 2000, by President Gordon B. Hinckley.

LDS Historic Sites in Hilo Area

Hilo is in the path of tidal waves, or tsunami, that occur all around the Pacific Ocean's Ring of Fire. The shape of Hilo Bay especially magnifies these events. Devastating tsunami have hit Hilo in 1868, 1877, 1946, 1957, 1960, and 1975. One member shares

---

21 Edward L. Clissold, "My Missionary Assignment in Kona in 1921," *Mormon Pacific Historical Society, Proceedings* (1982), 28–40; and Momi Bell, memories personally shared with Carolyn Depp on December 31, 1989, at Ainaola Ward, Hilo Hawai'i Stake. See also updated reprint of this article in Underwood, *Voyages of Faith*, 339–55.

22 Pack, *Building Missionaries in Hawaii*, 113–19.

23 "Stakes of Zion," *Deseret News 1976 Church Almanac* (Salt Lake City: Deseret News, 1976).

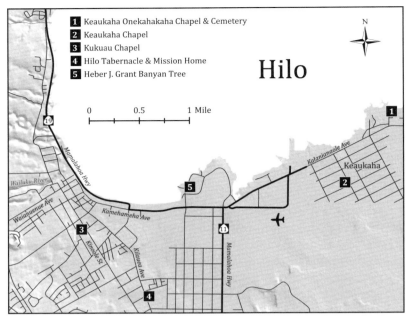

her story of surviving the April 1, 1946, tidal wave that killed 159 in Hilo. Sister Valerie Meyers Sewell's life was literally saved by oatmeal on that fateful morning. Valerie was a school girl in Hilo at the time, and, in spite of her Oriental heritage, her mother—district Relief Society president Chiyo Meyers—always served the children hot oatmeal on weekday mornings. She adamantly insisted that her children eat a nourishing breakfast before heading off to school, and Valerie's pleas that she would be late if she waited for it to cool did not sway her mother. "If I hadn't stayed behind to finish that oatmeal," Valerie explains, "I would have been walking right in the main path of the wave when it hit." She adds that she has not looked at *haole* hot cereal the same way since.[24]

President Spencer W. Kimball "visited Hawai'i in 1946, shortly after the tidal wave where walls of water, some forty feet high, struck Hilo." He reported as follows:

> I saw the devastation that resulted. Homes had been overturned and shredded, crushed into splinters like toothpicks; fences

---

24 Carolyn Depp, *Haole Kine from Hilo Side: Cross-Cultural Experiences from a Quarter Century of Life on the Big Island of Hawai'i* (Lehi, UT: CherishBound, 2009), 52–53.

and gardens were obliterated; bridges and roads were washed away. Bathtubs, refrigerators, mangled autos lay strewn all about the streets. Where one of our little chapels had stood, nothing remained but the foundation. More than a hundred people lost their lives; as many more were injured; thousands were left homeless. I heard many stories while there of suffering, of heroism, of salvation.

One woman told how she received a telephone message from friends to get out and leave—that a tidal wave was coming. She looked out to sea and saw the monstrous wave approaching, like a mountain. She and her husband picked up the baby and ran for their lives up the hill. However, two of their little girls were away from home playing near a clump of lauhala trees. They saw the wave coming, ran into the trees, and held tightly with their arms around the tree trunks. The first gigantic wave washed entirely over them, but they held their breath and clung with all their might until the water receded and their heads were again above the water. When the wave receded, they quickly ran up the hill before succeeding waves came. Together, the family watched from the safety of the hill as their home below disappeared under the pounding of the waves.[25]

1. Original Keaukaha Branch Chapel Site and Cemetery

Keaukaha, which means "the passing current," lies two miles east of Hilo. The Church has had a presence in Keaukaha from its earliest days on the Big Island. A prominent Church member of the community and *kumu hula,* "Aunty" Edith Kanakaole (designated a Living Cultural Treasure in her later years by Hawai'i's governor), recalled that there were two ancient Hawaiian temples, or *heiau,* in this area: a fishing heiau in Puhi, and another near the pond of the Kepoo family. She also recalled

Keaukaha Chapel at Onekahakaha. Courtesy of BYU–Hawaii Archives.

25 Ibid.

that there were two sharks, or *mano*, in the Puhi pond which the natives believed protected the families of that area when they would go to the beach.[26]

Abraham Nakapuahi Kahoilua gave property here for a chapel to be built by the Church in the late 1800s. The first structure used as a chapel was a grass hut. This "chapel" for the Keaukaha Branch, the second "official" branch on the Big Island, was located close to Onekahakaha beach. Then in 1906, a small red building, shared with a Protestant congregation, was constructed approximately 24 x 18 feet in size with benches on both sides of the room and an aisle in the center.[27] Momi Bell also recalled meetings held in this small shared building across from Onekahakaha Beach Park when her family moved into Keaukaha from Puna. The Protestants would meet first, followed by the Latter-day Saints, each hospitably staying to share the other's services. Classes were held out under the mango tree, and the temptation was strong for the younger children to sneak off and join the Sunday parties held nearby by Japanese beachgoers.[28] The red church was dedicated by Elder Eugene Neff, a missionary in the area at the time. In 1926, a new building, which came to be known as the "gray chapel," replaced the little red building. The gray chapel was also dedicated by Elder Neff, who by then had returned to Hawai'i as mission president.

By 1940, the gray chapel's roof leaked so badly that for a time the members held their meetings in the Keaukaha School building or the Kawananakoa Hall in the Hawaiian Homes subdivision. Then in 1946 the grey chapel was destroyed by the April 1 tidal wave that devastated Hilo. The foundation and stair steps of this early branch chapel are still visible by a grassy area.[29] A small cemetery for Latter-day Saints was also provided close by on the *mauka* side of the park.[30]

---

26 Rhea Akoi, *Ku'u Home I Keakuakaha* (Hui Ho'omau O Keaukaha Penaewa, 1989), 5, 22. (hereafter Akoi).

27 Roy G. Bauer to Mary Jane Woodger, email, October 14, 2009, in possession of Mary Jane Woodger; and Akoi, *Ku'u Home I Keakuakaha*, 92.

28 Momi Bell, Memories personally shared with Carolyn Depp on Dec 31, 1989 at Ainaola Ward, Hilo Hawai'i Stake.

29 Akoi., 93.

30 Andrew Jensen, "Report of 1928."

Directions to the Keaukaha Branch Chapel Site at Oneka-hakaha Park:

From the intersection of Highway 19 and Highway 11 near the airport, take Kalanianaole Avenue northeast 1.4 miles to Onekahakaha Beach Park and turn left, You will find the chapel site and cemetery. The chapel site was on the little hill in the middle of the park, and the cemetery is across Machida Lane *mauka* of the chapel site. Kawananakoa Halls in the Keaukaha homesteads on Baker Avenue next to the school.

2. Keaukaha Ward Chapel

The Keaukaha area of Hilo is a subdivision of homes built on Hawaiian Homes Land just north of the Hilo airport. To hold title in this area, property owners first had to document their Hawaiian ethnicity, defined as having at least fifty percent Hawaiian blood. This has stimulated many Hawaiians to research their genealogy, much of which has been collected by the Latter-day Saint church.

Latter-day Saints on the island contributed $60,000 as well as many hours of labor toward the construction expense of this new chapel across the park on Pua Avenue. Groundbreaking for

Last Keaukaha Chapel. Courtesy of BYU–Hawaii Archives.

the large tropical-style chapel occurred on November 2, 1953, and it was dedicated on November 21, 1954 by Elder George Q. Morris. It had an open and spacious design with a pronounced oriental flair. It was designed by Church architect Harold Burton, who designed several chapels around Hawai'i in this style in the 1950s. The chapel was built on land leased from Hawaiian Home Lands. When the building became termite-riddled to the point of having to be entirely rebuilt, the Church chose not to rebuild on land it could not own. The property was returned to Hawaiian Home Lands, and the Keaukaha Ward began meeting in the new, spacious Hilo Stake Center.[31]

> *Directions to the Keaukaha Chapel site:*
> From the Hilo International Airport, turn right on Kanoelehua and continue for a half a mile, then turn right on Kamehameha Ave. Go 50 yards and then turn left onto Kalanianaole Avenue. Continue for one mile to Keaukaha Park and then turn right on Pua Avenue. The address is 226 Pua Avenue across from the elementary school on the corner of Pakele Lane.

3. Kukuau Chapel, Mission Home, and Amusement Hall

The Church owned a substantial meeting house at Kukuau, which was built in 1896, along with a mission home and amusement hall. Andrew Jenson was with Mission President Matthew Noall when he bought the property for $250 on June 20, 1895. The meeting house, with a seating capacity of three hundred, was centrally located on Kino'ole Street. The mission home had seven rooms the amusement hall in 1928 was described as "new and commodious, . . . fitted with

Kukuau Chapel. Courtesy of BYU–Hawaii Archives.

31 Riley Moffat, interview with Jay Akoi, January 6, 2010, notes in authors' possession.

showers, dressing rooms and baptismal font; it is one of the best halls in the city of Hilo."[32] By April of 1952 it needed to be replaced, and the Hilo Saints began meeting in the Waiakea School; the Kukuau property was sold in September for $30,000. This building was the main chapel on the Big Island until the "tabernacle" on Kilauea Avenue was built in 1954.

Early missionary Castle H. Murphy, who served four missions in Hawaiʻi, as both mission and temple president, recorded that a young boy named Sam Johns used to come frequently to their meetings in the Hilo chapel on Kukuau Street and became very much interested in the gospel. One day Johns asked Brother Murphy to sit with him under this large banyan tree in the chapel lot, and he sincerely asked Brother Murphy if the things he had said about Joseph Smith the Prophet and the Savior were true. "In answer, I told little Sam Johns that if I didn't know those things were true, I certainly would not have left my home, my family, my business, and paid my own way to come to far-off Hawaiʻi to preach those things to the people." The boy's heart was touched, and he brought his father to the mission home to meet Brother Murphy the next day. Two days before Brother and Sister Murphy were to return home to Utah in 1913, Sam Johns Sr. and his two young sons were baptized and confirmed members of the Church—due in part to a sincere testimony shared under the historic banyan tree.[33]

Directions to Kukuau Branch Chapel, Mission Home, and Amusement Hall:
The branch building was located on the present site of Borthwick Mortuary at 570 Kinoʻole Street in Hilo, just north of the current DMV office and Police Station.

4. Hilo Stake Center (Kilauea Chapel) and Mission Home

A new chapel at Hilo, which could be used jointly as a branch and district meeting house, was for years a goal of local leaders and mission presidents alike. In March 1949, property was purchased from Territorial Senator Doctor W. H. Hill for this purpose

32 Andrew Jenson, "Report of 1928."
33 Castle H. Murphy, *Castle of Zion: Autobiography and Episodes from the Life of Castle H. Murphy* (Salt Lake City: Deseret Book, 1963), 70–71.

Hilo Mission Home, 1949. Courtesy of BYU–Hawaii Archives.

on Kilauea Street in Hilo through the efforts of Mission President E. Wesley Smith and others. The eight-acre parcel included a mission home and spacious grounds for a future chapel. The home had previously belonged to Mr. Henry H. Padgett, manager of the Waiakea sugar mill, and his family, and was considered one of the finest homes in Hilo at the time.

This original property was dedicated by Elder Matthew Cowley on March 12, 1949. Elder Cowley told the Saints assembled at the Mission Home that day,

> We must put a building here that people will come up here to visit when they come to Hilo. So we will preach the gospel with this building. . . . We are going to build something to add to the beauty of this magnificent piece of ground. We must put up a magnificent building. . . . You are blessed here at Hilo, and you are going to bless Hilo. You are going to bless the people here. You are going to bless the community. This is going to be a wonderful addition to the city of Hilo. The people are going to be proud of it.[34]

Hilo Chapel. Courtesy of BYU–Hawaii Archives.

34 Henry A. Smith, *Mathew Cowley—Man of Faith* (Salt Lake City: Bookcraft, 1954), 255.

Elder Cowley's dedicatory prayer included the following:

Holy Father, we are grateful for this land which has been purchased for the blessing of thy people in Hilo and this entire
island. We thank thee for thy generosity, for thy love and tender
mercy. We thank thee for this building which is now our home
wherein thy servants dwell. Let thy holy Spirit be and abide here.
May all who enter the doors of this home feel thy presence. May
this place ever be a place sanctified unto thee and dedicated to
thy name's honor and glory. May it be open to thy people and
our friends. May they come here and mingle socially as well as
in the spirit of the work.

May there be a center of salvation in this island, that people
may be glad to come here and partake of the spirit which will
be and abide here. . . . May thy all-seeing eye ever be upon this
property.[35]

On July 27, 1953, groundbreaking exercises for what was
known locally as the "Hilo Tabernacle" were held under the direction of Mission President Ernest A. Nelson. The original plantation manager's home in the back right corner of the property was
remodeled to serve as the mission home. Local Latter-day Saints
labored diligently night after night, as well as many Saturdays and
off days, to complete these building projects. Their service will
stand as a great, lasting tribute to their love and devotion to the
Church.[36] This chapel was built on hard lava, which had to be leveled with dynamite. A visiting landscape expert from Japan, Nagoa
Sakurai, was so impressed with the design of the chapel that he
delayed his trip home to Japan and offered his services, without
charge, to design the chapel's landscaping.

The interior of what became the Hilo Stake Center after
1968 was furnished primarily in Philippine mahogany, which
was both beautiful and durable. The chapel ceiling, designed like
an overturned boat, emphasized both a "seafaring" and "Pacific
Islander" openness and hospitality in a way that was both inspiring and beautiful. On November 21, 1954, this new structure, with
its oriental-style exterior designed by Church architect Harold

35 Ibid., 253–60.
36 Dedication Program of the Hilo Tabernacle, June 10–13, 1954, original in possession of Carolyn Depp.

Burton, was dedicated by Elder George Q. Morris of the Quorum of the Twelve.[37]

A variety show was held on Thursday evening (June 10), an open house on Friday (June 11), district conference on Saturday (June 12), and the dedication itself on Sunday, June 13, 1954. The Dedicatory Prayer was offered by Elder LeGrand Richards of the Quorum of the Twelve, followed by a youth conference in the afternoon and a closing session of district conference that evening.[38] Unfortunately, like all wooden buildings in this wet, tropical climate, it was not destined to last forever, and the weather and bugs eventually took their toll on the unique chapel.

A new rebuilt Hilo Hawai'i Stake Center, constructed along the Church's standard plan, was dedicated in July 1995 on the site of the original Kilauea Chapel. Several wards currently meet in this building, which also houses Hilo Stake offices, a large cultural hall, a baptismal font, a Family History Center, and a little apartment for the missionaries in back.

Directions to the Hilo Stake Center and mission home:
The address is 1373 Kilauea Avenue. The large mission home was located in the back right corner of the property.

5. Heber J. Grant Banyan Tree

On the Big Island, a tradition was established in Hilo to honor celebrities, dignitaries, and other respected figures by inviting them to plant a banyan tree along Banyan Drive, also called the "Hilo Walk of Fame." Long aerial roots dangle from the limbs of these banyan trees, which are often covered with orchids and ferns. Today there are over fifty trees along the drive.[39] The first tree was planted in 1933, shortly after park commissioners decided to invite celebrities to plant banyan saplings along the peninsula. The first tree was planted by Cecil B. DeMille, who was filming a movie on the island. Other celebrities who have planted trees on Banyan Drive include Amelia Earhart, Babe Ruth, Franklin Delano Roosevelt, and Richard M. Nixon, and in 1935, Latter-day Saint

37 Akoi., 92–93.
38 Dedication Program of the Hilo Tabernacle.
39 "Banyan Drive," *Downtown Hilo*, http://www.downtownhilo.com/Places/BanyanDrive/tabid/415/Default.aspx.

President Heber J. Grant, who was visiting the Big Island after organizing the Oahu Stake.[40]

Momi Bell remembers being in Primary in Hilo when President Heber J. President Grant visited. During his talk, he looked down and declared, "Some of you will be living during the Millennium."[41] Hilo city officials gave him the opportunity to plant a designated banyan tree.[42] A plaque at the base of the tree identifies it as the Heber J. Grant Banyan Tree. After planting his banyan tree, he often referred to it in his talks.

Directions to the Heber J. Grant Banyan Tree:

From the Hilo International Airport, turn right on Highway 11. Continue straight across its intersection with Kamehameha Ave. (Highway19) onto Banyan Drive, which forms a circular route counterclockwise around the peninsula. Before you arrive at Reed's Bay you will see this distinct banyan tree, planted by Heber J. Grant.

Other LDS Historic Sites on the Big Island

6. Aleamai Chapel

The Kailimai family were among the early converts to the Church who formed the first branch in Kahuwa or Aleamai, just north of the Papeekeo plantation. Samual Kailimai and Kauahi Kanakaloloa Kailimai were baptized a month apart, in December 1873 and January 1874.[43]

David Keola Kailimai, born March 6, 1873, was later active in the Aleamai Branch. In 1913 the Kailimai family accompanied Elder Castle

Aleamai Chapel, 1910. Courtesy of BYU–Hawaii Archives.

---

40 Ibid.
41 Momi Bell, Interview with Mary Jane Woodger, October 22, 2015, Hilo Hawaii, transcription in authors' possession.
42 "Stake No. 114," *Time*, July 22, 1935, 28–29.
43 "Records of the Hilo District, Hawaiian Mission 1896–1923, Family History Library, Salt Lake City, Utah, microfilm 128851.

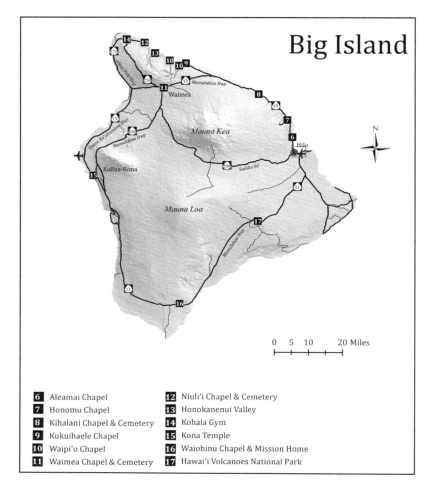

6	Aleamai Chapel	12	Niuli'i Chapel & Cemetery
7	Honomu Chapel	13	Honokanenui Valley
8	Kihalani Chapel & Cemetery	14	Kohala Gym
9	Kukuihaele Chapel	15	Kona Temple
10	Waipi'o Chapel	16	Waiohinu Chapel & Mission Home
11	Waimea Chapel & Cemetery	17	Hawai'i Volcanoes National Park

Murphy back to Utah to receive their endowments and be sealed in the Salt Lake Temple.[44] Elder Murphy even named his son, born in Hawai'i in 1912, "Keola," after Brother Kailimai.[45] David Kailimai, recognized as "one of the most influential leaders and able speakers in the Hawaiian Mission," participated in the vision during the visit of President David O. McKay at the Pulehu chapel in Maui in 1921.

44 Britsch, *Unto the Islands*, 162–63; Murphy, *Castle of Zion*, 42, 138–39; Abbie Kailimai (granddaughter of David Keola Kailimai) to Roy Bauer, May 2007; and Roy Bauer to Mary Jane Woodger, email, October 21 and 22, 2009.
45 Murphy, *Castle of Zion*, 42.

In 1928 the Aleamai Branch was one of the largest on Hawai'i, with two hundred members. It was not far from the seashore near the Papaikou post office.[46] After the 1850s, the Latter-day Saint Church in Hawai'i was known as a Hawaiian church, so branches were organized where the Hawaiian members lived. Along the Hamakua coast especially, as the many sugar plantations were developed, the Latter-day Saint branches became associated with the plantations, and later on with the Hawaiian homestead areas. As the labor needs of the plantations diminished due to mechanization after World War II and the general movement of members to towns, the Aleamai Branch was combined with the Hilo Branch on August 27, 1961.

Directions to the Aleamai Branch site:
Go north from Hilo on Highway 19 about 4.5 miles past Papaikou and turn right on to the Old Mamalahoa Highway. Go about 1,000 feet, and the chapel site will be on the left.

7. Honomu Chapel

According to Sister Abbie Kailimai, the first chapel in Honomu was built in 1924 and stood out in the middle of a sugarcane field. Then the branch moved into town and held meetings in a store before constructing the chapel seen now.[47] Just a few years later the

Honomu Chapel. Courtesy of BYU–Hawaii Archives.

Honomu Branch built a chapel in the town of Honomu, which is about a half-hour drive from Hilo up the Hamakua Coast via Highway 9.[48] When a new chapel was built, noted LDS sculptor Jan Fisher (see his statue of Duke Kahanamoku in Waikiki and of

---

46 Riley Moffat," Andrew Jenson's Big Island Tours of 1895 and 1928," *Mormon Pacific Historical Society, Proceedings* (2001), 9.
47 Abbey Kailimai, "History of the Honomu Chapel," *Mormon Pacific Historical Society Proceedings* (2001), 25.
48 Andrew Jenson, "Report of 1928."

Joseph F. Smith's "Hawaiian Mother," Ma Naoheakamalu Manuhi'i (1832–1919) in the gardens beside the Laie Hawai'i Temple) retired from BYU–Hawaii and rented the building because of its high ceilings and used it as a studio and residence.

The old Honomu chapel that was built and dedicated by Mission President William M. Waddoups on June 24, 1928 still exists. As transportation improved, a number of the small rural branches were combined to strengthen them, and the members in Honomu were assigned to the Hilo Branch on February 25, 1962. But as the years passed, membership along the Hamakua Coast grew, and the Honomu Branch was reorganized and a new chapel built.[49]

Directions to the Honomu Chapel:

From Hilo, head north on Highway 19 for 11 miles to the turnoff for Honomu, which is also the turnoff for Akaka Falls. After a quarter mile going into toward town, turn left again on Old Mamalahoa Highway. Continue for about a block. On your left you will see the old wooden chapel, which sits up kind of high just north of the Ishigo building.

8. Kihalani Chapel

The Kihalani Branch included those members living on the Laupahoehoe Peninsula as well as the surrounding plantations. The tidal wave (tsunami) that devastated Hilo on the morning of April 1, 1946, also destroyed much of

Kihalani Chapel. Courtesy of Leonie Poy.

the peninsula, including the school where twenty-four students and teachers lost their lives. The house of the branch president, John Akiona, was washed away, including the branch records and

---

49 Abbie Kailimai, "History of Honomu Chapel," *Mormon Pacific Historical Society, Proceedings* (2001), 25.

collected tithing. One of the students who drowned that day was fifteen-year-old Daniel Akiona, a grandson of President Akiona. President Akiona's wife, Lucy, barely survived. Later that afternoon, David Kailimai and others, with great difficulty and at great peril to themselves, were able to launch a small boat to rescue the survivors floating offshore.

The following experience was related to Elders Glenn S. Smith and C. Myron White by Sister Lucy Akiona of Laupahoehoe, Hawai'i, when they were holding a cottage meeting with her in November, 1946. (The meeting was held at Brother and Sister Akiona's home for the benefit of investigators.)

This experience happened April 1, 1946, April Fool's Day, at which time nineteen school children and four school teachers lost their lives at Laupahoehoe Point on the Island of Hawai'i.

Sister Lucy Akiona, while preparing the morning meal, was interrupted by the confusion taking place at the seashore. The school children and some teachers had gathered to watch the unusual action of the ocean as one could see the bare ocean bed for quite some distance. Sister Akiona, sensing danger, told her children to run toward the hills for safety, but they were too entranced by the ocean. John Jr. told the school teachers in the cottages of the ensuing danger, and since the children wouldn't flee, Sister Akiona grabbed Billy Matsu, the son of Seichi and Florence Matsu, and took him to safety at a Mrs. Malani's. The other children at the house were frightened because the entire house had become surrounded by water, but they finally reached safety. Sister Akiona returned to the house to save more valuables, and as she was fleeing from the seashore, a huge, gigantic wave came from the south side and swept her out to sea. The house had overturned on Daniel (a grandson), killing him instantly, and then the house was washed out to sea.

Brother John Akiona during this time was on the highway waiting for a bus to bring some pork from Hilo. He heard of the disaster and became hysterical, so his children took him to Paauilo so he wouldn't try to swim after his wife.

Sister Akiona managed to hold on to a one-by-twelve [board] all day, from approximately 7:00 A.M. to 5:00 P.M. After fervent prayer, she saw a door floating towards her as an answer to her prayer that she might have something more substantial to rest upon. She managed to get to the door, but had much difficulty getting on it, since it was broken and capsized easily. She prayed earnestly that she would be able to be protected through the night, and a foot cushion was floating towards her as she opened her eyes. She fastened this cushion fairly secure to the door and then, after a bitter struggle, managed to get on the door. She found that her entire body was extremely bruised except for that portion where her temple garments touched.

She had a gash in her right foot which caused her entire foot to be numb. It was raining bitterly and a cold wind was blowing and she prayed that she might be able to be warm and rest during the night. She immediately felt warm all over her body, as if hot pads were placed around her, and she shortly fell off to sleep. The next morning she awoke and heard the five o'clock whistle of the plantation blow and could see it was getting light. She touched the water and noticed it to be hot, so she knew sharks were in the area. She prayed once again that she might be protected. One shark's fin pierced the underside of the door, and part of her garment was hanging over the side of the door and a shark clasped his teeth into it. The shark immediately let go and the entire school of sharks left the area.

Realizing that she was in the midst of an area of rubbish about one-half mile in diameter, she thought of making a flag. So she tore off a piece of her nurse dress and then was confronted with finding a stick to put it on. She was searching the area, when she noticed a huge wave coming towards her and she felt this was certain doom, so she prayed fervently again and also asked for a stick to hoist a flag. She was so frightened because of the wave that she turned her back and closed her eyes and to her surprise the wave broke just before reaching her, instead of going to shore as it usually does. A stick approximately two inches wide came floating toward her door as an answer to her prayers. She obtained the stick and forced the cushion on an end of the door, hoisted the stick through the center of the cushion and after much difficulty, raised the pole. She was very weak from loss of blood, cuts, and exhaustion.

The first relief was an inter-island plane that circled her and then went towards Hilo. She had difficulty with the pole and it fell, the cloth floating away. She tore off another piece of her dress to put on the pole. She sighted a plane and P.T. boat coming towards her. She hurriedly hoisted the pole and the plane spotted her and circled several times. The P.T. boat failed to see her, so her spirits were lowered again.

Finally she sighted an LST [landing ship tank] that had been undoubtedly notified, and it came towards her. She shouted and waved the flag and they saw her signal. Since she was in the midst of debris, she prayed that she might be able to reach the LST—immediately after saying Amen, all the debris left her and she couldn't believe her eyes. Then she seemed to float directly to the boat since they had stopped the boat because of the debris. They threw a rope to her, but she couldn't tie herself because her strength was exhausted. She floated on around to the rear of the ship, and they threw her a Mae West. She held on to the Mae West [life preserver], and when they were raising her, she just could not hold on because she was so weak, hence she fell into the sea and immediately a sailor dove to keep her from drowning. The sailor and Sister Akiona then tried to climb the ladder on to the ship, but failed. She told them she would be helped on the ship with God's help somehow. A huge wave caught her and lifted her to the anchor, to which she held firmly until the sailors helped her on the ship. She only had a few clothes on her body and she was given artificial respiration, which caused a continuous flow of salt water [to come] from her mouth and lungs. They gave her blankets to keep her warm and applied iodine to her numerous cuts. Since the cuts were so numerous the application of iodine was extremely painful. She was injected with a drug and immediately went to sleep. She didn't awake until the next morning, about 4:00 A.M. in a Hilo Hospital. The first words she said to her husband in the hospital were, "I know God hears and answers prayers and that temple work is of God."[50]

The Kihalani chapel was torn down on November 13, 1956, and the members were combined with Honomu. The Kihalani Branch also had its own cemetery, which still exists. When the new Mamalahoa Highway was constructed it was built right over the site of the chapel, which was on the ocean side of the old Mamalahoa Highway. The new highway was actually cut below grade as it passed through the site of the chapel.

50 Quarterly Historical Report, Hawaiian Mission Manuscript History, December 18, 1946.

Directions to the Kihalani Branch site and cemetery:

The Kihalani chapel was located close to the Laupahoehoe dispensary 200 yards on the Hilo side of the Minit Stop store at 36-2266 Mamalahoa Highway. The new highway was built right through the site of the Kihalani chapel. The Latter-day Saint cemetery is located just on the ocean side of the new highway where many of the Latter-day Saint members are buried.

10. Kukuihaele Chapel

The original 16' x 20' Kukuihaele chapel was built in 1912 by Waipio Branch President Solomon K. Poliahu and his son John K. Kealoha. It was torn down in June 1952 to make room for a new, larger chapel (42' x 24') that incorporated

Kukuihaele Chapel. Courtesy of Leonie Poy.

building materials from the demolished Kalopa and Waipi'o chapels. It cost $3,600 and was dedicated on February 15, 1953. When the April 1, 1946, tidal wave drove most of the members out of Waipi'o Valley and the branch there closed, the former Waipi'o members moved up to the Kukuihaele area. This caused the membership of Kukuihaele Branch to increase from twenty-eight to eighty-three members and necessitated the larger building. Kukuihaele school principal John Keoni Thomas became branch president in November 1947, and by the time that branch merged with the Honoka'a Branch on Maile Road in 1956, there were 199 members.

Directions to the Kukuihaele Chapel Site:

The Kukuihaele Chapel site is located at 48-5464 Kukuihaele Road. From Kaliua-Kona, drive 53 miles northeast to Honoka'a on Highway 190 and Highway 19. Turn northwest on Mamane Street (Highway 240) toward Waipi'o Valley Lookout for 7 miles. Take Kukuihaele Road toward Kukuihaele for another mile. The chapel stands on the north side of the road.

It has been converted into
a family residence and
painted blue.

11. Waipi'o Chapel

Waipi'o Valley, with its
myriad of taro patches on
the flat valley floor and steep
sides rising up 2,000 feet, and
1,500-foot Hi'ilawe Falls, is
particularly picturesque. His-
torically, Waipi'o had one of
the largest and densest pop-
ulations in the Islands. But
over time, disease and the isolated nature of Waipi'o Valley
has reduced its population to
almost nothing. During a visit

Waipio Chapel. Courtesy of BYU–Hawaii Archives.

in August 1877, Elder H. P. Richards said the branch there numbered 130. In 1895, Andrew Jenson described the Waipi'o Branch
with its eighty-four members as being the "most lively" branch in
the North Hawai'i District. The Waipi'o Valley is famous for its
involvement in Hawaiian history and legends. A chapel was dedicated probably in the village at the foot of Hi'ilawe Falls by Mission

Waipi'o Valley, 1919. Courtesy of BYU–Hawaii Archives.

President Samuel E. Woolley on November 5, 1911. President
Woolley recorded the following in his journal:

> I was called upon to dedicate the new house to the Lord. I made
> a few remarks stating how much the people had given (356.10)
> and the house had cost 456.10 so I had made up the 100.00 as
> we never give a house to the Lord till it is free from debt, so
> I opened the meeting and then offered the dedicatory prayer.
> All were as quiet as could be, after which we all sang Ha Kumu
> paa loa, and Bro. Eyre spoke a few moments, as did the Prest. of
> Pahoehoe, Kahohano, and prest of Kui, o Kumukoa. John Moa
> Prest. of Kealia, Kuahiwinui Prest. of Opihale. Then I spoke for
> an hour. They all gave me the very best of attention and the good
> spirit was with us and we surely had a good time. There were 121
> present, many of which are not members of the Church but I
> could see the tears drop from their eyes in spite of them.[51]

The gospel was brought to Waipiʻo by a convert, Paul Nakan-
elua, who lived in Waimanu Valley (the next valley north) in the
1850s; it had its own branch with fifty-six members in 1895.[52] By
land, Waipiʻo Valley was accessible only by a steep path winding
down the wall of the valley, which contributed to a sense of seclusion from the rest of the island.[53] This valley was once one of the
most densely populated areas in all the Hawaiian Islands, supporting thousands of people. It furnished a substantial percentage of
the poi used in the Hamakua District during the early 1920s. That
was when a Brother Poliahu was branch president and took particularly good care of the missionaries. The quarterly reports of the
Hawaiian Mission say that a new chapel was being built in September of 1941, probably down near the beach.

The tsunami of April 1, 1946, did much damage in the valley.
A 55-foot-high wall of water surged 3,000 feet up into the valley.
Some of the members survived by climbing trees and holding
on for dear life. Most of the residents moved out and the branch
closed. Kelly Loo remembers seeing his neighbor running over to
him on that fateful day while he was eating breakfast and yelling,

---

51 Samuel Woolley, "Journals," November 5, 1911, BYU–Hawaii Archives.
52 Delores Ramos, "History of Honokaa Chapel," *Mormon Pacific Historical
   Society, Proceedings* (2001), 28.
53 Andrew Jenson, "Report of 1928."

"Hey! Tidal wave!" Kelly replied, "No. It's April Fools, I know." But when he looked at his neighbor's face he knew that it was real. So Kelly followed him running up the mountain. As Kelly looked back at the beach he could see the fish jumping up from a dry bed and that the water had receded.[54] The Waipio Chapel was destroyed minutes later.

The members were reassigned to move up to Honoka'a and Kukuihaele and attend church there.[55] The damaged Waipio chapel, which was down by the beach, was torn down in July of 1947; the Waipio members went to the Kukuihaele Branch. The small Kukuihaele Branch merged with the Honoka'a Branch in 1956. A few taro farmers remain as permanent residents in this isolated valley; others commute in and out.[56]

Directions to Waipio Branch Site:

Go to the end of Highway 240 (Waipio Road), where you can park and enjoy the spectacular view into the valley. A precipitous and narrow 4-wheel drive track leads down into the valley and is *definitely not recommended* for other types of vehicles. Local tour operators, especially the Loo family, also offer guided tours down to the valley floor for a fee. The 1941 Waipi'o Chapel site is located at the base of the Waipi'o Valley. From Kaliua-Kona, drive 53 miles northeast to Honokaa on Highway 190 and Highway 19. Turn northwest on Mamane Street (Highway 240) toward Waipi'o Valley Lookout for 8.5 miles. Proceed down the steep Waipi'o Valley road for .75 miles. The chapel site location is on the west side of the road (south of first home on the road).

12. Waimea Branch Chapel

In 1928, about two hundred members of the Waimea Branch met in a frame meetinghouse situated 2,500 feet up on the saddle

54 Kelly Loo, Interview with Mary Jane Woodger, October 21, 2015, Waipi'o, Hawai'i, transcription in author's possession.
55 Margaret Loo, "Church History in Waipio," *Mormon Pacific Historical Society, Proceedings* (2001), 31.
56 Billy Bergin, *Loyal to the Land: The Legendary Parker Ranch* (Honolulu: University of Hawai'i Press, 2004), 159; and Joseph Brennen, *The Parker Ranch of Hawaii: The Saga of A Ranch and a Dynasty* (New York: John Day Co., 1974), 102.

between Mauna Kea and the Kohala Mountain within the Waimea Ranch district.[57] Also called Kamuela, Hawaiian for "Samuel," to distinguish it from the "Waimea" on Kaua'i and O'ahu, this community is the headquarters of the huge Parker Ranch, which dates back to 1847 and is still one of the country's largest working cattle ranches.

Waimea Chapel. Courtesy of BYU–Hawaii Archives.

The ranching industry began when Captain George Vancouver brought cattle over from California in 1794. A *kapu* was placed on them, and they multi-

Waimea 1956 Chapel and 1938 Gym. Courtesy of BYU–Hawaii Archives.

plied rapidly, thereby creating a source of meat and hides. Many of the early members of the Church in Waimea were *paniolo*, or cowboys, on the ranch. Now, many of the members work for the fancy hotels in Waikoloa along the beach between Kawaihae and 'Anaeho'omalu.

In 1871, Jonathan Napela's only child, Harriet Panana Napela, married Colonel Samuel ("Kamuela") Parker, the ranch's owner. They would often represent their close friend King Kalakaua and the Hawaiian government in its dealings with the Church, such as checking on La'ie and how the Saints at Iosepa in Utah were doing.

There have been three different chapels in Waimea. A wood-frame chapel described by Jenson, which later included a large separate cultural hall, was replaced by a much larger chapel, which still exists on the village's "Church Row." Mission President

---

57 Andrew Jenson, "Report of 1928."

D. Arthur Haycock laid the cornerstone on June 21, 1955; it was dedicated by Elder Spencer W. Kimball on February 10, 1956. This second Waimea chapel was similar in design to the Keaukaha chapel in Hilo. These older buildings, designed by Church architect Harold Burton, were beautifully distinctive, with a pleasing Oriental-Islander ambiance to their design: grey-weathered, wooden exteriors, and practical Island-wise adaptations, such as covered, open breezeways, central atriums or *lanai*, and wooden jalousie windows for flow-through ventilation. The associated gymnasium, the largest Church gym on the island and the only gym in Waimea, was a very popular venue in the community for dances and athletics. It was dedicated by Elder John A. Widtsoe on November 20, 1938. During World War II, it was taken over by the U.S. Marines and used as part of their Camp Tarawa training facility. When they returned it to the Church after the war it was trashed and had to be refurbished. The 1956 chapel has in turn been replaced by a more modern chapel on Kapiolani Road behind Waimea Park.[58] There is also a Latter-day Saint section in the cemetery behind the old chapel near the Imiola Congregational Church. When the Church built the new chapel on Kapiolani Road, the Evangelical Hope Chapel bought the distinctive 1956 Burton chapel.

Directions to Waimea Branch Chapel Site:

"Church Row" is on Mamalahoa Highway just east of the Parker Ranch Shopping Center. If you are driving through Waimea from the east on Mamalahoa Highway, the area nicknamed "Church Row" will be on your right before you approach the central part of town. This building (painted blue) now belongs to the Hope Chapel, a local evangelical organization.

13. Niuli'i Cemetery and Chapel site

Some of the earliest converts to the Church on the Big Island were found in the Kohala area. On June 15, 1853, two branches of the Church were organized in Kohala, one with thirty-four

58 Barbara Robinson and Sister Keliikoa, "The Church in Waimea," *Mormon Pacific Historical Society, Proceedings* (2001), 63.

members, and another with sixteen members. As the years went by, many more branches were established in Kohala, each within walking distance of where the members lived: Mahukona, Kokoiki, Puakea, Honomakau, Halawa, Niuli'i, and in the valleys of Pololu

Niuli'i Chapel. Courtesy of BYU–Hawaii Archives.

and Honokanenui. Besides Niuli'i's little frame chapel, a social hall was added on July 10, 1937. All of Kohala's branches have now been combined into the Kohala Ward located in Hawi.[59] The seven sugar plantations that operated in Kohala are now shut down as well, as is the railroad that took the sugar from the mills to the harbor at Mahukona. But the Kohala ditch (which the Sproat family supervised), which brought water from the eastern valleys to the thirsty cane, is still running. The Niuli'i Cemetery, which is known as the Latter-day Saint cemetery by local citizens, was next to the Niuli'i Branch chapel. In 1994, as part of his Eagle Scout Project, Brent Kamaka Cornillez prepared an alphabetical directory of burials here, including previously unmarked graves, which he identified, numbered, and added to his survey. The property was formerly owned by the Church but is now maintained by living descendents of some of the members buried here.[60] Bill Sproat and his family, who lived at the end of the road overlooking Pololu Valley and managed the Kohala Ditch trail for forty years, were an integral part of this branch and cemetery.

After the construction of the large Hawi chapel in 1959, all the small branches in North Kohala, such as Niuli'i, Honomakau, and Mahukona, were combined into one branch in Hawi.

Directions to the Niuli'i Cemetery and Kohala Chapel Site:
The Niuli'i Cemetery is located 6.5 miles past the small village of Hawi. Go north on Highway 250/Hawi Road until you reach Hawi. Turn right on Highway 270/Akoni Pule Highway

59 Jimmy Tohara, "Church History in Kohala," *Mormon Pacific Historical Society, Proceedings* (2001), 41.
60 Susan Raymond, "Niulii Cemetery," *Hawai'i Raymonds*, http://freepages.gene alogy.rootsweb.com/~wgidir/pages/raymond/niulii.html.

and continue 100 yards past Keokea Beach Road. The cemetery will be on the left, and the chapel site is just to the right of the cemetery.

14. Kohala Gym

The Kohala District is rich in LDS history dating back to the confontations with Reverend Elias Bond in 1853. Over time, at least nine branches have existed in the district. With modern transportation and the loss of members due to the demise of the sugar plantations, they were finally combined into one with the purchase of the full-size Kohala gym by Bill Sproat in 1962. But a problem was the limited nineteen parking places. The first services were held in the building on December 13, 1959, and the chapel dedicated by Elder Delbert L. Stapley on June 27, 1963. The Kohala Branch combined all the other branches in North Kohala, such as Niuli'i, Honomakau, Halaula, Kokoiki, and Mahukona. Upkeep was a challenge, and various stake presidencies would alternately decide to fix it up or sell it. Eventually, in 2001, the Church built a new chapel on the street above it. But the Kohala gym has always been a center of activity for the community, especially for the youth.

Directions to the Kohala Gym:
The gym is located on Hawi Road (Highway 250) a block south of Akoni Pule Highway.

15. Honokanenui Valley

On July 27, 1853, Hawaiian Elder John W. Kahumoku died at the age of twenty-six and was buried in Honokanenui Valley. Elder Kahumoku had just baptized some new converts, and when he was returning to his home, he was caught in a cloudburst. He caught cold from this exertion and the resulting chill. A high fever ensued, and although fasting and prayers were sincerely offered for him, he passed away peacefully. He was buried in Honokanenui Valley in a stone sepulcher about 150 yards from the sea and the same distance from the bluffs. The entrance was sealed with a stone.[61]

---

61 Dorothy L. Behling, "Love for Ohana Helps Bring the Temple," *Mormon Pacific Historic Society*, Proceedings (May 21, 1988), 32.

Honokanenui (right) and Honokaneiki Valleys. Courtesy of Longbach Nguyen.

Elder Henry P. Richards was visiting the Honokane Branch in September of 1877 to organize the Hui Manawale'a (Relief Society) in that branch. On September 26, Queen Kapiolani arrived and offered to help with the organization. Elder Richards journalized as follows:

Thursday September 27th

> After breakfast I again bid the good Saints at Honokane farewell and proceeded on to Pololu with Kekuewa and quite a number of the natives from Honokane stopt [sic] a short time at Mokuilima's house where the Princess Kinoiki the Queen's younger sister came over to escort me to the house where her Majesty was stopping, The Queen received me very kindly, and as she was about to take breakfast she invited me to eat with her, which I declined as I had already been to breakfast at about 11 am. The people assembled together in the school house after being called to order. I opened the meeting by prayer when her Majesty proceeded to organize one of her "Hui hoola a Hooulu Lahui." In the course of an hour the organization having been completed I helped the queen eat a very fine watermelon when her majesty and suite started on for Puehuehu when she intended stopping for the night. I bade her adieu with the understanding that I should again join her party at night unless I could get on board of a schooner during the day bound for Honolulu.[62]

---

62 Journal of Henry P. Richards, September 26–27, 1877.

In the late 1800s, almost the entire population living in this valley were Latter-day Saints, and they had their own chapel. Honokanenui and Pololu Valleys are now deserted and are accessible only on foot. Visiting Honokanenui Valley should be considered a strenuous full- or at least half-day hike that requires food and water, even though it is only three miles as the crow flies.

Directions to the Honokanenui Valley:

Drive to the end of Highway 270 in Kohala past Niuli'i to the end of the road at the Pololu Valley Overlook. Hike down into Pololu Valley and across the mouth of the valley and up and over the pali on the other side along the Awini Trail into Honokanenui Valley.

16. Pu'uanahulu Chapel and Cemetery

The members that moved onto this small block of Hawaiian Homestead lands met in homes in 1928. An unused chapel was moved from Pahoehoe in South Kona on May 11, 1940. The first meeting was held on September 15, 1940, and the chapel was dedicated November 17, 1940. The Puuanahulu Branch was combined with the Kailua Branch on May 27,

Pu'uanahulu Chapel. Courtesy of Mary Jane Woodger.

1962. A small cemetery associated with the chapel contained fifteen graves as of January 5, 1965. The chapel is now the blue house across from the Baptist church.

Directions to Pu'uanahulu Chapel and Cemetery:

The Pu'uanahulu Chapel site is located at 71-1534 Hawai'i Belt Road. From Kaliua-Kona, drive 18 miles north on Highway 190. The chapel stands on the west side of the road and has been converted into a family residence, painted blue. Stained glass windows were added by former residents.

The cemetery lies in a field 40 yards directly behind the chapel. Approximately 10–15 people are buried at this site; some headstones are still visible.

17. Kona Hawai'i Temple

The Kona Temple was prophesied, and seen in vision, decades before its physical construction was ever announced by President Gordon B. Hinckley. As early as 1979, faithful members were receiving powerful assurances from the Lord that a temple would indeed someday be built on their island. Many of these special and sacred revelations remain too personal to be widely disseminated, but they are recorded and documented in the Kona Temple History. Island members were also told it would be smaller than other temples then being built, that it would be on a hillside facing the ocean but visible from the main highway, and that the site had been consecrated to that very purpose in ancient times.[63]

When Philip A. Harris was called as president of the Kona Hawai'i Stake, he prayed to know what the Lord would have him accomplish as stake president. He recounted, "One night I dreamt there was to be a temple in Kona. I woke and told my wife. . . . I took my dream to be a direction for me as a stake president that I was to [help] my people to become temple worthy and temple

Kona Hawai'i Temple. Courtesy of the Church of Jesus Christ of Latter-day Saints.

63 Philip Harris, Personal Kona Temple History, transcription in authors' possession.

ready." Initially, President Harris thought his dream meant that the people needed to be spiritually prepared, not that there would be an actual temple built in Kona. However, when President Gordon B. Hinckley announced the construction of small temples in 1998, President Harris knew the temple he had dreamed of would be built in Kona.[64] In 2014, he was called as president of the temple.

When the Kona Hawai'i Temple was announced, many Latter-day Saints wondered whether the Kailua village planning and design committee would give the Church permission to build a temple. John Pharis, the architect for the temple, asked President Harris to arrange for a show of community support for the temple among his stake members. Three hundred Saints showed up at a planning hearing. The whole hearing room was filled to capacity. Some people were outside looking in through the windows, while others stood in the corridors, and even more packed the sidewalks. Committee members, astonished and impressed by the community's support, granted permission to the Church to build the Kona Hawai'i Temple.

Ground was broken on the seven-acre site for the Kona Hawai'i Temple on March 13, 1999, with more than 1,200 people attending the ceremony. A combined choir from both the Hilo and Kona Stakes provided the music, and Primary children had the honor of turning some of the dirt after the dedication and groundbreaking. Elder John B. Dickson of the First Quorum of the Seventy presided over the ceremony.

Miraculous experiences were reported during the construction of the Kona Temple. Mark Kealamakia, while working on the baptismal font, felt the presence of early settlers of the Island who wanted their temple ordinances performed for them. Experiences like Kealamakia's increased Latter-day Saints' anticipation of the completion of the temple. Another miracle took place when Myron Lindsey was repositioning a mobile crane on the temple construction site. When the weight of the crane threatened to topple the machine, the crane miraculously righted itself. After Lindsey's experience, Hawaiian Saints fasted and prayed that another

---

64 Chad S. Hawkins, *The First 100 Temples* (Salt Lake City: Eagle Gate Publishing, 2001), 192.

crane used to lift a nine-thousand pound spire would be able to handle the weight. When the time came for the spire to be lifted, the crane started to bow as the spire was being raised. Yet despite the bow of the crane, the spire cleared the roof (by one foot), and the crane was able to put the spire in place.[65] This feat can be seen as a milestone in Kona, because as a structre, the temple is still somewhat distinctive, in spite of much progress on the island in the construction field. Before the temple was constructed, there were no tall buildings in Kona.

The Kona Hawai‘i Temple rests on a hillside flanked by Mount Hualalai to the east and the Pacific Ocean to the west. The 10,700-square-foot temple is set on 7.02 landscaped acres and houses two endowment rooms and two sealing rooms; its finish is a white marble veneer. The architect of the Kona Hawai‘i Temple, John Pharis, as he was reading the biblical parable of the wheat and the tares, felt inspired to include a sugarcane leaf motif both on the benches outside and on the interior walls of the temple. Wheat is not commonly grown on the Island, and so Pharis used the similar sugarcane motif instead as its local equivalent.

Many visitors were impressed by the spirit of the temple during the Kona Hawai‘i Temple open house in December 1999. President Harris reported that some mothers stopped and embraced their children while standing in the celestial room of the temple. Locals, even nonmembers, use the steeple and its angel Moroni as a navigational beacon when sailing into Kailua Bay. They call him "our angel." The lit spire is also used as a landmark by large cruise ships coming into the harbor.[66]

The Kona Hawai‘i Temple was dedicated by President Gordon B. Hinckley on January 23, 2000. Hundreds of potted red poinsettias decorated the front of the temple for the dedication, and many prayers of gratitude were offered. After the dedicatory services, more than a thousand Latter-day Saints gathered in front of the temple to await President Hinckley's departure from the building. As he appeared, the Kona Saints sang "We Thank Thee, O God, for a Prophet." Then, as President Hinckley got in his car

---

65 Ibid.
66 Phil Harris, Personal Kona Temple History, 1975–2000, transcription in possession of authors.

and waved to the congregation, the Saints sang "Aloha Oe," the traditional Hawaiian song of love and farewell, written by Queen Lili'uokalani.[67] The Kona temple stands next to the stake center that was built on the same land.

Directions to the Kona Temple:

The Temple is located at 75-230 Kalani Rd, Kailua Kona, Hawai'i. From the Kona International Airport, take Keahole Airport Road, then go right and head south on Queen Kaahumanu Highway/HI-19. Continue on Queen Ka'ahumanu Highway until Palani Road, and then go left. Continue on Palani Road until Kuakini Highway and then turn left. Turn left at Kalani Street. The temple is just above the stake center. The office telephone number of the Kona Hawai'i Temple is 808-331-8504.

18. Kailua Chapel

Before the recent tourist boom in Kona, Kailua was a sleepy little town, though rich in Hawaiian history. An early chapel was located on Hawaiian homestead land at Kalaoa a few miles north of town on the upper road, Mamalahoa Highway. The mission home in Kailua was moved from the back of the lot on December 26, 1940, to make room for a new chapel, but the Kailua Branch was still meeting in the Kalaoa chapel as of April 1958. Finally, construction on the new Kailua chapel began in

Kailua Kona Chapel. Courtesy of Fred E. Woods.

September 1959 on the mauka, or mountain, corner of Kuakini Highway and Hualalai Road. The Kalaoa Branch was combined with Kailua in the new chapel on July 11, 1961. This little chapel was replaced in the 1990s by the stake center that sits just below the temple.

---

67 See Appendix C.

Directions to Kailua Chapel

The Kailua Chapel was on the mauka, or mountain, corner of Kuakini Highway and Hualalia Road. The chapel site is now the West Hawai'i Community Health Center.

19. Waiohinu Chapel and Mission Home Site

The first official branch of the Church on Hawai'i was organized in Waiohinu in the Ka'u District, which is located between Hilo and Kona on South Point Road. Elder John S. Woodbury spread the gospel in this area in 1852. A branch was later organized here, and in the late 1800s a small Latter-day Saint chapel, typical for that day, was constructed. This was followed by another meetinghouse on Konohiki Road about one hundred yards off the highway to the south and dedicated by Mission President William M. Waddoups on October 22, 1928. A social hall was added in 1950 with materials provided by the Kahuku Ranch. The third building was constructed by labor missionaires in 1962 in nearby Na'alehu and dedicated by Elder Gordon B. Hinckley on November 2. It is still being used as the Ka'u Ward meetinghouse.[68] On August 21, 1950 the elders living at the Waiohinu mission home felt as if their lives had been spared when they felt inspired to go to Pahala to spend the night. During the night a terrible earthquake occurred, which hit the hardest at Waiohinu. It broke the refrigerator, letting all the ammonia gas escape into their sleeping quarters; had the elders remained home, they most likely would have died.[69] Electricity did not reach Waiohinu until 1953.

Directions to the Waiohinu Branch Chapel Sites:

Na'alehu is about 65 miles south of Hilo on Highway 11 toward South Point. Upon arriving at the south end of the island, drive south on the South Point Road approx. 4 miles. The original Waiohinu Branch first chapel site is located on the east side of the road before the road forks off to Ka'alu'alu Road. The site is marked by a white metal bar gate with a short lava rock wall. Beyond the white gate are some logs remaining from the foundation of the chapel.

---

68 Woodbury, Journal. See Roy G. Bauer to Mary Jane Woodger, email, October 14, 2009, in authors' possession.

69 Quarterly Historical Report, Hawaiian Mission, August 21, 1951.

Waiohinu is about 67 miles south of Hilo on Highway 11 toward Naʻalehu. Upon arriving at the south end of the island, turn south on Konohiki Street. The second site of the Waiohinu Branch chapel is located about 100 yards down Konohiki Street on the west side. The site is now an empty field; a few trees surround the property.

20. Hawaiʻi Volcanoes National Park

Hawaiʻi's volcanoes are particularly visitor friendly in that they seldom erupt explosively but rather ooze out lava, which usually flows like a molten river toward the sea, adding more acreage to Hawaiʻi. The spectacular power of the eruptions around Kilauea, however, has awed and inspired Church leaders for over a century and a half.

Kilauea Volcano. Courtesy of BYU–Hawaii Archives.

During his world tour of missions in 1921, Elder David O. McKay visited the Kilauea Volcano and there experienced a miracle through his obedience to promptings of the Spirit. One night while viewing the Kilauea volcano, Elder McKay reported that he and his company stood on the rim of the fiery pit, while a cold wind swept down from the top rim of the volcano.

> Tiring of the cold, one of the elders discovered a volcanic balcony about four feet down inside the crater where observers could watch the display without being chilled by the wind. It seemed perfectly sound, and the "railing" on the open side of it formed a fine protection from the intense heat [of the volcano], making it an excellent place to view the spectacular display.
>
> After first testing its safety, [Elder McKay] and three of the elders climbed down into the hanging balcony. As they stood there warm and comfortable, they teased the others . . . to take advantage of the protection they had found. For quite some time

... all watched the ever-changing sight as [the group's members] alternately chilled and roasted.

After being down there in their protected spot for some time, suddenly [Elder McKay] said to those with him, "Brethren, I feel impressed that we should get out of here." With that [Elder McKay] assisted the elders to climb out, and then they in turn helped him up to the wind-swept rim. . . . Almost immediately the whole balcony crumbled and fell with a roar into the molten lava a hundred feet or so below.[70]

Nothing was said as the elders walked down the slope. They all knew they had been saved by inspiration from a fiery death.

The beautiful black-sand beach village of Kalapana nearby, which once had a small chapel, has in recent years been completely buried by lava.

Directions to the Hawai'i Volcanoes National Park:
From the Hilo International Airport, turn left on Mamalahoa Highway/HI-11 for about 28 miles. At the Kea'au Junction, keep right following signs toward Glenwood, Kurtistown, and the National Park. Turn left at Crater Rim Drive, and then right at the Volcano Art Center.

---

70 David O. McKay, *Cherished Experiences from the Writings of President David O. McKay*, comp. Clare Middlemiss (Salt Lake City: Deseret Book, 1976), 52–53.

Kaua‘i

Kaua‘i is geologically the oldest and fourth largest of the eight main islands in the Hawaiian archipelago. The island emerged five million years ago from a volcanic "hot spot" in the depths of the ocean; then, over time, erosion created the spectacular landforms seen today. Located some 2,400 miles from the nearest landmass, Kaua‘i, like all of Hawai‘i, was one of the last places on earth to be inhabited. Ocean voyaging Polynesians formed the first colonies when they arrived around AD 400–600, according to archaeologists. Kaua‘i also boasts mountaintop bogs, rain forests, deep canyons, tangled valleys, coral reefs, and sandy beaches. At over 5,000 feet, Kaua‘i's Mount Wai‘ale‘ale is the wettest place on the planet; it has an average annual rainfall at 468 inches.[1] Appropriately, Kaua‘i is known as the Garden Isle.

The Hawaiians on Kaua‘i had inhabited the fertile valleys of Hanapepe and Waimea for centuries before Captain Cook arrived in 1778 on the island's southeast coast on his way north seeking a northwest passage. Kaua‘i was the last island to capitulate to Kamehameha I in 1810, without the shedding of blood. In 1816, Russian traders from Alaska unsuccessfully attempted to colonize Kaua‘i. Their fort can be seen across the river from Waimea. Christian missionaries arrived in Waimea in 1820, and in 1835 the first sugar plantation in the Hawaiian Islands was founded in Koloa.

At first, Hawaiians were asked to work on the plantations. However, the Hawaiians' lifestyle of living off the land was not conducive to working on a plantation, and other workers had to be found. Immigrants brought in to work on the sugar plantations came from the China, Japan, Portugal, and the Philippines. Later, many of these people became entrepreneurs and helped develop the Kaua‘i we see today. Following World War II, mechanization reduced the demand for labor, and high production costs forced

---

1 Joesting, *The Separate Kingdom*, 5–6.

the closing of the sugar plantations one by one. With the closing of the sugar plantations, Kaua'i became dependent on tourism. This dependency was demonstrated in the aftermath of Hurricane Iniki in 1992, when much of the tourism infrastructure was damaged. Kaua'i is also famous for, and promotes, movies that are filmed on the island. The Church's film *Testaments* was filmed in Kaua'i along Highway 50 between Kapa'a and Anahola. Tourism and its ancillary activities fuel Kaua'i's economy and help support Kauai's 67,000 residents (see the the 2010 census).

Latter-day Saints in Kaua'i

On December 21, 1850, missionaries William Farrer and John Dixon arrived on Kaua'i. Having no success, they returned to Honolulu a month later.[2] Of all the Hawaiian Islands, only on Kaua'i and Ni'ihau were Utah missionaries not initially successful. Instead, on these two islands, the first investigators and convert baptisms were made by local Hawaiians who had been taught the gospel on other islands by the Utah elders. LDS historian Lance D. Chase tells us that "it was not until hundreds of the local people of Kaua'i had been taught the gospel and dozens baptized and confirmed members of the Church that the Utah missionaries returned to Kaua'i to share in the responsibility of the missionary work."[3]

One of the major factors that helped missionary work get started on Kaua'i was the baptism and subsequent ordination as an elder of P. H. Kaele, a district judge on Kaua'i, who heard the gospel in Honolulu and was baptized. Upon his return to Kaua'i he began to teach the gospel. Kaele baptized about ninety people. Finding it difficult to fulfill his judicial responsibilities and teach the gospel simultaneously, he wrote and asked that elders be sent to help him with the work.[4]

2 Linda Gonsalves, *The History of the Church of Jesus Christ of Latter-day Saints on Kaua'i* (Kauai, HI: Kauai Hawai'i Stake Relief Society Ad-Hoc Committee, 1997), 2 (hereafter cited as Gonsalves, *Kaua'i*).
3 Lance D. Chase, *The Beginnings of Mormon Missionary Work on Kauai, 1850–54* (Lihue, Kauai: Mormon Pacific Historical Society, 1995), 26.
4 P. H. Kaele, as cited in Gonsalves, *Kaua'i*, 4.

In response to Kaele's request, on July 9, 1853, Mission President Phillip B. Lewis sailed for Kaua'i with companion Elder J. W. Hosea Kauwahi.[5] By the end of August, between three and four hundred people had been baptized by these missionaries on Kaua'i. At a conference in October 1853, Farrer was again appointed to preside over Kaua'i, to be assisted by Elder William McBride.[6] On December 11, 1853, Elder George Q. Cannon went to Kaua'i for two months to work with Elder Kauwahi to check the manuscript of the translation of the Book of Mormon. A conference in 1854 reported 654 members on Kaua'i, out of a population of 6,900.

A few Kaua'i Saints joined the gathering at Palawai on Lana'i. When that settlement failed, another site was sought, and High Chief Levi Ha'alelea, who had leased Palawai to the Church, offered the land of Lumahai on the north coast. In 1853, Ha'alelea had offered the *ahupua'a* of Kealia on Kaua'i's windward side, but the elders chose Palawai, more desolate and also more remote, for their gathering place. But La'ie on O'ahu was chosen instead.[7] By 1883, there were eight branches in Kaua'i with 458 members; in 1895, Andrew Jenson counted seventeen branches with 783 members on Kaua'i.[8]

One of the most influential Kaua'i Latter-day Saints of the 1800s, whose life straddles the breadth of the history of the Church on Kaua'i, is Lilia Wahapa'a.[9] She was born December 27, 1835, in a grass house near the spot where the Waimea and Makaweli Rivers join. At this spot she was also baptized and confirmed

Lilia Wahapa'a, 1919. Courtesy of BYU–Hawaii Archives.

5 J. W. Hosea Kauwahi, as cited in Gonsalves, *Kaua'i*, 4.
6 Chase, *Mormon Missionary Work*, 30.
7 Gonsalves, *Kaua'i*, 8.
8 Manuscript History of the Hawaiin Mission, July 13, 1895.
9 Leon Huntsman, "The Evidence of Things Not Seen," as cited in Gonsalves, *Kaua'i*, n.p.

a member of The Church of Jesus Christ of Latter-day Saints by a Hawaiian missionary named Kualaulau, who was assigned to Kaua'i by Elder George Q. Cannon. For the next seventy-three years, Lilia Wahapa'a was one of Hawai'i's most faithful members. For thirty-three continuous years she served as the Relief Society president. She was called in 1893 at the age of fifty-eight and released in 1926 at her own request due to advanced age.

Her home was located at Haikioa, four miles from the chapel where she attended church meetings. "When it rained she would carry her shoes past the second swinging bridge near Menehune ditch. There, she would wash her feet, put on her shoes, and walk to church in Waimea. On the way home she would carry her shoes and walk in the mud."[10]

She survived "three husbands and all but one of her nine children. Sister Wahapa'a read her fine-print Bible daily without the aid of eyeglasses." She had an amazing memory, which included memories of the beginnings of the Church in Kaua'i. She passed away on November 12, 1944, at the age of 109.[11] With the efforts of converts like Lilia Wahapa'a, the Church steadily grew during the twentieth century in the Waimea-Makaweli area.

Another stalwart over the years on Kaua'i was Brother A. Burnham, who was converted on Maui and came to Kaua'i in about 1853 to work on one of the plantations. For decades, missionaries could count on the Burnhams at Lihu'e for sustenance and support.

Kaua'i was the last of the Hawaiian Islands to be incorporated into a stake. The creation of the Kauai Hawai'i Stake in July 1977 marked a milestone: all Hawaiian Islands became encompassed in stakes. At present, there are on the island of Kaua'i five wards and one branch, with a total membership of over three thousand.

10 Florence Kajiwara and Hattie Blackstad, as cited in Gonsalves, *Kaua'i*, n.p.
11 Virginia Bennett Hill, "Wahapaa, 106, To Get Her First Plane Ride," as cited in Gonsalves, *Kaua'i*, n.p.

LDS Historic Sites in Kaua'i

1. Kapaia Chapel

In the late 1880s, the Kapaia Branch was one of the largest branches in Kaua'i Conference, consisting of Latter-day Saints in the town of Kapaia, situated in a valley about three miles north of the Nawiliwili Bay, about midway between the sugar plantations of Hanamaulu and Lihu'e on the east coast of Kaua'i.[12] The Kapaia chapel originally stood just below where the G. N. Wilcox Hospital now stands.

Then in the 1920s the Lihue Plantation decided to construct a building for the Latter-day Saints in Kapaia, right at the foot of a hill, on the present-day site of the Hongwanji Buddhist Mission. On July 14, 1929, Mission President William M. Waddoups

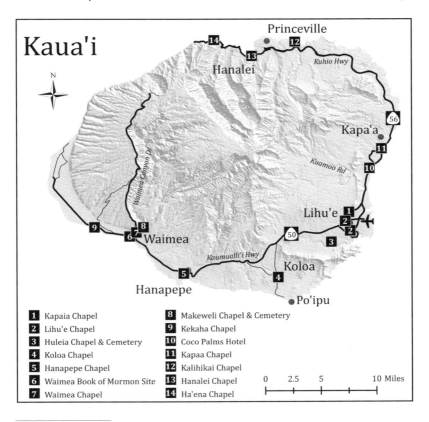

Kaua'i

Princeville

Hanalei

Kuhio Hwy

Kapa'a

Waimea Canyon Dr

Kuamoo Rd

Lihu'e

Waimea

Kaumualli'i Hwy

Koloa

Hanapepe

Po'ipu

0   2.5   5   10 Miles

1 Kapaia Chapel
2 Lihu'e Chapel
3 Huleia Chapel & Cemetery
4 Koloa Chapel
5 Hanapepe Chapel
6 Waimea Book of Mormon Site
7 Waimea Chapel
8 Makeweli Chapel & Cemetery
9 Kekaha Chapel
10 Coco Palms Hotel
11 Kapaa Chapel
12 Kalihikai Chapel
13 Hanalei Chapel
14 Ha'ena Chapel

---

12 Jenson, Manuscript History, July 12, 1895.

dedicated this chapel at Kapaia, Kauaʻi, with 240 in attendance.[13] Members had to do a lot of walking to get to their meetings at this chapel in Kapaia, but in spite of this hardship, members were faithful.[14]

Kapaia Chapel in Lihue. Courtesy of BYU–Hawaii Archives.

This chapel was the building moved in just eight hours on September 18, 1955, to Hanalei on George Koga's taro truck. The building was then connected to a chapel that was moved from Kalihikai. The two buildings were joined to form a new chapel in Hanalei.[15]

Directions to the Kapaia Chapel Site:

The site of the original Kapaia Chapel is in the valley below the Wilcox Memorial Hospital. Go north of Lihuʻe on Kuhio Highway past Wilcox Memorial Hospital, then down into the valley. The 1929 chapel was where the Lihuʻe Hongwanji Mission is now, on the right at 3-3530 Kuhio Highway.

2. Lihuʻe Chapel

In November 1950 the Lihuʻe branch leased the large Rice home on Rice Street and held their meetings there. Branch President Michael Yoshinaka was then given instructions by Mission President D. Arthur Haycock to look for a large piece of property for a new church building.

President Yoshinaka asked Mr. Caleb Burns, the manager of the Lihuʻe Sugar Plantation, to give the Church the Isenberg Gym and its property for the Lihuʻe chapel. With the development of the labor union, the plantation owners could not afford to maintain the gym for its workers. "Mr. Burns could not comply with this request, since he did not own the property, so President Yoshinaka

13 Ibid., July 14, 1929.
14 Ibid., October 3, 1853.
15 Diana Spencer, "Relief Society Journal," original in possession of Diane Spencer, Hanaleiʻi, Hawaiʻi 1997, as cited in Gonsalves, *Kauaʻi*, n.p.

turned to his friend Mr. Charlie Fern, an associate of the sugar plantation's board of directors. Mr. Fern expressed interest in the Isenberg property and gym on behalf of The Church of Jesus Christ of Latter-day Saints." Mr. Fern

Isenberg Gym and Lihu'e Stake Center. Courtesy of Riley Moffat

called President and Sister Yoshinaka and explained that the Lihu'e Sugar Plantation would sell the property.[16] The Church purchased the property for much less than the plantation could have gotten elsewhere. The gym portion of the current chapel is part of the original purchase.

In 1958, the employer of Branch President Libert K. Nakaahiki Sr., who worked as a heavy equipment operator, allowed the employees to use the "company's crane to place the tall beams in the chapel and the necessary equipment to pave the parking lot. Many members worked on the building. The Relief Society sisters provided meals."[17]

Directions to the Lihu'e Meetinghouses:

The original meeting place for the Lihu'e Branch was in the Rice home, at 4121 Rice Street. It is now the Kalapaki Villas condominiums. The chapel that includes the old Isenberg gym is on Ehiku Street. Turn east from Kuhio Highway on to Ehiku Street at the Walmart and go two blocks to 4580 Ehiku Street.

3. Hule'ia Chapel Site

The Hule'ia (sometimes spelled Hula'ia) Branch consisted of members living along the Hule'ia River in the Hule'ia valley a mile and a half upstream from what is known as the Menehune Fishpond near Nawiliwili Harbor. Missionaries would arrive at Nawiliwili Harbor and then walk to Hule'ia. Baptisms were held at the

---

16 Libert K. Nakaahiki, Sr. "Waihona Hoomana'o." 1997, as cited in Gonsalves, *Kaua'i*, n.p.

17 Ibid.

Alekoko or Menehune Fishpond 1912, Hule'ia chapel one mile upriver.
Courtesy of BYU–Hawaii Archives.

muliwai (river) edge here.[18] In 1895, the tiny Hule'ia chapel was dedicated. This chapel, which no longer exists, measured just 24 x 14 feet and was painted green outside, with wooden benches inside and a small cemetery adjoining the chapel. A conch shell was blown to call members to services. It was remodeled for $360 and dedicated by William Waddoups on October 29, 1928.[19] This Hule'ia Chapel was used into the 1950s, when this branch was combined with the Lihu'e Branch.

Directions to the Hule'ia Chapel Site:

There is no access to the Hule'ia chapel site and cemetery. It is on private land on the Hule'ia Wildlife Refuge about a mile upriver from the Menehune Fishpond. An excellent view of this area is from the overlook on Hulemalu Road. From Kaumuali'i Highway west of Lihu'e turn south on Puhi Road about ¾ mile, then left on Hulemalu Road about one mile to the lookout.

---

18 *Healani Trembath* as cited in Gonsalves, *Kaua'i*, n.p.
19 Jenson, Manuscript History, May 1, 1928; and Linda Gonsalves to Mary Jane Woodger, email, July 16, 2009.

4. Koloa Chapel)

Elder George Q. Cannon joined Elders Lewis, Farrer, and McBride and native missionary J. W. H. Kauwahi at Koloa on December 15, 1853.[20] It was near Koloa that these early missionaries

Koloa Chapel. Courtesy of BYU–Hawaii Archives.

held a prayer, blessing the island that the work would go forward. Koloa became an early meeting place for the Latter-day Saints. At Koloa, the missionaries received a hearty welcome from native members. At this time the branch in Koloa already had sixty-nine members.[21] Many members worked at Koloa, Hawai'i's oldest sugar plantation town.[22]

Later in the 1870s, branch members met in a meetinghouse that held between thirty and forty people.[23] At Koloa, some of the plantation workers were "South Sea Islanders" from the Gilbert Islands, now called Kiribati. At least forty were baptized by Elders James H. Gardner and Isaac Fox in 1883 and they met in a new frame meetinghouse described as being 20 x 30 feet. A year later, most of the Gilbertese returned home while others stayed on Kaua'i and had large families. By the 1920s, missionaries reported that this old church looked, felt, and smelt of the dark ages and needed to be replaced, but it was not torn down until March of 1943, according to the quarterly report of the Hawaiian Mission.[24]

---

20 Gonsalves, *Kaua'i*, 115.
21 Ibid.
22 Gonsalves, *Kaua'i*, 2.
23 John Stillman Woodbury, Journal, November 11, 1877. 2 volumes; William Farrer, "Biographical Sketch, Hawaiian Mission Report and Diary," December 2, 1853; and typescript in L. Tom Perry Special Collections, Harold B. Lee Library, Brigham Young University, Provo, Utah.
24 Gonsalves, *Kaua'i*, 29.

Directions to the Koloa Plantation and Meetinghouse Sites:
Though the Koloa Chapel no longer exists, the address for the former site is 3358 Waikomo Road and is now a Kingdom Hall of the Jehovah's Witnesses. From downtown Koloa at Maluhia Road and Koloa Road, turn left half a block to Weliweli Road; then turn right one block to Waikomo Road and turn right one block to 3358.

5. Hanapepe Chapel

During the late 1800s, Hanapepe town boomed because it was located near the harbor at Port Allen. The Hanapepe Latter-day Saint branch consisted of members residing in the town of Hanapepe and vicinity, located twenty-two miles southeast of Lihu'e on the south coast of the island. Members were often baptized in the Hanapepe River.[25]

On September 8, 1883, a small frame building (20 x 30 feet) was dedicated by Mission President Edward Partridge as the Hanapepe chapel.[26] This building served the Hanapepe Branch until it was replaced in 1919.[27]

Hanapepe chapel

25 Ethel Buchanan, "Waihona Hoomana'o," as cited in Gonsalves, *Kaua'i*, n.p.
26 Jenson, Manuscript History, September 8, 1883; and Family History Library microfilm #01288688 (pre-1900) and #0128869 (1901–1930), Church History Library.
27 William M. Wadoups Journal, October 20, 1919, transcription, "Missionary Journal," Church History Library.

In 1928, "the chapel in Hanapepe was across the Hanapepe River bridge where a ball field was located." The frame building had the capacity to seat 200 people. In 1940, two classrooms were added to the Hanapepe Chapel.[28] As the congregation grew, a recreational hall was needed for the youth, along with a larger chapel. The neighbor on the west side of the frame chapel was willing to sell his land, and some state-owned land behind it was also available. It was thought that if the Church could obtain these two lots there would be enough land to build a recreational hall. In seeking authorization for the sale, the First Presidency sent Elder Gordon B. Hinckley of the Quorum of the Twelve in 1965. When he examined the property on the west side and in back, he said, "We have enough room if we have those." When he turned to see the back of the chapel, he saw a brown stripe on the wall right across the back of the chapel. He asked, "What is that line there?" The answer was flood water from the Hanapepe River. Elder Hinckley continued, "You mean this chapel was two feet under water?!" When the branch president said yes, Elder Hinckley said, "President [John Ham Young], you'd better move to higher ground!" And a search for new property was initiated.[29]

The chapel referred to above, located at 4507 Puolo Road just off Kaumuali'i Highway, still stands and is now used by the Hanapepe Missionary Baptist Church. Local leaders then chose a property for a new building in Kalaheo, and the First Presidency sent Howard W. Hunter of the Quorum of the Twelve to approve the site.[30] The Kalaheo Chapel was dedicated in 1975.

Directions to Hanapepe Chapel:
The 1919 chapel is on the west, or mauka, side of Puolo Road near its junction with Kaumuali'i Highway, on the west side of the Hanapepe River. The address is 4507 Puolo Road.

6. Editing the Hawaiian Book of Mormon Manuscript at Waimea

Elder George Q. Cannon arrived by steamboat on Kaua'i in December 1853. The main reason George Q. Cannon came

---

28 Jenson, Manuscript History, May 1, 1928 and September 1940.
29 Charles Kwai Chung Fu, as cited in Gonsalves, *Kaua'i*, n.p.
30 Ibid.

to Kaua'i was to review his trans-lation of the Book of Mormon with Elder J. W. H. Kau-wahi. Elder Cannon became so popular among the Kaua'i Saints that his time to work on the man-uscript became very limited. On Decem-ber 21, 1853, Elder Cannon, along with

Book of Mormon editing site. Courtesy of Riley Moffat.

Elders Farrer, McBride and Lewis, journeyed to Waimea, where a local member, Brother Samuela, had prepared a place for the missionaries.

Interestingly, the place Samuela chose for the conclusion of this phase of the Book of Mormon translation was the recently vacated jail in Waimea. One wonders if Samuela knew that some of the greatest revelations recorded in scripture could be called "prison literature," such as those written by Joseph Smith and the Apostle Paul while being imprisoned. Built partially underground, the thick walls provided a cooler environment. Cannon and the others had cots set up in the various cells for sleeping. J. W. H. Kauwahi assisted Cannon in the review process because of his knowledge of both the Hawaiian language and English. The work began on Christmas Eve, 1853, and by January 31, 1854, the review was completed.[31] This translation published by the Church is still being used.[32]

Though the prison no longer stands by itself, it's found under-neath another structure. In November 1945, Lilia Wahapa'a told her grandchildren that the location of the former jail could be vis-ited by crossing the second swinging bridge in the Waimea Val-ley and then walking about a mile along a path that follows the base of the mauka (inland side) pali (cliff) of the Makaweli stream.

31 Gonsalves, *Kaua'i*, 115.
32 "Hawaiian Edition of Book of Mormon," *Church News*, November 22, 2008, 15.

The path passes numerous stone ruins of house sites, including Lilia Wahapaʻa's and J. W. H. Kauwahi's.[33] However, this description matches the site of the Makaweli Branch chapel. According to Brother Joe Manini, the jail cell site is in the basement of a large, old building near the Waimea hospital under a massive monkey-pod tree at 9567 Huakai Road.

Directions to the Waimea Site of the Retranslation of the Book of Mormon:

The jail cell spot where Elder Cannon worked with J. W. H. Kauwahi is at 9567 Huakai Road, which can be reached by turning up Waimea Canyon Drive two blocks, then going left on Huakai Road one block to a large monkeypod tree on the right. In 2013 the building was fenced off and looks abandoned.

7. Waimea Chapel Site

In 1928 the Waimea Branch had a new frame meetinghouse that seated 150 and a small amusement hall constructed from boards taken from the Makaweli chapel. This chapel

Waimea Chapel, Christmas, 1919. Courtesy of BYU–Hawaii Archives.

served until December 10, 1961, when the Waimea and Kekaha branches merged and met in Kekaha.[34] This is the chapel Sister Wahapaʻa would have walked to in her later years.

Directions to the Waimea Chapel:

Coming from Lihuʻe on Kaumualiʻi Highway in Waimea, turn right on Menehune Road about one-half mile toward the Kiki a Ola footbridge across the Waimea River. The chapel site

---

33 Clarice B. Taylor, "Little Tales All About Hawaii," *Mormon Centennial; Kauai Landmark* no. 13 (1949); "The Revision Completed," *Star Bulletin*, May 19, 1949.
34 Joseph Punilei Manini Sr., as cited in Gonsalves, *Kauaʻi*, n.p.

is on private property; the cultural hall is now an abandoned home.

8. Makaweli Chapel Site and Cemetery

A number of Latter-day Saints, such as Lilia Wahapaʻa, lived in the lower Makaweli River valley among numerous taro patches. The site of the historic grass meeting house where George Q. Cannon preached was located in Kakalae or the arch of Lae, also called Hakioa. On this same spot, the grass meetinghouse was replaced with a frame meetinghouse, which was remodeled in November 1900. It also featured a small amusement hall.[35] Over time, many members moved out of the valley to Waimea, and much of the land was turned over to growing rice by Chinese. The Makaweli and Waimea Branches met together as one until the Waimea Chapel was completed. Several members are buried on top of

Makaweli Chapel at base of bluff. Courtesy of BYU–Hawaii Archives.

Kanekula cemetery, Makaweli Chapel site below on left. Courtesy of Riley Moffat.

---

35 Jenson, Manuscript History, May 1, 1928); and Family History Library microfilm #01288688 (pre-1900) and #0128869 (1901–1930), Church History Library.

the bluff that separates the Waimea and Makaweli Rivers in the Kanekula Cemetery.

Directions to Makaweli Meetinghouse Site:

From Kaumuali'i Highway in Waimea, turn right up Menehune Road about one mile to the swinging bridge. The chapel site and cemetery are up the Makaweli Valley on private property accessible only by four-wheel-drive vehicle. Kanekula Cemetery is up a trail behind the chapel site.

9. Kekaha Chapel

In 1919, a small frame chapel, open-sided social hall, and missionary apartment were located near the beach where St. Theresa's Catholic Church is now. Later, a larger wooden chapel was built away from the beach, which served until labor missionaries built a block chapel on the property in 1964. A brass bell from the frame chapel now hangs in the courtyard of the current chapel.

Kekaha Chapel, 1919. Courtesy of BYU–Hawaii Archives.

Directions to Kekaha Chapel:

The first chapel is on the beach at 8343 Kaumuali'i Highway. The second and current chapel can be reached by turning right off Kaumuali'i Highway on to Amakihi Road two blocks to Iwipolena Road, across from the school.

Kekaha Chapel, 1940. Courtesy of BYU–Hawaii Archives.

10. Coco Palms Hotel

The Coco Palms Resort, popularized in the Elvis Presley movie *Blue Hawaii*, opened in 1953 on the banks of the Wailua River. In 1954, a group of Latter-day Saints from Kapa'a began performing at the Coco Palms Hotel as a fund-raising activity. Over the next thirty years, many members participated in the Coco Palms shows. In addition to performing three nights a week, members made flower and seed lei to sell here. This group eventually toured on the mainland, the first tour group in 1960 and the second in 1965. While touring the continental United States, the group visited early Church history sites between performances.

Called the Coco Palms Ambassadors, this singing group sent members on missions and provided necessities for the different wards, including a piano for the Hanalei Branch and classroom renovations at the Kapa'a chapel. Performances at Coco Palms ended in the mid 1980s.[36] After Hurricane 'Iniki in 1992 destroyed or damaged most of Kauai's hotels, plans to rebuild the Coco Palms Resort were scrapped when it was found that the hurricane had damaged the foundation.

The Coco Palms Choir influenced the public for many years. The performances were initially offered as fund raisers, but they were most effective as an introduction to the Church by a group of extremely talented singers and entertainers. So far, efforts to rebuild the hotel have not been successful.

Directions to the Coco Palms Hotel:
The hotel is located at 4-241 Kuhio Highway in Wailua just north of the Wailua River bridge on the left.

11. Kapa'a Chapel

On June 25, 1912, Mission President Samuel E. Woolley dedicated a new chapel at Kapa'a.[37] The building was a frame meetinghouse with a seating capacity of two hundred.[38] This chapel was so narrow across that only three people could sit on a pew. At that time the "Kapaa Branch consisted of Latter-day Saints residing

36 Germina Quereto, as cited in Gonsalves, *Kaua'i*, n.p.
37 Jenson, Manuscript History, June 25, 1912.
38 Ibid., May 1, 1928.

Kapa'a Chapel, 1919. Courtesy of BYU–Hawaii Archives.

from the Wailua River through Anahola, about five miles past the town of Kapa'a, which is situated about thirteen miles north of Lihu'e and was the headquarters of the Kauai District." Members had previously met in a large grass meetinghouse up in Kealia.

In 1932, a new chapel was constructed and dedicated on Christmas Day by Mission President Castle H. Murphy. Its unique design is similar to that of the Ho'olehua, Moloka'i Chapel, and is probably the oldest chapel still in use in Hawai'i. The Kapa'a Chapel had an old organ that

> needed to be pumped to get it going. It was quite an antique, but it produced good music. There was a beautiful painting of *The Last Supper* that adorned the back wall of the choir loft. It had

Kapa'a Chapel, 1940. Courtesy of BYU–Hawaii Archives.

a maroon velvet curtain that could be drawn [over the picture]. When the chapel was renovated they removed the painting. . . . The Sacrament table was located in the front of the podium and there were high back [hand-carved] chairs for the Sacrament officiators with the same maroon velvet covering of the seats and backs.[39]

The Kapa'a social hall or amusement hall had been dedicated earlier, in 1924. Later, in 1940, showers, dressing rooms, and a stage were constructed. Adjoining the Kapa'a chapel, the social hall's ceiling was raised five feet in the center to make room for playing basketball.[40] By 1960, the "hall had gotten old, the windows were missing panes, the doors sagged, the roof leaked," and there was a need for a new facility.[41] An extensive building program was taking place throughout Hawai'i in which new chapels were constructed with cultural halls inside the building, which took the place of the former social halls that had been built separately. To help pay for the new cultural hall at Kapa'a, the branch organized an entertainment group that performed at the Coco Palms Resort. The group had so many performers that it eventually split in half. One half went to Poipu, the other half to the Coco Palms Hotel.[42] The new Kapa'a Branch cultural hall was dedicated by Elder Marion D. Hanks on December 19, 1965.

Directions to the Kapa'a Meetinghouse:
The Kapa'a Chapel is located at 4561 Ohia Street in Kapa'a. Coming from Lihu'e on Kuhio Highway, cross the Waiakea Bridge and turn left on Ohia Street at the Kapa'a shopping center.

12. Kalihikai Chapel

The name *Kalihikai* comes from the Kalihikai Reef, which dominated the seascape along the beachfront. This reef is the longest on Kaua'i. The water inside the reef is calm and makes one of the best swimming, snorkeling, and spear-fishing areas on Kaua'i. Anciently, torch fishing was also common inside the reef. The

39 Evelyn Ohai Fernandes, as cited in Gonsalves, *Kaua'i*, n.p.
40 *Kauai Komments*, February 1940, as cited in Gonsalves, *Kaua'i*, n.p.
41 Evelyn Ohai Fernandes, as cited in Gonsalves, *Kaua'i*, n.p.
42 Germina Quereto, as cited in Gonsalves, *Kaua'i*, n.p.

Kalihikai Chapel. Courtesy of BYU–Hawaii Archives.

entire beachfront community was also called Kalihikai. The name has changed over the years. It is now called Anini Beach.

The Kalihikai District, as it was referred to in the 1950s, covered the north end of the island of Kaua'i from the plantation camp of Moloa'a to Ha'ena, a distance of about twenty-five miles. Kilauea, a small town in this district, had a sugar mill and was a typical "sugar town" during the first four decades of the 1900s. The Kalihikai, Kalihiwai, and Anini Branches were in this same general location just a few miles apart. Eventually the Kalihiwai Branch combined with the Kalihikai Branch. The first chapel mentioned in this area was the Hanapai Branch chapel, dedicated by Elder Henry P. Richards on January 19, 1879. No one seems to know exactly where this chapel was built; a small cemetery on the hill supposedly contains the remains of some of the old members. A Latter-day Saint chapel was built in 1906 in Kalihikai with P. K. Kuhi, a nephew of King Kalakaua, as branch president.[43] In 1928 the Kalihikai Branch of the Church was described as being a frame chapel seating 150. "The chapel was located on Kalihikai Beach Road. It was a typical church building of the time, . . . with a central chapel and a small classroom on either side."[44] The boys rang a bell at the chapel to call the members to meetings. Diana

43 Gonsalves, *Kaua'i*, 25.
44 Kalihikai District, n.p.

Spencer recalled that the chapel was packed every Sunday, some Church members sitting on the lawn outside. Everything was done in Hawaiian, even the minutes.[45] A new or remodeled Kalihikai Branch chapel was dedicated by President David O. McKay on February 3, 1935.

On April 1, 1946, a very severe tsunami hit Kaua'i. At that time, no one living had experienced such a disaster, and people were not prepared. Loss of life and much property damage resulted. Miraculously, the Latter-day Saint chapel at Kalihikai Beach escaped damage, even though it was only fifty yards from the beach. One observer said, "It seems like the waves went around the building."[46] Damage to the missionaries' home was minor. Most other structures in the neighborhood were destroyed. After the tidal wave, Church membership at Kalihikai began to decline, while membership in Hanalei increased.

In 1955, the Church decided to tear down the Kalihikai and Kapaia chapels, move both to Hanalei, and rebuild a combined, larger structure to accommodate all the members on Kaua'i's north shore. Kaua'i Church leaders discussed ways to move the chapels. One proposal was to move the chapel by barge, but the pier at Hanalei had deteriorated so badly that there was no way to load the building on a barge anywhere on the Kalihikai coastline. Another suggestion was to use an industrial helicopter to move the building in sections. This was the most feasible suggestion but very expensive. Another plan was to move the chapel overland. In Kaua'i, buildings of this size had been moved on public highways, but this scheme presented two obstacles: the main highway and the Kalihikai Beach Road were narrow and winding; and the road was obstructed by an old (1912) one-lane bridge over the Hanalei River. The final proposal was to cut the building into sections small enough to navigate the Hanalei Bridge by truck. Thus the Kalihikai Chapel was cut into sections on September 24, 1955, and rebuilt in Hanalei, and the Kapaia branch building was added to

---

45 Diana Spencer, "Waihona Hoomana'o," as cited in Gonsalves, *Kaua'i*, n.p.
46 Ibid.

it.[47] This patchwork chapel didn't last long; a small standard-block chapel replaced it in 1966.

Directions to the Kalihikai Chapel Site:
The former chapel was located on Kalihikai Beach. From Kuhio Highway, past the Kalihiwai bridge, turn down Kalihiwai Road, then turn left onto Anini Beach Road 1.2 miles to Kalihikai Beach. According to local informants, the chapel was on 3509 'Anini Road on private land.

13. Hanalei Valley and Chapel

Hanalei is a beautiful valley below magnificent mountains, with a river on one side. It had been a Protestant mission station since the 1830s, and the Wai'oli Church and mission house date from that time. In the late 1800s, "on one side of the river close to the bank [was] a large sugar mill . . . [and] on the other side about 300 acres of rice fields worked by the Chinese." Now much of the land grows taro.

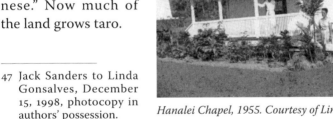

---

47 Jack Sanders to Linda Gonsalves, December 15, 1998, photocopy in authors' possession.

Hanalei Chapel, 1955. Courtesy of Linda Gonsalves.

Hanalei Valley, 1919. Courtesy of BYU–Hawaii Archives.

It was in this valley that Elder George Q. Cannon and other early missionaries preached and rebaptized members. While watching an ordinance performed on February 12, 1854, Elder William Farrer said that ordinances "had been administered improperly in consequence of the awkwardness and ignorance of the persons officiating: the body not being always covered or immersed in the water." The missionaries rebaptized ninety and baptized six new members, with Elder Cannon officiating and Elder Farrer and Elder Paku confirming at the water's edge. They also reordained all priesthood officers that day and then held a sacrament meeting that afternoon at Hanalei.[48]

In 1955 it was decided to move the chapels at Kalihikai and Kapaia to Hanalei. During the demolition and reconstruction period, an unused chapel from Kapaia was first moved to Hanalei to provide a meeting place while the Kalihikai Chapel was being moved.[49] On September 18, 1955, the first meeting in Hanalei was held in the former Kapaia chapel. Seven days later, the Kalihikai chapel was cut into sections and then reconstructed at Hanalei. This combined chapel was dedicated on February 6, 1957, by Elder Hugh B. Brown.

A new standard chapel was built in Hanalei in 1965 and dedicated on July 8, 1966. It took eight months to complete this building, the work being done by members and labor missionaries of the Church.[50] This chapel still stands in the center of Hanalei town. On any given Sunday, visitors usually outnumber local members. Another small branch called Hanalei Uka existed three miles up Hanalei River; its grass meetinghouse was dedicated in 1907.

Directions to Hanalei Chapel:
The chapel in Hanalei is on Kuhio Highway on the right just after the shopping center and before Malolo Road.

---

48 William Farrer Diary, February 12, 1854, photocopy, "Diary of William Farrer as LDS Missionary in the Hawaiian Islands, Largely on Kauai," 5:143, L. Tom Perry Special Collections, Brigham Young University, Provo, Utah.
49 Jack Sanders to Linda Gonsalves, December 15, 1998, photocopy in authors' possession.
50 Diana Spencer, "Waihona Ho‘omana‘o," as cited in Gonsalves, *Kaua‘i*, n.p.

14. Ha'ena Chapel

Ha'ena is at the end of Kuhio Highway where the Na Pali cliffs begin. "The branch consisted of a few members residing on the northern extremity of the Island of Kaua'i, and is nine miles west of

Ha'ena Chapel. Courtesy of BYU–Hawaii Archives.

Hanalei Valley."[51] It is just past Lumahai Valley that was offered to the Church by High Chief Levi Ha'alelea in 1864 as a replacement for the loss of Palawai Valley on Lana'i. On October 27, 1928, with thirty-five members in the congregation, Mission President William M. Waddoups dedicated the little Ha'ena Chapel. The building, measuring 16' x 26', was constructed at a cost of $714.00. Its high foundation provided a room underneath for classes.

During the tidal wave of April 1, 1946, many people in the area ran for safety into the Ha'ena Chapel, which was not being used for church services at the time. They must have felt safe, because the chapel was three hundred yards from the shore. The wave damaged the chapel and the roof collapsed, injuring a number of people, including one elderly lady who lost a leg.[52] The homes of ten members in Wainiha were also destroyed.

Directions to Ha'ena Chapel:

The chapel site is at 5-7257 Alamihi Road on private land at the corner of Kuhio Highway, about five miles west of Hanalei.

---

51 Jenson, Manuscript History, July 12, 1895.
52 Letter from Jack Sanders to Linda Gonsalves, November 20, 1998. Transcription in author's possession.

Ni'ihau

N i'ihau, which is privately owned, is known as the *Forbidden Island*. It is famous for its isolation, fine *makaloa* mats, and shell necklaces. In January 1864, Kamehameha V sold the island to Elizabeth Sinclair of New Zealand for $10,000 in gold, which prompted the Hawaiian leg- islature to ban the king from

Ni'ihau. *Courtesy of Auckland War Memorial Museum.*

selling any more of the Crown lands. Sinclair's descendants, the Robinsons, have owned the island outright ever since and exert total control over the island; approximately 130 pure Hawaiians live there. Their paternalistic management has helped preserve the traditional culture, but at the price of restricting access to many modern technologies.[1] Andrew Jenson offered this description of Ni'ihau in 1895, and things have not changed much since then: "The island is celebrated for its small white shells, which are strung together for necklaces. The mats manufactured on [Ni'ihau] are of extremely fine textures. . . . The manners of the natives on this island, and their style of life are said to be more primitive than [those] on any other island of Hawai'i."[2]

Ni'ihau residents are nearly all of pure Hawaiian blood. They generally work for the Robinsons, who tightly control all access

---

1 Riley M. Moffat and Gary L. Fitzpatrick, *Surveying the Mahele* (Honolulu: Edi- tions Limited, 1995), 2:108; Ruth M. Tabrah, *Ni'ihau: The Last Hawaiian Island* (Kailua: Press Pacifica, 1987), 91–100; Rerioterai Tava and Moses K. Keale, Sr., *Niihau: Traditions of a Hawaiian Island* (Honolulu: Mutual Publishing Com- pany, 1989), 47; and Hugh Laracy, "The Sinclairs of Pigeon Bay and the Roman- tic 'Prehistory' of the Robinsons of Ni'ihau," *Journal of Pacific History* 36, no. 2 (September 2001): 183–199.
2 Jenson, Manuscript History, July 13, 1895.

to the island. Electricity is only by solar power. Transportation is by horse or bicycle. The Robinsons deliver supplies by barge. An elementary school is conducted in Hawaiian, but older students must leave the island to continue their education. One of the few opportunities for outsiders to set foot on Ni'ihau is to go there by helicopter or to book a custom hunting adventure.

Latter-day Saints at Ni'ihau

At Mission President Phillip Lewis's suggestion, P. H. Kaele traveled to the island of Ni'ihau to preach the gospel. He was the first native to hold the Melchizedek Priesthood on Kaua'i. As a district judge he rode the circuit and stayed in people's homes and baptized many.[3] In 1854, Brother George Raymond was appointed to preside over the district from Nualolo to Hanapepe with an Elder Hosea to assist him and also for them to take a trip to Ni'ihau.[4] In 1895, Andrew Jenson reported eight members on Ni'ihau, who were assigned to the Kekaha Branch. Other than that, The Church of Jesus Christ of Latter-day Saints has not had a presence on this private island since the 1850s, except for a short time during World War II when a Sunday School was organized.[5]

---

3 J. W. Hosea Kauwahi, 1853, as cited in Gonsalves, *Kaua'i*, 4.
4 George Raymond, Kalawaia, and Kamakahohano, 1854, as cited in Gonsalves, *Kaua'i*, 10.
5 Hawaiian Mission Quarterly Reports, June 1943.

Appendix A

Hawai'i Branches
according to Andrew Jenson, 1895

⌂ *has a chapel*

	# of members		# of members
Oahu		Kipahulu	22
		Keoneoio	38
⌂ Honolulu	677	⌂ Lahaina	69
⌂ Laie	364	⌂ Kanaula	54
⌂ Kahana	154		
⌂ Kaalaea	27	**Molokai**	
Kaneohe		⌂ Kalawao	78
Kailua	32	⌂ Kainalu	54
⌂ Waimanalo	21	⌂ Kalaupapa	149
Kalaekao	23	Palawai, Lanai	13
Halawa	17		
Waikele	25	**Kauai**	
⌂ Kawaihapai	20	Kekaha	39
⌂ Waialua	43	Waimea-uka	11
		Makaweli-uka	16
Maui		⌂ Makaweli	73
⌂ Waihu	56	Hanapepe-uka	36
⌂ Wailuku	132	Wahiawa	49
⌂ Waikapu	85	⌂ Koloa	87
⌂ Pulehu	149	⌂ Hulaia	47
Paia	19	Lihue	113
⌂ Peahi	56	⌂ Kapaia	79
Pauwela	24	⌂ Kealia	73
⌂ Kamaole	58	Papaa	14
Keanae	41	Kalihiwai	62
⌂ Ulaino	29	Hanalei-uka	20
⌂ Hana	46	Waioli/Waipa	33

	# of members			# of members
Wainiha	15	🏠 Weloka		47
Haena	16	Wailea		36
		🏠 Kahuwe		71
Hawaii		🏠 Aleamai		95
🏠 Puakea	22	Hilo		48
🏠 Honomakau	83	Waiakea		35
Halaula	53	🏠 Keaukaha		31
🏠 Halawa	27	🏠 Koae		19
🏠 Niulii	59	🏠 Kalapana		51
🏠 Honokane	48	🏠 Pahala		101
Kawaihae	5	Hinakukui		32
Kalala	8	🏠 Naalehu		86
Waimea	13	Puueo		30
Waimanu	56	🏠 Papa		58
🏠 Waipio	84	Opihale		40
Honokaa	70	Kaohe		46
Paauhau	17	🏠 Keokea		26
Aleakila	31	Kahaluu		28
🏠 Kihalani	26			

Hawai'i Mission:
Districts and Branches
according to Andrew Jenson, 1928

🏠 *has a chapel*

	# of members

Honolulu District

🏠 Kalihi
Kalihi-kai
Niuhelewai
Kauluwela
Papakolea
🏠 Makiki
🏠 Kakaako
Kalia
🏠 Waikiki

Laie District

🏠 Watertown
🏠 Pearl City
🏠 Wahiawa
🏠 Laie
🏠 Laie-maloo
🏠 Kahana
🏠 Waialua

Kauai District

Halehaku
🏠 Kapaa
🏠 Kalihikai
Haena

	# of members

🏠 Koloa
🏠 Hanapepe
🏠 Waimea
🏠 Kekaha

West Maui District

🏠 Wailuku	250
🏠 Waiehu	50
🏠 Waihee	40
🏠 Waikapu	
🏠 Kihei	35
🏠 Kahului	150
🏠 Paia	
Haiku	
🏠 Peahi	50
🏠 Pulehu	35

East Maui District

🏠 Hana	200
🏠 Nahiku	150

Molonai District

🏠 Olowalu	60
🏠 Lahaina	150
Honokohau	
🏠 Hoolehua	250

# of members

⌂ Kainalu 50

Kalaupapa District

⌂ Kalaupapa 95

Hilo District

⌂ Hilo 300
⌂ Keaukaha 200
  Olaa 50
  Kapoho
⌂ Kalapana 27
⌂ Aleamai 200
⌂ Honomu 150
⌂ Kihalani 200

South Hawai'i District

  Kau

# of members

  Puuanahulu
⌂ Kalaoa
⌂ Keei 100
⌂ Pahoehoe
⌂ Papa

Kohala District

⌂ Niulii 80
⌂ Honomakau 20
⌂ Kokoiki 100

Hamakua District

⌂ Waimea 200
⌂ Kalopa 150
⌂ Honokaa 75
  Kukuiau 50
⌂ Kukuihaele
⌂ Waipio

Appendix C

Hawaiian Mission President's Records of Church Buildings, September 1952

(List excludes property on Oʻahu, which was part of the Oahu Stake.)

Branch	Address	Property
Kauai District	**Island of Kauai**	
Kapaa	Kapaa, Kauai	Chapel, Hall, Elders (district and branch use)
Kalihikai	Kalihikai, Kauai	Chapel
Lihue	Lihue, Kauai	Large Home Leased for Chapel-Elders Home
Koloa	Koloa, Kauai	Chapel, Small Hall
Hanapepe	Hanapepe, Kauai	Chapel, Elders Home
Waimea	Waimea, Kauai	Chapel, Small Hall
Kekaha	Kekaha, Kauai	Chapel, Small Hall, Elders Home
Molokai District	**Island of Molokai**	
Hoolehua	Hoolehua, Molokai	Chapel, Elders Home
Kaunakakai	Kaunakakai, Molokai	Chapel
Kainalu	Kainalu, Molokai	Chapel, Hall
Kalaupapa	Kalaupapa, Molokai	Chapel, Hall (used by LDS but owned by Territory)
Mauna Loa	Mauna Loa, Molokai	(Community Buddhist Hall rented)
Maui District	**Island of Maui**	
Lahaina	Lahaina, Maui	Chapel

Honokahua	Honokahua, Maui	Chapel
Kahului	Kahului, Maui	Chapel, Elders Home
Wailuku	Wailuku, Maui	Chapel, Sisters Home & Relief Society Home
Waiehu	Waiehu, Maui	Chapel
Waihee	Waihee, Maui	Chapel
Waikapu	Waikapu, Maui	Chapel, Small Hall
Kihei	Kihei, Maui	Chapel
Paia	Paia, Maui	Chapel, Hall
Peahi	Peahi, Maui	Chapel
Haiku	Haiku, Maui	Chapel, Hall, Elders Rooms
Pulehu	Pulehu, Maui	Chapel
Keanae	Keanae, Maui	Chapel
Nahiku	Nahiku, Maui	Chapel
Hana	Hana, Maui	Chapel, Hall, Elders Home
Ulupalakua	Maui	Chapel (no branch and not used much)

Maui District	**Island of Lanai**	
Lanai	Lanai City, Lanai	Chapel, Hall, Elders Home

Hilo District	**Island of Hawaii**	
Kukuau	Hilo, Hawaii	No Chapel (using Community Center Hall)
Keaukaha	Hilo, Hawaii	No Chapel (using Keaukaha Community Hall)
Olaa	Olaa, Hawaii	No Chapel (using a Plantation Hall)
Aleamai	Aleamae, Hawaii	Chapel, Elders Home
Honomu	Honomi, Hawaii	Chapel
Kihalani	Kihalani, Hawaii	Chapel, Elders Home

Hilo Mission Home, 1373 Kilauea Avenue, Hilo, Hawaii

Hamakua District	**Island of Hawaii**	
Honokaa	Honokaa, Hawaii	Chapel, Elders Home

| Kukuihaele | Kukuihaele, Hawaii | Chapel |
| Waimea | Waimea, Hawaii | Chapel, Large Gym |

Kohala District[1] **Island of Hawaii**

Honomakau	Honomakau, Hawaii	Chapel, Small Hall, Elders Home
Kukuihaele	Kukuihaele, Hawaii	Chapel
Waimea	Waimea, Hawaii	Chapel, Large Gym

North Kona District **Island of Hawaii**

Puuanahulu	Puuanahulu, Hawaii	Chapel
Kalaoa	Kalaoa, Hawaii	Chapel, Hall
Kailua	Kailua, Hawaii	Home used for Meeting House and Elders Home

South Kona District **Island of Hawaii**

Keei	Keei, Kona, Hawaii	Chapel, Elders Home
Kealia	Kealia, Kona, Hawaii	No Chapel (meet on porch of member's home.)
Opihali	Opihali, Kona, Hawaii	Chapel

Kau District **Island of Hawaii**

| Pahala | Pahala, Hawaii | No Chapel, meeting in school building, Elders Home |
| Waiohinu | Waiohinu, Hawaii | Chapel, Hall, Elders Home |

---

1 Source: Hawai'i Mission Presidents Records, LR 3695 21, reel 3, box 1, folder 9, Church History Library, Salt Lake City.

Appendix D

Hawai'i Mission Branch and District Membership as of January 1, 1956

(Excludes wards and branches in the Oahu Stake.)

Hamakua District 500

Honokaa	147
Kukuihaele	138
Waimea	215

Hilo District 1,530

Aleamai	166
Honomu	92
Keaukaha	612
Kilauea	440
Olaa	105
Kihalani	115

Kau District 230

Pahala	90
Waiohinu	140

Kauai District 1,570

Hanapepe	216
Hanalei	156
Kapaa	370
Kekaha	217
Koloa	121
Lihue	320
Waimea	170

Kohala District 450

Honomakau & Mahukona	294
Niulii	156

Kona District 460

Kailua	120
Kalaoa	82
Puuanahulu	47
Keei	164
Opihali	47

Maui District 1,570

Haiku	57
Hana	99
Honokahua	57
Kahului	181
Keanae	27
Kihei	83
Lahaina	190
Lanai	62
Paia	164
Peahi	48
Pulehu	88
Waiehu	53
Waihee	64
Wailuku	397

Molokai District 600

Hoolehua	443
Kainalu	49
Kalaupapa	28
Kaunakakai	47
Maunaloa	33

Source: Hawai'i Mission Presidents Records, LR 3695, box 5, folder 4, Church History Library, Salt Lake City.

Index

missionary work of, in Kula District, 117–118, 119
missionary work of, in Maui, 20, 94–95, 97–99
missionary work of, in Wailuku, 108–110
prayed about missionary work, 95
set apart as missionary and sailed for Hawai'i, 10–11
told Hawaiians they needed sealing blessings, 60
translated Book of Mormon into Hawaiian, 111–113, 115, 203, 211–212
traveled to Hawai'i in canoe, 166
visited ex-queen Liliuokalani, 28
Cannon, Hugh J., 119, 120
Castle, James B., 73, 91
Castle, Julia, 91
Castle & Cooke, 149
cemetery
I Hemolele, 56–57
Kahana, 39
Kanekula, 215
Kauhaku Crater, 148
Keaukaha, 170
Kihalani Branch, 183
Nahiku, 125
Niuli'i, 190
Papaloa, 147–148
Pu'uanahulu, 193
Waialua, 43
Waimea, 189
Waiola Church, 106
Central Pacific Mission, 14
chapels
Aleamai, 177–179
general construction patterns of, 14
Ha'ena, 222–224
Hanalei, 221–222
Hanapepe, 210–211
Hawi, 190
in Honolulu, 21
Honomu, 179–180
Hule'ia, 207–208
I Hemolele, 25, 52–55, 62
Kahana, 39–40
Kailua, 197–198
Kalaupapa, 143–146
Kalawao, 146–147
Kalihi, 32–34
Kalihikai, 218–221
Kapa'a, 216–218

Kapaia, 205–206
Kaunakakai, 135
Keaukaha Branch, 169–171
Keaukaha Ward, 171–172
Kekaha, 215
Kihalani, 180–184
Kilauea, 173–175
Kukuau, 172–173
Kukuihaele, 184–185
Lahaina, 106
La'ie, 52
La'iemalo'o Branch, 68–69
Lana'i, 157–159
Lihu'e, 206–207
Makaweli, 214–215
Nanakuli, 41
Niuli'i, 189–191
"one-eyed" church, 22
Pearl City, 37
Pulehu, 117–122
Pu'uanahulu, 193–194
Wahiawa, 41–42
Waikapu, 108
Waikiki Branch, 31–32
Wailuku, 115
Waimea, 213–214
Waimea Branch, 187–189
Waiohinu, 198–199
Waipio, 185–187
Chase, Lance D., 65
Choy, Sam, 76
Church College of Hawai'i (CCH), 15, 51, 82–87
City of Joseph, 12, 151, 155, 157
Clark, Hiram, 11, 20, 94, 95
Clark, J. Rueben, 121
Clawson, Rudger, 63
Clissold, Edward L., 83, 88, 91, 167
Cluff, Harvey H., 70
Cluff, William Wallace, 13, 46, 100–105, 154
Coco Palms Ambassadors, 216
Coco Palms Hotel, 216
Conde, Daniel T., 108–109
Congregationalists, 108
Cook, James, 3–4, 17
Cooke, Maude, 91
Cope, Marianne, 138
Cornillez, Brent Kamaka, 190
Cowley, Matthew, 80, 88, 121, 142, 174